HOW TO HOLD YOUR AUDIENCE
WITH HUMOR

How to Hold Your Audience with HÜMOR

A Guide to more EFFECTIVE SPEAKING
by
Gene Perret

Writer's Digest Books   Cincinnati, Ohio

Library of Congress Cataloging in Publication Data
Perret, Gene.
    How to hold your audience with humor.

    Includes index.
    1. Public speaking. 2. Wit and humor. I. Title.
PN4066.P46   1984   808.5'1   83-25989
ISBN 0-89879-136-7

Design by Christine Aulicino

To Joanne

Wit ought to be a glorious treat
like caviar. Never spread it
about like marmalade.

NOEL COWARD

CONTENTS

ers on serious themes have employed wit with their wisdom . . . the important relationship between a speaker and an audience . . . an audience is a collection of *minds* . . . a touch of comedy can enhance a sober theme by relieving tension.

Being funny is not enough . . . the material must suit the presenter . . . comedy is an individualistic art . . . even the professional comedians can't do one another's material . . . how to find your individual style . . . what styles you have to select from . . . tricks for introducing humor into your speech.

Humor should look effortless, but it isn't . . . the pros work hard at their comedy . . . speakers must, also . . . done well, comedy is exhilarating; done poorly, it's disastrous . . . a list of areas which require your application.

PART TWO: GATHERING HUMOR

Several ways for a speaker to generate comedy material . . . suggestions for researching and applying material . . . ways that listening to others may stimulate your own creativity . . . how to use joke books and services . . . the pros and cons of writing original material or working with a writer.

Writing humor isn't as difficult as you think . . . a speaker's humor doesn't have to be professional quality . . . an exercise that will show you that you can write comedy . . . writing funny material requires preparation . . . how to find the slant to produce funny lines . . . a list of "shortcuts to humor."

TAILOR YOUR MATERIAL TO FIT YOU

George Bernard Shaw said, "Good writers borrow. Great writers steal" . . . borrowed, stolen, or original, your stories should be indelibly stamped as *you* . . . some hints on selecting material . . . three ways to tailor your material so that it becomes uniquely your own.

TAILOR YOUR MATERIAL TO FIT YOUR AUDIENCE

Your audience will decide what is funny . . . find out what your audience wants to hear and then say it in a clever way . . . study and research your listeners . . . some questions you might ask about your audience . . . how to use that information to generate your comedy.

SHOULD YOU HIRE A WRITER?

Employing a writer doesn't take all the burden off you . . . there may be communication problems and differences between your concept and the writer's execution . . . writers can supply different material and a steady supply . . . how to find and select *your* writer . . . how to work with and keep a good writer.

TIMING AND PACING

What is "timing?" . . . you'll probably have to learn it the same way the masters did, by trial and error . . . the rules of economics apply to comedy timing . . . the punch line must be strong enough to justify the time invested in it . . . what is "pacing" and how does it differ from "timing?" . . . suggestions for positioning your humor.

PART THREE: DELIVERING HUMOR

joke doesn't get laughs . . . a speaker's purpose in
using humor is not solely to generate laughter . . .
prepare for the failures . . . audiences don't judge
you on the basis of one joke . . . avoid changing
your routines on the basis of one piece of humor
that didn't work . . . sometimes we lose audience
reaction because we don't wait for our laughs.

LEARN FROM YOUR SPEECHES
Each new speech and each new audience is a learning experience . . . don't be too severe on yourself
for the weak ones, or too complacent with the
strong ones . . . learn from your own performance,
the audience make-up, and even the working conditions . . . you can select from several methods of
review.

HOW TO HOLD YOUR AUDIENCE
WITH HUMOR

AUTHOR'S PREFACE

I WANT TO START this book with this important message: Humor is such an essential tool for a speaker who wants to captivate an audience that it cannot be reserved for professional humorists only. If it were, there would be no laughter at family gatherings or hardly any gaiety at parties and a lot of good fun would be missing for all of us.

Laughter is much too valuable a commodity to be entrusted to just a few people. It belongs to everyone. Everyone should and can enjoy it and use it.

HUMOR BELONGS IN *YOUR* SPEECH

The purpose in writing this book is not to make you a better *humorist*, but to make you a better *speaker* through the effective use of humor.

Some people fear using humor in a presentation. This is the main cause of the resistance I face when conducting seminars on humor. "I'm not a comedian. Don't try to turn me into one," objecting listeners will say. Some are even more pointed in their remarks. They say, "Don't make me a buffoon."

These are genuine concerns, and they should be. *Let me reassure you that transforming you into a comedian is definitely not the intention of the book.* Most of my comedy writing is done for comedians who work in nightclubs and on television. Believe me, I have my hands full turning the professionals into comedians without attempting to convert the masses.

Anyone who does any speaking at all has a statement to make and that statement should not be overpowered even by humor.

Your message must be important to you for you to work as hard as you do to communicate it to others. The purpose of humor is to enhance your message and to get people to listen to it more attentively and remember it much longer. Humor has that power. It is so popular that when people hear it, they want to listen, and it is so graphic that it sets your message firmly in the minds of the listeners.

YOUR HUMOR CAN AND SHOULD FEEL NATURAL

You are an important part of *your* humor. Each person has some comics that he likes and some he dislikes. "Heaven forbid," you mutter to yourself, "if the guy writing this book tries to turn me into a Richard Pryor!" Now I don't mean to belittle Richie's talents, which are considerable (although, even he would admit that some of his stuff wouldn't go over too well at the company's annual stockholder's meeting).

No, I'm not going to dictate any one style of comedy for everybody. In fact, a major premise of this volume is that comedy is subjective. Each person has a natural, individualistic, unique style that is peculiarly his or her own. That tendency should be developed and maximized. The kind of comedy that you like and do best—not the style of someone else—should be included in your talks.

YOU *CAN* USE HUMOR

At conventions, I'll converse with other speakers in the hotel lobby. The song I hear over and over again is, "I can't do comedy." I disagree, but they are adamant. "No sir," they say, "I don't have a funny bone in my body. I can't remember jokes and I can't tell a joke." Then enters a friend from Chicago that this person hasn't seen in six months. They embrace, shake hands, pat each other on the back. Then my reluctant comic will do six fantastic jokes about his friend's sportcoat, four great jokes about how much this man has had to drink already, another three tremendous lines about how bad his sales were this year, then he'll introduce him to me with four put-downs on why I wouldn't want to know him in the first place. All this from a man who can't do comedy.

None of these lines got by our friend from Chicago without some clever retort. This windy city-an was a worthy foe in the ad-lib department. Now I'm introduced to him as a comedy writer and his next sentence is, "I don't know how you guys do it. I couldn't write a funny line if my life depended on it."

We've just had a gross of laughs from two guys who *can't do comedy.*

Most people *can* do comedy and do it very well. Being a comedy writer isn't a requirement. In fact, one of the most embarrassing sights is a comedy writer on a talk show *trying* to do comedy. That's a solid example of someone who really *can't do comedy.*

When good friends get together, humor blossoms and laughter is generated. It's good comedy because it's natural and unaffected. It's not forced. It isn't there simply to get a laugh; it's there to further camaraderie and communication. It's likable.

That's the humor that the book wants to introduce into your speaking. Don't tell me you can't do it *because I've heard you do it* in hotel lobbies across the country.

YOU CAN RESEARCH AND CREATE YOUR OWN FUNNY MATERIAL

There are plenty of good books on the market that offer thousands of one-liners for all occasions. There are books full of celebrity stories and insult jokes. You can even subscribe to joke services that provide topical material.

My profession is writing new jokes for clients. That becomes an almost impossible task when my mind is cluttered with old jokes. So I stay away from joke books. Nevertheless, they're a superb source of comedy material for speakers who can't afford writers. (If you *can* afford writers, call me.)

You may pick up some stories from this book that you can include in your own speaking engagements. We will be using illustrations throughout and will have some anecdotes that you may consider worth borrowing. With a change of a word here and a word there, almost any anecdote may become *your* anecdote. You're welcome to it. In fact, I'll even tell you how to do it in Chapter 8. But the primary purpose of this book is not to supply you with material for your talk, but rather, to help you gather material or write your own. My main concern is to help you include humor that feels as if it's yours and belongs in your speech, *and in your speech only.*

HUMOR DOES REQUIRE SOME EFFORT

Humor is worthwhile and belongs in your talk. I'd like to help you spice up your speaking with comedy that is both comfortable for you and effective in your presentations. However, right from the start, you should know that this is not going to be a case of simply plugging in a word here and a phrase there, or lifting a joke from this or that book and popping it into your lecture, and then having the audience spring to their feet with a deafening explosion of applause. (They'll do that. That's one of the explicit guarantees of this book: If you follow the precepts set forth here, you will get a standing ovation within one year even if I have to hot-wire the audience's seats personally.)

Creating humor takes some effort. It's not *hard* work, mind you, but it does take some premeditation and some application.

These chapters will tell you what to meditate on and where to expend the effort, but they can't eliminate either. If you're going to stand in front of a crowd on a podium, behind a lectern, with a spotlight on you, a live microphone crackling in anticipation, and every pair of ears in the auditorium just waiting for your wisdom, you'd *better* spend some time in preparation. Since you're going to devote energy to preparing and giving your speech anyway, why not allot more time to improve your presentation with good, solid, workable humor?

HUMOR GOES WITH EVERYTHING

Humor belongs in almost every speech, and blends well with practically any message. To prove it, I'll convince you that comedy is well within your scope and that you *can* do it. (I fully realize that once I've convinced all of you of that, I'll have no one to talk to in hotel lobbies anymore, but. . . .) Before you close the back cover you'll know how to create humor that is both a reflection of you and will be appreciated by your listeners. These pages will give you pointers on delivering your comedy effortlessly and successfully. All of this combined will teach you to enjoy your speaking as much as your audiences will.

Many of the examples and anecdotes throughout the following pages are from the world of show business. There are other reasons for that besides the obvious one that show business is the world I work and live in and am most familiar with. First, most of you are familiar with the people I'll cite so you not only can read the stories as written, you can almost "hear" them being spoken as well. I feel this makes the examples more valuable to the readers.

Second, the frame of reference is more universal. Stage comics work to the whole world, so their topics have to have a broad appeal. Using illustrations from the business world or from industry often requires an explanation that destroys the intended effect.

Most of these examples can be paralleled in your own field. In fact, they usually become stronger because comedy is much more effective when it applies directly to its audience. An inside joke always gets a bigger laugh than a "general" gag. Because you always know your audience better you can be funnier in your own arena than any of the "name" comedians.

FOREWORD

Laughter has always been very important to me. That glorious sound coming from an audience starts my juices flowing, makes my heart beat faster, and gets most of my bills paid on time. All my life I've said funny things and people laughed. That makes me a comedian. If ı said funny things and they didn't laugh, I'd be a politician.

Humor is not limited to the professional comedian. It's a powerful tool that's available to everyone who ever has given or ever will give a speech. Everyone can have a one-liner or two for his or her listeners—that includes the new president of the PTA, a business executive addressing the employees, and yes, there's even a joke or two in Washington. You should know that—you voted for some of them.

Humor is the welcome mat between a speaker and his audience. A short joke, a quick laugh, breaks the ice between you and that sea of strangers. When they laugh they're immediately on your side. The laughter makes them your friends. It's the most powerful ammunition you can carry. David could have saved himself a lot of trouble if he'd just told Goliath the one about the giant farmer's daughter.

"Powerful" is the right word for the ammunition that humor gives you. I've seen a clever gag or story accomplish more than all the ranting and raving in the world could.

This book is a good example of that. The author's kind of sneaky.

There's good solid information packed in these pages, but it's made more appetizing with funny stories and anecdotes. (I know because I'm the target of some of them, but I'll get Gene for that.)

Gene Perret must know something about comedy. He's been writing it for the "biggies" out here in Hollywood for many years. Once in a while, in his spare time, he even jots down a couple of witticisms for yours truly. He's written and produced scads of TV shows and this is his third book. Not bad for a guy who's supposed to be writing for me. (Incidentally, that's why I read this book—because Gene writes for me. I wanted to see if he was saving the best material for himself.)

But this book wasn't written by a guy standing in the wings as you and I take our chances up there at the microphone. For the last few years Gene has been slipping out from behind his typewriter every so often to give talks around the country. He knows what it's like to be up there. I figured that out one day when he called me to ask what was the best way to remove tomato stains from gabardine.

Perret is a born teacher who enjoys helping others achieve their goals through humor. That's exactly what he's done in this book— shared with you the secrets he's learned. Gene never could keep a secret, which is why I never let him keep score for me in golf.

All of you who are trying to put a touch of humor in your speaking have my encouragment and my sincere best wishes. Study this book and refer to it often. You'll quickly realize that humor can become your strongest ally in winning and holding an audience. More important, you'll be bringing laughter to a world that has never needed it more.

Bob Hope
Toluca Lake, California
October 11, 1983

PART ONE:
USING HUMOR

A little levity will save many a
speech from sinking.
Samuel Butler

Humor and Dignity

WHILE UNASHAMEDLY TRYING to drum up some speaking engagements, I suggested my humorous talk as a luncheon feature to a gentleman who was booking a convention. He listened to my proposition then said, "No, these executives are pretty high up on the corporate ladder. I don't think they would enjoy anything humorous." WOW! I was stunned and saddened; not because I didn't get the work, although that always saddens me, but because of this mentality.

What exactly was this man saying? That upper level executives don't have fun? If he believed that, why did he book a fine resort hotel for the convention? one that had a great golf course, tennis courts, pleasant cocktail lounges, showrooms, and other fun spots? If the big shots don't like to have fun, then he could have held the meetings in an abandoned prison.

Could he have meant that top executives don't have a sense of humor? I doubt that.

I hope he didn't mean that this group didn't like to laugh. What a terrible thing to say about anyone.

This man's statement said more about him than it did any of the executives he was hosting. He feared these people. He tried to put the blame on them but it was he who was guilty. *I don't want to take any chances of doing anything silly or foolish in front of these folks. I want them to think well of me. I want them to think that I'm as important as they are. I don't want them to picture me as a buffoon* is what he was really thinking.

If I had said, "I'll do the gig for no pay," he still would have refused the offer. *Remember, these are busy, hard-working executives. They don't have time for anything as childish as laughter,* would have been his rationale.

This gentleman's hesitation is based on the same fear that keeps many speakers from using humor: "I don't want to be thought of as a buffoon."

Some transfer the liability to the audience: "Oh, this group is much too dignified to enjoy comedy." There is no audience in the world that doesn't enjoy a laugh. Nevertheless, many think of humor as the opposite of dignity. That's a myth.

One way to dispel a myth, or at least to test it, is with empirical data: Experiment and see if it's true or not. My mom always taught me to turn a clock in a clockwise motion when resetting it. Turning it counter-clockwise supposedly would have broken it. I subscribed to this all my life. Why take a chance? If mom had been right and I tried to prove her wrong, I would have had a broken clock on my hands. One day, though, in a fit of bravado (the clock was off by only five minutes. It was either move it five minutes forward or 11 hours and 55 minutes back.) I did move the hands of the clock in an heretical counter-clockwise direction.

The minute hand didn't break off in my grasp. Springs didn't fly out of the works and bounce on the floor. The timepiece just kept functioning.

There is also a tag that hangs, enticingly, from most mattresses and upholstered furniture. It warns: "Do not tear this tag off under penalty of law." I never did. I've known people who were meticulous about everything on their person and in their home. They would break out in a cold sweat if there were a piece of thread hanging from their clothes. Yet these folks would allow this ugly piece of white cloth to hang obtrusively from their furniture because they believed it was illegal to tear it off.

Never have I seen a house surrounded by police with guns drawn, a sergeant with a bull horn, saying, "We have the place surrounded. We know you've torn the tags off. Come out with your hands up."

If these dire results don't happen, then we can probably assume that these myths are false. So, let's attack the fear of humor from the speaker's platform in the same way.

Think of all the speakers you've heard over the years. That could include entertainers, after-dinner speakers, preachers, teachers, and the like. Can you recall one that you personally labelled a buffoon purely because he used some comedy?

If, then, we can't think of anyone we have immediately tuned out because of humor, why do we persist in fearing humor? Trust me, you won't destroy all your timepieces by winding them backwards. You won't go to jail for tearing off tags despite the ominous warning. You won't be considered the town idiot for introducing a touch of wit to your presentations.

Let's return to a time when you heard a speaker who did use humor. (Isn't this fun? It's like analysis.) If possible, try to visualize that certain someone who surprised you with his sense of humor. Recall: Was he or she someone you thought was "above" humor? too dignified for it, if you will? Maybe it was a superior where you work, or a dignitary, or a stately, older woman. Now try to recall your feelings when that first touch of humor was introduced. Was it a negative or a positive feeling? Did you consider the person a *whacko* or, more likely, warm and likable?

I remember listening to a manager in my office who spoke at his retirement party. He began by complaining about having to leave the work he loved and to which he devoted most of his adult life. Now he wondered what was open to him. The audience withdrew, thinking that they were in for a bitter tirade about the unfairness of forced retirement. The speaker said, "When a racehorse is no longer useful, he's retired to stud. Hey," he added, "That's not a bad idea."

That gag got a tremendous positive response. I was, first of all, surprised and relieved. The line was set up so beautifully that it wasn't expected. It was also a nice feeling to suddenly realize that I wasn't going to have to squirm in my chair and hear a bitter executive complain about losing his job.

I also remember thinking that this gentleman, who had been *The Boss* for so long, was very down-to-earth and approachable. I had never worked with him enough to get to know him well, but now I could see that his attitude was consistent with his leadership through the years. I now recall him as being warm and likable. I hope the example you recalled was similar.

Contrast this, though, with what I had feared. Had my example continued on in a humorless fashion and spent his entire "farewell speech" berating society and the system that forced him to leave work at a youthful 65, my feelings would have been different. Again, I'm not taking sides or arguing for or against a specified retirement age. I'm simply confessing to my honest reactions to a speech that could have left a negative memory, but didn't.

There is one sin that audiences won't tolerate: It's not the sin of being humorous, or even the sin of telling bad jokes. It's being dull. If you must offend, offend on the side of fun.

We've been analyzing this from a subjective point of view. How have *we* felt about speakers *we* have heard. Now let's ask how society feels about humorists. Does our culture label them as buffoons?

Only one nonpolitician is immortalized with a statue in the Capitol Building in Washington, D.C.: Will Rogers. We may, from time to time, put some clowns into the Capitol, but not their statues.

Will Rogers was 99 and $^{44}/_{100}$ths percent a humorist, and was probably the most beloved entertainer in history. Was he considered a fool? An anonymous statesman once told Eddie Cantor that every member of Congress was keenly aware that his constituents paid more attention to what Will Rogers said than to the pronouncements of the· Supreme Court.

In dedicating the Will Rogers Memorial in Claremont, Oklahoma, Lawrence J. Peter remarked that, "Will Rogers mastered every medium of public communication of his day." He added, "In my view, Will Rogers was probably the greatest communicator of all time. He could communicate to every class of people with the same message. No one has ever come near him." The revered cowboy-philosopher communicated with humor.

In 1983, Queen Elizabeth II sailed along the West Coast on her yacht, *Britannia,* on her ten-day tour of America. The United States welcomed her regally both as a tribute to her royal rank and to repay her for the welcome she extended earlier to President Reagan.

Many influential people tried to call in their markers and pulled whatever strings they could to be included in some of the official ceremonies. Politicians, millionaires, philanthropists, all wanted to meet Her Majesty. One of those invited onto the Royal Yacht for dinner was Bob Hope, a comedian of some renown.

Mr. Hope has also been honored by America's "royalty." President Kennedy presented him with the Congressional Medal of Honor. He's one of the few entertainers, if not the only one, to stay overnight in the White House. He slept in the Lincoln Room. It was a bit of a problem, he told me. He had to get up twice during the night to shave. Then sometime around three o'clock, he woke up and freed all his writers.

Some may argue that these examples are exceptions; that Will Rogers and Bob Hope are extraordinary entertainers who transcend the word, "humorist." Perhaps they are exceptional but I still maintain that America—no, the world—loves those who make us laugh.

We revere our clowns: Red Skelton, Carol Burnett, Lucille Ball, George Burns, Jack Benny . . . the list goes on and on. These are people who are genuinely loved.

You may add a few whom you respect. You may even argue with the choice of some of those whom I've included. That's fair enough. Some of these may be people you don't find particularly funny. That's OK, too. The point is, there are very few humorists or comedians whom we would call buffoons.

For speakers, the fear of humor is unfounded. It's a myth that I hope this chapter has dispelled. Comedy and dignity can obviously be compatible. Wit belongs in every environment. It belongs in your presentations. Can you work some into your talk, make it natural, and not destroy your dignity? In as dignified a manner as I can say it: "You bet your buns you can!" That's what the rest of this book is about.

Why Use Humor in a Speech?

RECALL SOME GREAT SPEAKERS who have really impressed you. They might be television performers, people who spoke at your company convention, or even friends who are great conversationalists. Didn't they all bring a touch of wit to their speaking?

As a speaker, I have been to many corporate conventions and listened to other speakers. I'm also a bit sneaky; blending in with the crowd and listening to the reviews these other speakers get. I have heard honest and unbiased critiques given in men's rooms immediately after the speaker concludes. No doubt, the same criteria are voiced among the ladies in the powder rooms. (One thing that all speakers can do—good or bad and with or without humor—is to chase an entire assemblage to the rest rooms at the conclusion of their lectures.) Most of the good reviews I hear are a paraphrase of, *"Boy, that guy was really good. He's funny."* How much a speaker amuses an audience often determines his evaluation.

Rarely do listeners comment on the substance of the talk. This doesn't mean that they consider the content unimportant or that they ignore it completely. Rather, they take it for granted that there'll be something substantive said because it's assumed that a speaker wouldn't approach the podium unless he or she had something to say. Consequently, the evaluation of a good speaker is determined as someone who makes that obligatory lesson enjoyable and, therefore, memorable. The listeners measure that by how pleasant the speaker made the listening. A sense of humor is what makes all the difference.

There's a saying that is repeated at almost every gathering of the National Speakers Association. Since it's been attributed to many, I'll attribute it to none. It goes like this:

"Does a speaker have to include humor in his talk?"

"No. Only if he wants to get paid."

What magic power does humor have to raise a speech from the ordinary to the excellent? What spell does it cast over an audience to have them favor that performer who adds just a dash of wit to his message? Let's analyze that power.

HUMOR COMMANDS AUDIENCE ATTENTION

I recently attended a speakers' showcase. It was three solid days of *listening* from eight in the morning until seven at night. People spoke on self-improvement, managerial how-to, self-motivation, sales, fashion coordination, personal computer usage, and what-not and other know-hows. It was a marathon of listening endurance for the audience. However, they were auditioning these "performers," so they had good reason to stay and hear us all. I listened to all of them because I wanted to observe what other speakers were doing and how they were doing it. In short, study the competition, so to speak (and maybe steal a few of their good stories).

I not only observed the performers on the platform but the audience as well. As the hours crawled by, and we all began to experience fatigue, the audience's reactions became much more obvious.

As lecturer succeeded lecturer with dry, although no doubt, important technical information, the audience became visibly wearier. But when a peppering of humor was introduced, the audience perked up and was revitalized. This was not a condemnation of the information that was being projected. Most of the points were valid, worthwhile, and usable: But people have a definite attention span that can't be stretched. Humor helps to bring that span back into line by refreshing the listener's interest.

Admittedly, this example is extreme. You won't often have to talk to people who have been listening for two or three days straight.

Nevertheless, it illustrates the principle. Educators recommend that students take a periodic break from their studies for the same reason. They suggest getting away and listening to records or doing something else that is fun and different, helps the student return to his or her studies with renewed interest.

Playwrights have used a similar trick for centuries. It's called "comedy relief." They realize that serious, heavy drama can be wearisome work for an audience. So, they interject some lighter moments into their work. Why? Is this done as a favor to the audience? Do they want to prove that they can write comedy as well as drama? No. It's to refresh the audience. The author wants them to be bright and sharp again so they can better perceive and appreciate the drama still to come. He brings them to that refreshed state with a sprinkling of fun.

A recent TV documentary concerning an experiment that studied the effects of lack of sleep reinforced this point in my mind.

Several volunteers were given varying tests while they endured 72 hours of sleeplessness. Some of the experiments were totally physical, such as jogging or walking on a treadmill. Others tested their recall abilities, for example, by periodically asking them to recite a poem they had memorized. Another interesting test measured their capacity to concentrate on boring assignments. They were to sit at a machine which beeped at irregular intervals. The volunteers had to record the occasional shorter beeps by pushing a button.

Surprisingly, the lack of sleep seemed to have no negative effect on the body's physical abilities. In fact, athletic prowess appeared to improve. One would expect the drowsiness to intensify as the experiment wore on, but whenever the participants gathered together for pure fun, for games and for camaraderie, the weariness seemed to disappear. The group became lively and awake again. The most dramatic evidence of the effect of the deprivation of sleep was during the vigilance test. It became almost impossible for the volunteers to stay awake listening for the variance in the beeping sounds. (Apparently beeping and sleeping go well together.)

There is a correlation here between this test group and your audience. They can tire mentally just listening to a message drone on. But like the people in the experiment, they will respond to a moment of fun which can refresh their minds and restore that listening power that both you and they want.

HUMOR HELPS LISTENERS RETAIN WHAT THEY HEAR

Companies send their employees to meetings, seminars, workshops, and conventions so that they will learn tricks of the business that they can bring back and put to good use in the office. Speakers are there to impart this knowledge and motivation. However, none of it does anyone any good if the essential message is left in the convention hotel with the towels (or most of the towels). It has to be brought back to the main office to be used as it was meant to be.

A speaker speaks to communicate—to convey information. He or she is passing on knowledge. But why bother lecturing if after the audience opens the banquet room doors for a coffee break, everything that was said floats off into the ether? It would be like running your heart out in a relay race, passing the baton on to your teammate, who, instead of running with it, gives it to someone in the stands as a souvenir. If you as a speaker don't help your audience to remember your lessons, then you're wasting everyone's time.

Humor, even used sparingly, can help accomplish that needed retention. How? Well, comedy is largely graphic. A funny image appears in the mind of the listener. We may paint this picture with words, but the real joke is in the image that each person sees. It's equivalent to going to an art museum to look at a picture. You don't go to see paint; you go to see a painting. Paint is merely the medium that the artist used to create the work. The image is what you see in that work.

Let me illustrate this point with some jokes about a skinny person. If I say, "He was so skinny that he had to wear snowshoes in the shower so he wouldn't go down the drain," you can visualize that. It produces a graphic image in your mind.

GRAPHICS ARE MORE EASILY REMEMBERED

Now, if I were to joke that, "She was so skinny she looked like a flesh-covered bronchoscope," most people would have trouble with that. They couldn't picture it. That's because a bronchoscope is a long, slender medical instrument that most of us either have never seen or recognize from the name. The potential imagery is applicable, but since we can't easily create the image itself in our minds, the humor is lost. Comedy, as I said, is graphic, and the mind seems to remember graphics much more readily than it does abstractions. A column of numbers is more difficult for the mind to fully absorb than is a pie chart or a bar graph. Even with graphs, we try to make them more vivid by using familiar images of men or houses or boats to represent our comparisons. Most memory systems convert abstract ideas to familiar images because they are impressed upon the mind more easily and are retained longer.

Since images are more easily remembered than are abstract ideas, and since humor is largely visual, it stands to reason that using comedy in an illustration will help people remember the ideas you are conveying longer and better.

Let me give you an illustration of what I mean. At the speakers' showcase that I mentioned earlier, one speaker, Danny Cox, taught us how to improve managerial effectiveness by fostering team-relation-ships. One point I'll probably never forget is that an executive will invariably have some unpleasant or difficult tasks to get done. Danny's advice was to attack them, finish them, and get them out of the way. Another memorable point was that sometimes a manager will have to admit that there are some people who simply won't or can't accept a team situation. As disagreeable as it might be, those people will have to go.

I'm not a manager, so I was not that interested in learning those skills. Yet the lecturer got these two points home to me in such a way that they will stay in my memory for a long time. Why and how? He did it with graphic humor that impressed his message into my memory.

To reinforce his point about not postponing unpleasant tasks, Danny said, "It's like we used to say back home . . . if you got a frog to swaller, don't look at it too long."

What a vivid, funny picture! I laughed aloud at the silliness of it. But then the idea clicked that if I ever did have to swallow one of those slimy creatures, the longer I looked at it the more repugnant it would become. The imagery is *expressive, graphic* and *unforgettable!*

Another image solidified the second point. Speaking about eliminating those people who won't subscribe to the team spirit, the speaker said, "We used to say on the farm that you can't teach a pig to sing. It wastes your time—and it irritates the hell out of the pig."

This capsulized in an easily understood and very funny way exactly what the man wanted his audience to learn and remember.

Another important point should not be overlooked here. These down-home epigrams were not the information that was being imparted. We had already been told in somewhat more clinical terms what the important points were. These were just small jokes that took hardly any time at all to tell, but which served to solidly imprint that information in our minds.

HUMOR MAKES YOU MORE APPEALING AS A SPEAKER

I began my comedy career at a large industrial plant in Philadelphia, Pennsylvania. During my working hours I was, initially, a drafting apprentice, then a draftsman, then an engineer, and finally, I reached the lowest rung on the managerial ladder, I became a supervisor. In the evenings I was the resident comedian, emceeing many retirement and 25-year parties that the plant would hold.

Shortly after I became a supervisor our plant was faced with the possibility of a strike. The upper echelons of management, the lawyers, and sundry other bigwigs spent most of the time meeting together to try to discover some means to prevent this threatened walkout.

One day they called on me, a lowly supervisor, to advise them on the best ways to handle the communications with the unionized employees in order to prevent a work stoppage. I dutifully gave them my recommendations. I was curious, though, as to why I was called to this committee. I asked my manager. He said, "The jokes you tell at the company banquets are always right on the nose. We thought you would have your hand on the pulse of the workers." I was at once dumbfounded and complimented.

Management recognized that there is wisdom in wit. Audiences will appreciate that, also, if you include a sampling of humor in your speeches. Instinctively, they'll realize that you're a person worth listening to.

A sense of humor implies that you possess three attributes:

1) The ability to *see* things as they are.
2) The ability to *recognize* things as they are.
3) The ability to *accept* things as they are.

If you can keep those three items in mind you'll always have a sense of humor about yourself. If you have a sense of humor about yourself, you can have one with others. However, if you lose sight of any one attribute your sense of humor is weakened. So be alert and guard these attributes well.

The best example I can give to illustrate these three points is somewhat grim, but very vivid. A doctor explained to me why so many people are struck down with apparently sudden heart attacks. Some of them never have any warning. There simply are no advance symptoms. They have no way of *seeing* the problem.

Some have symptoms, but misread them. A chest pain is thought to be a pulled muscle. These people don't *recognize* the trouble.

Then there are those who do know exactly what the problem is, but refuse to see a doctor because they fear the consequences. They may tell themselves, "This will go away,"—or "This can't be happening to me." They refuse to *accept* the reality of the situation.

The person who feels the symptom, recognizes the potential danger, and sees a doctor is able to get the best remedy.

The value of possessing these attributes is duplicated in our personal and business lives. The person who can *see, recognize,* and also *accept* the reality of a situation can select the best way to handle it.

Audiences are not dummies. When they find a sense of humor in someone they intuitively *see* much that is contained within the person. If you have that sense of humor they will respect you for it. Do I have to tell you that speaker is off to a great start if he earns the respect of his listeners?

There is a story about Abraham Lincoln debating an opposition candidate for office during an election campaign. Lincoln's opponent spoke first and devoted much of his oratory to *haranguing* Lincoln. Mr. Lincoln sat calmly while his adversary called him a "double-dealing politician totally devoid of scruples." Time and again during the debate, the first speaker referred to Lincoln as a "two-faced politician." When Lincoln stood to speak he began by saying, "Friends, I ask you, if I were two-faced, would I be wearing this one?"

Did the crowd consider this tall, thin, gangly-legged lawyer a buffoon? Hardly. They recognized that with this well-chosen, humorous beginning, he not only nullified his opponent's entire premise, but he endeared himself to these now sympathetic voters. Here was a keen, clever, resourceful man—a man *to be listened to.*

When that crowd got home, which do you think they remembered longer—the foe's ranting attack? or Lincoln's quietly humorous retort?

HUMOR IS FUN

It's invigorating for the performer. There are very few thrills (that are safe and legal) that can compare to the exhilaration you get when you step up to the podium and with just a sentence or two convert a suspicious, semi-hostile crowd into a receptive audience. It's more than that. They're not only friends now, but laughing, cheering, advocates. They came into this auditorium because the company said they had to. Most were not impressed by your appearance and some might have wondered what right you had to be behind the lectern while they sat unacknowledged among the audience. You were probably greeted by polite applause but there may also have been a smattering of sneers that silently but eloquently warned, "This had better be good."

But after hearing your first few sentences this emotional lynch mob exploded in laughter, appreciation, and, finally, sincere applause. Certainly, that's exhilarating. You have every right to inwardly pat yourself on the back (even though, that sounds like a physical impossibility). That's got to be a fun experience for a speaker.

I love a good, witty opening remark because it shows such a mastery of the audience; it's *performer psychology*. A funny, incisive beginning labels the speaker as a *pro* and certainly someone worth listening to. It says to an audience, "Hey, relax and enjoy. This is not going to be as bad as you thought." It also conveys to the listeners, in a very nice way, "You may have wondered why I'm on the podium, standing behind a lectern and speaking into a live microphone. But I think I've just proven to you *that I deserve to be here*." That's establishing a meaningful rapport with an audience; commanding their respect and affection in a very short period of time.

Here are some opening lines that I've enjoyed:

This first one was created by Pat McCormick, the rotund comedy writer and actor who has been seen on TV and in such movies as the "Smokey and the Bandit" films with Paul Williams. Pat wrote the line, but it was Johnny Carson who delivered it on February 9, 1971. The date is important because it was on that day that Los Angeles was rocked by a major earthquake that forced the city to come to a virtual standstill. Almost nothing was happening anywhere in L.A. as people reacted to the damage and panic caused by the quake.

Amid the after-shocks, the Tonight Show went on (of course). Johnny Carson opened his broadcast by saying, "The 'God-is-Dead' meeting that was scheduled for tonight has been cancelled." It was the ideal punchline for a set-up that had registered a frightening 6.5 on the Richter Scale.

Bob Hope had another good opener. The straight line for this one wasn't inspired by a natural catastrophe, but rather by a man-made disaster that cost, incidentally, several hundred million dollars. This was back when Russia had successfully entered the space age with the launch of *Sputnik*. The United States had been struggling, literally, to get their rockets off the ground. Front pages of newspapers everywhere kept up a steady stream of reports on our many failures.

On the day of one particular Hope telecast, another one of our launches was aborted with the rocket falling into the ocean. It was a demoralizing situation. Despite this, however, Bob Hope had the courage—and the wit—to open with this line: "I guess you've all heard the good news from Cape Canaveral. The United States just launched another submarine." The line provided a boost in our national spirit just when the country needed it most.

Comedian Joey Bishop had a great opening line many years ago when his show first premiered in the late-night time slot opposite two already established powerhouses—Johnny Carson and Merv Griffin. (Actually, this is what made the line so good, as I'll show you.) The Bishop show faced formidable odds in trying to dislodge either of its competitors from their hold on the higher ratings. The premiere had been highly publicized in advance and critics had already doubted, in print, that the new show had much of a chance against mighty champions of late-night television.

On the opening telecast Bishop was introduced and confidently marched to center-stage while the band played his theme. When the music stopped and the applause died down, Bishop calmly asked, "Are the ratings in yet?"

While accepting an award once, Helen Reddy used an opening line that was greeted with laughter and applause by the audience, and later quoted in many newspapers and magazines. The singer, who is a well-known champion of women's rights, said, as she accepted her statuette, "I'd like to thank God. I couldn't have done it without Her."

Modesty be damned: I'll also include a favorite opening line I wrote. Phyllis Diller had been on a tour of Australia when she suffered a minor injury to her shoulder that required her to wear a cast for several weeks. She called me because she was to appear in Las Vegas soon and wanted some sort of opening line that would explain the reason for the cast and then get the audience to ignore it afterwards so that she could go on with her regular act.

The next week she was introduced to her audience in Las Vegas. When she walked on stage, they were surprised to see the cast. Phyllis said, "I'd like to begin with a public service announcement. If there is anyone in the audience who has just bought the new book, *The Joy of Sex,* there's a misprint on page 206."

After the laughs died down, she followed up with, "It'll break your arm, but it's worth a try."

These examples are classics that I've collected from the show business world and I use them as illustrations because the frames of reference are universal. But I've heard some great openers in the business world also.

I attended a meeting of the "100 Per Cent Club" of a small company. These people, who made their quota, were given an expense-paid trip to a nice resort and then inducted into the club. This year, though, business was down. In order to make attendance worthwhile, the employees were given two extra months to make their quota.

The president of the company greeted them at the opening session with this remark:

> "All of you should be proud of yourselves because this wasn't an easy year to make your 100 percent of quota. I asked someone in the lobby how to get to the banquet hall and he said, 'Go down this corridor and turn left. You can't miss it. But it takes 14 months to get there.' "

If you can come up with short, witty, openers like these, I guarantee you're going to feel good and feeling good—having a good time—is as important to your presentation as your message.

Picture some entertainers whom you consider outstanding show-men. Now, analyze them for a moment. Are their skills *that* extraordinary? Probably not. Don't misunderstand. That is not to say that the show business giants don't have talent. Obviously they do. However, there are many folks in the same profession with comparable ability, yet they never break into that super star stratosphere. What sets the fantastic show people apart from the journeyman performers?

My theory is that the real greats thoroughly enjoy what they do in front of an audience. They're having fun up there. Sometimes, even when they're not having fun, they're professional enough to *appear* as if they are. That spirit of fun infects the audience. *That's what makes the difference.*

That's what you want to do: First you have to fill yourself with spark, crackle, and vitality. Feel good about yourself so that this good feeling will overflow onto your listeners. Then, if you're having a good time, and your listeners are enjoying themselves, the perfect atmosphere has been created in which your message will be received.

Humor Is Compatible with a Serious Message

FOR MOST SPEAKERS, with the exception of humorists and comedians, humor is simply a tool that is used to more effectively convey a message and help listeners to remember it. It's one way that a speaker can sell a point-of-view. The humor shouldn't overpower the message, but the impact of the message shouldn't rule out the use of humor.

When John Fitzgerald Kennedy was campaigning, he wanted to convince every voter that he was *the* person who should be elected President in 1960. Every speech and press conference he gave was peppered with humor.

Rather than shy away from potentially embarrassing issues, he attacked them with wit. One such issue was the charge that the Kennedy family's wealth was used to buy the Presidency. When a reporter asked, at a post-election press conference, why the vote was so close, Kennedy replied, "I didn't want my Daddy to pay for a landslide."

He also silenced criticism of the appointment of his younger brother, Robert, as Attorney General of the United States with honest humor: "I want him to get some experience before he hangs up his shingle."

Abraham Lincoln governed our country during its most serious turmoil. Probably no single President had to make more momentous and far-reaching decisions than Lincoln. He may have been our greatest President. He was certainly among the wittiest.

My favorite Lincoln story concerns the time he was riding a strange horse. The more he tried to control the creature, the more it jumped and bucked. Finally, it reared so much that it got its hind foot caught in its own stirrup. The President said, "That settles it. If you're getting on, I'm getting off."

The story may be apocryphal, but it illustrates the fact that Lincoln used humor liberally not only to convey his philosophy but to sustain him during trying periods.

Rarely will the content of a speech be so overwhelming that it will preclude the use of humor. Yet some speakers object. "The substance of my lecture," they may say, "is so important that humor would be inappropriate." The opposite is more often valid. The "heavier" a speech is, the more it demands to be lightened by some comedy relief.

To help justify the statement I just made, let's first analyze the relationship between a speaker and his audience. I do this in my comedy seminars by asking two questions:

1) What is a joke?
2) What does every entertainer share in common?

Think a bit about your replies before going on to look at my answers.

The answer that I try to get from the assembly is that *a joke is anything that makes people laugh*. It can be a series of words or one word. It can be a yelp, or a shrug, or a facial expression. If it gets a laugh, it's a joke.

Now for the answer to the second question: Every entertainer has *an audience*. Some may argue that film performers and authors don't have an audience. But they do. A movie audience or a readership qualifies even if the actor or the writer is never in physical contact with the moviegoer or the reader. Few of us would perform if no one ever appreciated what we did.

The point these questions and their answers makes is that the audience is very important. Speakers, because they stand in the front of a room, high on a podium and assisted by a microphone, may feel that they are the important part of most lectures. They are not. The people seated out there are. They are the reason for the lecture in the first place.

They come to learn what you have to teach.

When you speak you are, as they say in show business, *working to people*. However, it's important to know that an audience is not only a collection of people's bodies; it's also a collection of people's minds.

Boy! Was that lesson forcefully brought home to me one time. I had done a show for a local service club in my neighborhood, and did a terrific job. They not only loved every joke I told, but they invited me back to entertain at a dance they would be holding later on. I accepted eagerly. When a comic is blessed with a crowd like this, he doesn't want to lose them.

I invited my mom and mother-in-law to my repeat performance. Let them see firsthand, I thought, that this venture of mine into comedy was not just a pipe dream; the kid really had talent!

My family sat right there at ringside and listened to every word I said. They were the only ones in the audience who did. I bombed. It was a devastating night for me. What happened to those people who loved me just a month ago?

After the show I found out what happened: A local college basketball team was playing for the National Collegiate championship that evening and television monitors were set up around the auditorium. I couldn't see them or hear them from the stage, but everyone else could so no one was paying much attention to me. There was a crowd of people's bodies in the auditorium, sure. But their minds were in Madison Square Garden.

I've bombed other nights for other reasons, but this fiasco illustrates my point. An audience is not just a collection of people. An audience is also a collection of people's minds.

Since a lecturer must reach people's minds, he or she should learn something about the psychology of an audience. The successful humorist has to know what his audience is thinking and what they want to hear, and then say that in a unique, funny way.

If we investigate how a speech can affect an audience, we'll see that humor can help convey the message of even a serious lecture in several ways.

HUMOR RELIEVES TENSION

Tension often has a negative effect on the ability of people to listen. I'm guilty of something that many other people also admit to; I forget names very easily. But that's a simplification that lets me off the hook too readily. I really *can* remember names because when I meet people who are important to me I make it a point to learn their names *and to remember them*. However, I'm a bit shy at parties. I'm tense when introduced to strangers and I've noticed that I do not actually forget the person's name: I never even hear it.

As bizarre as that seems, I've caught myself being introduced, shaking hands, and saying right after the introduction, "I'm sorry, I didn't catch your name." Anxiety made my mind go blank.

That's a momentary lapse. But apprehension can cause mental blanks that last for longer periods. I see this frequently happening in my work as a comedy writer for television. Comedy writers are usually quick-witted. They love to ad-lib and rarely hesitate to throw a good line regardless of where they are or who is there at the time. I recall an occasion on *Laugh-In* when the writing staff was on its way to a group lunch. We stopped by the producer's office to pick up one of our writers who had wandered in there. We all barged in, did our *shtick,* and left. The writer we barged in on was somewhat upset. When we asked why, he told us that he was concluding a business deal with the producer when we invaded the office and caused him to end his negotiations. We asked why he didn't just ask us to leave. He said that he had tried, but couldn't be heard above all the jokes that were flying around the room. Another writer said, "Why didn't you just tell us to shut our big, fat mouths?" The offended writer answered, "I think I did and somebody topped me."

The point is that although comedy writers are not inhibited souls, we always ask about a writer, "Is he good in a room?" That means, when we get together as a group and have to come up with lines quickly and under pressure, is that writer able to be funny at that time? Many, especially newer writers, are not. They may be brilliant and creative with only their typewriters as witnesses to their wit, but in a room with veteran writers, with a few performers, some crew members, and perhaps the star of the show, they may be terrified. It's not that they're inhibited or shy. They could throw a line if one occurred to them, but they just can't *think.* Their minds have gone blank under all this tension.

That's the way I was during my first few years in television. I dreaded writer's "emergency meetings" because I couldn't think of anything funny. I'd say, "Let me go to my office, close the door (maybe lock it), and I'll be back shortly with 25 lines. You can take your pick."

The producers would say, "We need the line and we need it now. We'll all stay here until we get it." So I'd be quiet for the rest of the meeting. I didn't want to be. It was just that my mind became like a clogged-up drain.

Your audience may have the same problem. The intensity of your speech may create enough tension to cause some of them to withdraw mentally. Each may think, "I'd rather not be here." And so each one leaves; not in body, but in mind. Humor is the greatest antidote in the world for tension. Just a touch of it often can relax an audience so that people will really listen to you and absorb what you're telling them.

I once emceed an unusual 25-year party. The guest of honor had been given his "lay-off" notice and would be with the company only another few weeks. Since both management and labor were attending, there was some tension abroad in the assemblage. Instead of allowing it to smolder, I attacked it directly at the start of the ceremonies. I said, "We're going to do something different because of the nature of this party. Rather than do the usual monologue, the guest of honor has asked, instead, that I write him a nice resume."

It worked nicely.

HUMOR ESTABLISHES PERSPECTIVE

There is a fine line between a message that is legitimately serious, and one that's full of pomposity. Comedy writers continually exploit this situation. Butlers are fair game for ridicule because they appear to be so stuffy. Most authority figures are lampooned because we see their authority as inflexible. The original commanding officer in the film, *M*A*S*H*, was an imbecile, while the regular surgeons were hip and bright. The hit TV show *Hill Street Blues* has many real characterizations, but the police lieutenant who thinks fighting urban crime should follow along the lines of his combat experience in Vietnam is a laughable, pompous ass. Notice also that he is the only character on the show with no sense of humor.

Television sometimes gives the impression that every boss, every politician, every police chief—damn near everyone in authority—is a caricature figure. Obviously, that isn't true. Comics, though, have always capitalized on this imagery. Charlie Chaplin was the champion of the "little guy." Much of his comedy tended to deflate authority or pomposity. The biggest laugh-getter was hitting the rich guy with the pie or pushing the overweight dowager into the swimming pool.

What the comics were really deflating was the inflated image that they themselves created. Their rich people were always made to look silly first; that made them much easier to mock. The dowagers were always overweight which made for a much funnier *splash* when they hit the swimming pool bottom first.

We've all met wealthy folks and most are not all that stuffy. It's not fair to generalize about people that way. But people do it. They'll do it to you. If you want to hear some sniggers, just put in a convention brochure that you'll be speaking at lunch—"on the yellow throated titmouse and how its perilous migration patterns parallel the executive-decision making process." The allusion to executives making decisions will get some big laughs in the restrooms during program breaks.

The more serious your subject is, the more likely it may be unfairly categorized as pompous even before it's heard. It's your obligation to prevent the loss of your audience's attention and to restore balance and perspective. The best way to do that is with humor.

HUMOR CAN HEIGHTEN THE IMPACT OF YOUR THEME

If the gist of your talk is extremely significant, you will surely want it noted *and remembered*. However, the gravity of your theme may lull an audience into a trance-like state. They may really be interested in what you have to say and may listen so intently that they become tired. It's like studying too hard: You reach a point where you can absorb no more information without some rest or diversion.

Boxers are finely conditioned athletes who expend a great deal of energy in a three-minute round. If they're to go at full strength for 10 or 15 rounds they need that one minute rest period between each round. It refreshes them. It revitalizes them and prepares them to answer the bell for the next round with renewed stamina.

In the same way, you give an audience some comedy relief with a sprinkling of wit and they'll be much more alert when you return to your important points.

During the height of the civil rights movement in the 1960s, I worked with a successful black nightclub comic. He was welcomed on most stages by most audiences. All they asked was that he be funny. However, they didn't want a "message" from him. They only wanted entertainment. If there was any hint that he was going to "preach" equality, the audience would not so much rebel as simply turn itself off. However, through humor subtle messages were conveyed without the audience turning away. In fact, they even enjoyed what they heard. The comic couldn't say, "I'm black and I've been treated unfairly for some time. From now on, how about just treating me like a human being." After all, these folks hadn't paid a cover charge to hear a sermon. But this gentleman said the same thing much more eloquently and got the attention he wanted from the audience, as well as their applause. For example, while speaking about James Meredith, the first black man to enter a university in Mississippi, the comic said, "I think James Meredith should be treated with dignity and respect. I'm not saying that because James Meredith is a Negro. I'm saying it because *I'm* one."

Remember: *humor doesn't have to overpower your message*. Good cooking is helped by a pinch of salt. It doesn't follow, therefore, that emptying the whole carton into the pot will make a tastier soup.

Chefs have a beautiful expression for that—"Add seasoning to taste." *Add humor to taste*.

Humor should serve a good speech the way a musical accompaniment assists a vocal performance. It highlights, enhances, and complements it. Very few singers would dare to work *a capella*. They need the chords and the counter harmonies to give depth to their own music. The accompaniment makes it easier to listen to the singer. Humor, used sparingly and skillfully, does the same for a speech; it makes it easier to listen to the speaker.

Some of my more argumentative readers may still insist that there are, indeed, speeches where humor is totally inappropriate. I agree. (Surprised?) They're right. I doubt if the President of the United States would open with a funny anecdote before announcing we were declaring war. A judge passing a life sentence on some hapless soul would be well-advised to avoid making any "knock-knock" jokes at that time. (I'm sure you can think of other instances.)

Most of these examples, however, are pronouncements; not speeches. There are people listening, certainly, but what is said is essentially a procedural conveyance of a message. There is no salesmanship or "convincing" being done. The decisions have been made and the announcement is a means of making them publicly official.

A college professor is an example of a speaker who doesn't have to convince his listeners of anything. He does impart knowledge, of course, but whether you believe it or not is not so important, from his point of view, as your learning it first. In fact, he may not even care how well you learn it. The burden is on the student, the listener, not the speaker.

Don't misunderstand. I'm not maligning professors. The good ones do care and do work hard to help their students learn. But they get paid regardless of how well you learn and retain the information and whether you eventually become a prominent lawyer or successful surgeon or not.

Humor can help to get any message across. For those speakers who have to not only transmit information, but also sell it to their listeners and guarantee that it will be accepted and used, humor is a valuable tool.

Comedy Must
Be You

THE FIRST LESSON A YOUNG comedy writer learns is: write for the comic. Being funny is not enough. The material must be witty, but it must also suit the person who is going to deliver it. Otherwise it is totally useless to that performer.

Without considering that important point, a writer could wind up doing nothing but rewrites. Comments come back from performers such as, "This is too jokey," "I don't do puns," "The set-up is too long," "I don't remind people of real problems." Understand, this could all be hilarious and brilliant material. But it's simply wrong for this one entertainer.

I kid about this in my own talks by saying that when I began writing comedy I used to come home from work and talk like the people I worked for. When I wrote for Jim Nabors, I'd sit around the dinner table saying *Gollee*. When I worked with Bill Cosby, I'd do a lot of "Fat Albert" imitations. I spent five years with Carol Burnett and I began dressing like her. I've got *that* pretty much under control now, though. It's down to just the weekends now.

In my travels with the National Speakers Association, I meet many platform performers who say to me, "I can't do comedy." As I've said before in this book, I don't buy that. But they're generally adamant about it. They say, "I've tried and it just doesn't work for me." That I believe. But what they really should be saying is, "I can't do *other people's* comedy."

They will hear a funny story on a record or on television (or heaven forgive them, from another speaker) and then try it during their appearances. *Bomb city!* They'll pick up a joke from a comedy service or a magazine and include it in their performance. *Stinksville!* They may even venture to write some of their own material. *Egg on the face time!* Does this mean the material wasn't funny? No. It was probably right for somebody, but not for them. Remember: Comedy has to be *you*.

We've all enjoyed listening to excellent comedians and we've all suffered through some really bad ones. What makes the difference? If you analyze the kid who bombed, you may find that his material wasn't pitiful; he was. He died on stage because he may have gathered his comedy from here and from there and from this person and that one. He had no real point-of-view. The audience never quite knew who he was or what he was trying to say.

Let's use the example of decorating a room. For it to work, the room has to have a sense of cohesion and a real personality. You can buy all kinds of fine, expensive furniture, but if it doesn't fit together to form an entity, the room can be a disaster. It's the same with humor. Comedy is a very individualistic art. It might seem that whatever is funny is funny, *but it's not*. It might be funny coming from one comedian, but it might merely be amusing coming from someone else.

For example, Joan Rivers and George Burns are both professional entertainers who have honed their individual styles to perfection. They both have excellent acts and use fine material. Yet if we asked them to perform for one night using each other's material, they'd be terrible. Why? Their professionalism remains intact. They both still have the same number of years of experience. The material they'll use is superb. It's the same material that has been getting laughs from audiences all over the world. So what has changed? Simple: They're each doing someone else's act; someone else's comedy characterization. *What comes through is not them.*

Let's try to forget for just a moment that George Burns has been in show business for some eight decades. Let's suppose this was his first appearance. He would have proven funny material, but he would bomb with it. He would come backstage and say, "I can't do comedy."

If so, he would be no more correct in saying that than the many speakers I know who also say it. Not even George Burns can do *other people's* comedy. No one can. But when he does comedy that is *his,* he's scintillating. And the same can be true for those speakers who tell me they can't do comedy.

When you do material that is truly *you, you* can get the acceptance you really want but hardly dared hope for.

Bob Hope has been the nation's jester for about half a century. He gets laughs from most crowds even before he speaks. Phyllis Diller gets roars just for the way she dresses. Jack Benny had one of the most well-defined characterizations in comedy history. His image of stinginess was legendary. His radio show boasted one of the longest sustained laughs of all time with a line that wasn't that funny in itself. But because it was the "miserly" Jack Benny who said it the line worked beautifully—

Imagine Jack walking down a dark street. A man jumps out of an alley and holds a gun on Jack and says, "Your money or your life." We hear only silence from the radio—then some audience laughter. As the laughs die down, the hoodlum repeats, "Your money or your life." Benny says, "I'm thinking. I'm thinking." Two solid minutes of audience laughter followed. The event remains a comedy classic. But the joke worked only because it was purely Jack Benny.

If there were a Hall of Fame for jokes, that one would certainly be in there. But use your imagination again. If that same set-up were done with other stars, the line would have gotten completely different responses. Martha Raye would have said one thing and Danny Thomas still another. Bob Hope would have had a different joke. But only Jack Benny could have gotten the record breaking laugh with the line he used. Remember: *Comedy has to be you.*

An error speakers often make is to force comedy material that they are not comfortable with into their talks. An audience senses this the same way a dog senses that a person is afraid. This tends to create tension. The speaker may become anxious that his or her material is not going over. More tension is produced when the listeners notice how the speaker is reacting; the spiral of anxiety continues to grow.

If you're afraid of a piece of material, drop it. If you're uncomfortable with one of your stories, omit it. But then you may ask, aren't we right back where we started? Doesn't this prove that people do have the right to say, "I've tried humor and I just can't do it"? Not really. Again, what has happened is that they tried to get laughs with other people's material; material that didn't fit them.

How then do you find that style that is right for you? You have to do some soul-searching, some self-analysis, some research and then have courage enough to try new material. It's not automatic.

Some of the great comics of radio and television discovered their comic characters only after years of trial and error. But don't let that frighten you. You're not really trying to make your fame and fortune as a monologist. You just want to liven up your platform presentation. Begin developing your style by some study and analysis.

WHAT KIND OF COMEDY DO YOU LIKE?

List your favorite performers and what you like about them. You may be a Jack Lemmon fan. Jack is a brilliant comedy actor who gets much of his audience reaction using gestures and looks more than words. A gesture, of course, can be as powerful as a statement.

Cataloging your favorite comics may give you a hint to the style of comedy you prefer. There are many different styles and many variations within each style. I'll list a few, but you may come up with others:

ONE LINERS: Bob Hope is the classic example of this style. There's also Will Rogers, Phyllis Diller, Rodney Dangerfield, and Joan Rivers, among others. One-liners are short jokes, usually no more than two or three sentences long.

STORY JOKES: Myron Cohen, Flip Wilson, and Danny Thomas tell these beautifully. These are longer than the one-liner, but they have a strong punch line. They're the kind of gags that begin with something like "These two guys were walking down the street. . . ."

STORIES: Bill Cosby and David Brenner are good examples of exponents of this form of humor. These are not necessarily jokes. They don't aim specifically at the heavy punch line. Rather, they have a comic life all their own. They're funny along the way.

INSULT HUMOR: This is a specialized form of the one-liner that puts somebody down. You can't mention this classification without mentioning Don Rickles as the present master of the form.

It may seem, at first, that this form would be used exclusively by entertainers and would be *verboten* to professional and corporate speakers. It's not true. The "insult" can be used advantageously by speakers. Audiences love to have their own organization, their fellow members as well as their officers kidded. I just did a show where I followed a vice-president of marketing who gave a presentation assisted by a live chimpanzee. When I opened I said, "I'm not upset by this. I've followed monkeys before. But this is the first time I've ever followed one that worked with a live chimp." The audience applauded it. (The vice-president didn't mind because I checked with him before I dared to say it.)

We'll be speaking later on how to use insult humor without truly offending anyone. For now, let's get on with our listings.

PLAYING THE CHARACTERS: The late Lenny Bruce was excellent at this form. It's a story that you not only tell, but actually act out, playing all the parts.

As an example, we may have a speaker talking about hanging out on the street corner when he was a kid and a guy comes out of his house to chase him. The speaker, with different vocal characteristics, now becomes both people. As we say in comedy, it probably goes something like this:

"Hey punk, how 'bout you quit hanging around my house, huh?" "What 'cha gonna do if I don't?" "How 'bout I hit you so hard I give your whole family a black and blue mark?"—and so on.

NONSENSE: Professor Irwin Corey is probably the most notable practitioner of this form although there are others such as the late Al Kelly who was superb at double-talk. Norm Crosby, who weaves some nonsensical malaprops into his funny stories, is another master of nonsense.

Again, this may seem like a style that would be useless on the platform, but I once saw a gentleman do a presentation of this type that was well received by a group of businessmen. This speaker made almost his entire presentation using redundancies. He said things like, "I once talked with three old ladies who were not only ancient, but also getting on in years." Or "I think the fact that I'm only going to say things once bears repeating."

PUT-ONS: Foster Brooks, the comic who plays such a great drunk, began his career as a put-on artist. I once saw him introduced at halftime at a basketball game as the commissioner of the league. People were stunned that this important official dared show up tipsy; then they realized it was a gag.

It's a popular form at conventions and business meetings and does provide good comedy relief.

As you make your list of favorite comedians you may notice that some of them combine two or more of these comic elements. Other favorites may use a style that is not mentioned here. However, as you go through your list you may begin to discover a pattern that will show you a comedy style that you will like and will want to adopt.

WHAT KIND OF COMEDY CAN *YOU* DO?

It's possible that the comedy you most enjoy is out of your range. Suppose, for example, you love to listen to Rich Little. Unless you're a gifted mimic, it might be suicidal for you to attempt to do the voices he does.

I enjoy Don Rickles. Yet there is no way that I could stand in front of a crowd and get laughs with his comedy style. His manner is aggressive. He attacks his audience. I simply don't have a forceful enough stage presence to permit that. Some of his lines may work for me, but only if delivered with a totally different style.

It fascinates me in working with top professional comics how well they recognize their own limitations. This is not to imply that they're not talented. They are. However, they know their shortcomings, avoid them, and thus emphasize their strengths. Many performers who seem multifaceted on the TV screen are really rather limited. Some will not do one-line jokes. They're simply uncomfortable with them. Others will not tell long story jokes. There are those who refuse to do dialects. Some want no humor that requires any physical movement. This doesn't mean that a performer who refuses to do one-line material is opposed to it. It simply means he doesn't do it well, and, therefore, refuses to do it professionally.

How do we know what is in our range? Investigate and study. Can you snap off a one-liner and get laughs with it? Or do you get groans? If you're always kidded about telling bad jokes, it might be because you tell jokes badly. If you do an impression of Humphrey Bogart and a listener points a finger at you and shouts triumphantly, "Edward G. Robinson," then mimicry is not your strong suit? If you tell a story with an Irish brogue and someone asks, "That's a funny story, but why did it have to be two Chinese?" you're probably not a dialectician.

Much of this is not so much a matter of skill as it is of confidence. Some professionals are dynamite in sketches, but back away from a one-line joke. They're afraid of the form. Consequently, they don't deliver it well. It's the proverbial self-fulfilling prophecy.

You, as a speaker, must find the style that you can do and that you have faith in. It's what you'll deliver best.

WHAT KIND OF COMEDY DO YOU *LIKE* TO DO?

Another thought to consider is what performing style you prefer. You may be like me; I'm a good audience. There are many forms of humor that I enjoy. You may be multi-talented, able to deliver many different styles of humor. The question, then, is which one do you favor?

This is important because humor is so "mental." All other things being equal, you'll probably do a better job with that style that you like most. Why? Who knows? I experience the same phenomenon playing tennis. There's a cross-court shot that I hit often because I like it and I have confidence in it. I can make it fairly frequently (which, for me, is good). There may be times when I have a choice between two shots—let's say, a down-the-line passing shot or my cross-court shot. The latter is the more difficult and because I prefer the harder shot, I may make it with more consistency. I'll blow the easier shot because, in my mind, I'm hesitant about it.

WHAT KIND OF COMEDY DO YOU DO *NATURALLY?*

Every person I know has tried for laughs when the situation warranted it. I don't necessarily mean just from the platform, but also with friends, over dinner, nursing a drink or two, somewhere, somehow, sometime or another, everyone has tried for the big ad-lib.

Study those humor attempts and you'll see that they generally form a pattern. One type of comedy or another will dominate.

One gentleman I know always does simple but very effective jokes that are a put-down of his own talents: "When I first started selling cars a man came in and asked what kind of car he should buy. I helped him as best I could. I told him to buy a green one." Later he was offered a job with a sprinkler company. The man asked: "What do you know about sprinklers?" This gentleman said, "I know they *phfft-phfft-phfft* squirt water like that."

This man's conversation is full of such lines, and so is his platform presentation, which is powerful. He blends a type humor that he does naturally along with a message that he delivers with intensity. It's something to behold.

As a writer, I'm always amazed at the metamorphosis that occurs in the middle of writing a screenplay, teleplay, or novel. At first, one struggles with the plot and the characterizations. What is going to happen and when and how and so on? The writer gets into the plot and the characters begin to come alive. Then the writer can't wait to get to the typewriter to find out what these characters are going to say next. The author almost becomes part of the audience, or at best a translator, who sits in his office and listens to the characters speak and then puts it into readable form.

Once you find your comfortable, natural comedy style, you won't have to hunt around for material or for ghost writers. The mood and the personality that you generate will inspire the lines. You'll utter them, and you may even be mystified as to where they came from.

Professional comics offer great examples of this point. When they're forced to ad-lib, most of them do it very well. Probably, though, if you gave them the straight line and sat them down before a typewriter, nothing would get on paper. However, stand them up before an audience and feed them the set-up, and their "character" takes over; it pulls inspiration from the ether and pronounces the funny line. This is the humor that comes naturally.

I've experienced this myself as a speaker and it never fails to amaze me. I can know that a presentation is going to be made to me, so I try to create a funny retort. Nothing happens. Then I stand there, and in the exultation of the moment, someone or something extracts the right response from my brain. When you do the humor that comes naturally to you, it will take over for you under pressure.

Once you study, investigate, and formulate your style of humor, how do you work it into your speech?

INTRODUCE NEW MATERIAL GRADUALLY:

It's deadly to write a piece of material, rewrite it, study it, be satisfied with it, and then throw it all into your speech. It's much safer to *ease* into it. Presumably, you have a talk that is working quite well. Good. Now you want to introduce some humor. Better. Don't add too much at one time, though.

This may be a seat-of-the-pants operation and you'll have to trust your own judgment, but add only just enough humor (or a little less) so that if it fails to work at that moment it won't destroy the entire talk.

(Watching those ski jumping contests on TV mystifies me. Those folks hurl themselves off a platform and fly through the air for what seems like a mile, then touch down ever so gracefully on the slope. How do they bring themselves to do that the *first* time? Surely, they start with smaller jumps.)

Add humor to your talk with care and caution. Then it won't be a lethal dose if it fails. Later, you may try again with the material that didn't work. You may change it slightly and give it a third try. If it still falters, drop it.

A percentage of your material will work. Some of it will work so well it will surprise you. Leave that in.

You can see what's happening. You're gradually building up your humor content with very little jeopardy to the effectiveness of your basic speech. Over a period of time you'll have the same powerful talk augmented with solid, proven humor.

This trial and error method, used wisely (that means sparingly at first), may not only build up your humor repertoire, but also dictate the style of comedy that you should use. Over many months, you'll probably begin to discover that certain types of gags work for you and others don't. That should tell you something, right? Once you notice that a particular style is successful for you, you'll gather more confidence in using it, and consequently, use it more effectively each time.

TRY OUT MATERIAL BEFORE USING IT

If you have a piece of material, whether it's a one-liner or a story or a piece of business, try it out among your friends and acquaintances. Sneak it into the lunch conversation. Tell it to the family over dinner. Give it a go at a party. You'll be able to tell from the response you get whether people enjoy it or not.

Someone once asked Doctor Charles Jarvis, one of the funniest speakers on the platform circuit and a great student of humor, how he got the courage to try out a new joke on an audience the first time. He said, "There is never any first time." Before he would tell a story in public, he would first tell it a hundred times or so in private. After he had polished it in that way, he would then introduce it on the platform. By that time it was ready to be told to his audience.

However, not all stories or gags lend themselves to that policy. Some of them make no sense unless done only from the podium. For example, I just saw an excellent program presented at the National Speakers Association winter workshop in Reno, Nevada, by Dr. Loretta Malandro. The presentation was entitled: "First and Lasting Impressions," and illustrated for the speakers how we project different attitudes to our audiences in nonverbal ways. Loretta would present different theories and then call on members of the audience to act these out. It was hilarious and very enlightening. But it needed audience participation. There was no way this material could be tested by three friends over dinner.

Incidentally, Dr. Malandro talked to me after the presentation and asked if she should hire someone to write jokes to make her speech even funnier. I told her that what she did had just the right humor content and that it was *her* humor. It was natural: It belonged in this production. If she changed her style to try to fit in book jokes, or gags written by someone who didn't know the subject as well, it could be awkward and might detract from the speech. [I tell you this just to reinforce what we've said before: Humor is not necessarily jokes; it's also an attitude.]

Now, back to the point. If you can try out humorous material privately, do it. It will tell you whether it's funny or not. It will give you confidence in the material. It will allow you time to polish your presentation and perhaps add a few ad-libs before you perform it publicly.

IMITATE YOUR FAVORITES:

Imitation is the sincerest form of flattery. It's also the cheapest form of thievery. Whatever, it's a great way to develop your own comedy characterization. Does that sound a touch unethical? It isn't. Johnny Carson admits that his boyhood idol was Jack Benny. Benny's influence is still visible in Carson's mannerisms. A few years ago, at a testimonial banquet, Woody Allen showed a film he'd made as a tribute to Bob Hope. In the film, Allen intercut scenes from his own films and scenes from Hope classics to show how much the Bob Hope *persona* influenced Allen's own. The reader can surely cite several other examples.

These copycats are not branded with a "P" burned into their forehead for "Plagiarist." Why? Because everyone in the business does it. Practically every great star has been influenced by another great performer and traces of that person's idol are often apparent in the student: Frank Sinatra begat Bobby Darin who begat Wayne Newton.

Then why aren't all the performers we see today just carbon copies of the ones whom we first saw years earlier? Because there is a gradual change in each new arrival, just as there will be in you as a speaker. At first new people simply imitate. Then they get comfortable with their performances and gradually introduce more and more of their own personalities into them. When I first saw Richard Pryor years ago on the Ed Sullivan show, I thought he was a copy of Bill Cosby. He was. But not today. Now he really is *Richard Pryor*. There's more of Johnny Carson in Johnny Carson today than there is of Jack Benny. In the beginning, it was probably just the other way around. Although most folks will argue that Woody Allen bears no similarity to Bob Hope, Woody himself says that he does.

When you emulate someone, whether it's a professional comedian or a speaker, you're building on a solid, already successful base. You're picking up good habits. Pros are well-schooled in the fundamentals. It's like imitating a good musician. If you can hit the same notes he hits, you're using fundamental musical principles. You may not know that you're playing chords built on the first, second, and fifth notes of the major key, but you are although you may have no technical knowledge of the mathematics of music.

Then from this solid base, you begin to introduce your own personality and your own nuances. What was originally a carbon copy performance may eventually bear no obvious resemblance to the original at all.

Some caution is advisable: (It was discussed earlier in this chapter, but bears repeating.) Be sure that you have the skills *necessary to imitate*. Don't try to parrot Don Rickles if you don't have that brash manner and quick wit.

Though comedy must be personal, imitation is recommended. It's not plagiarism, or something to be ashamed of doing. In fact, it's almost impossible to introduce humor into your routine without being influenced by someone. Just as surely, it's practically impossible to continue your imitation without gradually transforming your style from your mentor to yourself.

The above guidelines are included for your reference. Basically, however, the comedy that you like, feel comfortable with, and can present in the most relaxed and confident manner will be right for you.

HUMOR IS NOT NECESSARILY "JOKES"

It's important to remember that humor is not necessarily jokes. Although we defined a joke as "anything that makes people laugh," we also said humor is an attitude. The conclusion, then, is: Speakers don't have to make people laugh in order to add humor to their talks.

You don't have to generate belly laughs to be humorous in your lectures. You simply have to relax your audience and establish a spirit of fun with them. You're bringing a perspective and a balance to your lecture. The hint of humor that you introduce is telling your audience that you're aware of exactly how important your content is. Humor is not only jokes, stories, anecdotes, and such. It is also the attitude or spirit of fun, perspective, and balance that colors everything you say.

Billy Graham is a preacher who has a great sense of humor, yet I can't recall any jokes he's ever told in his sermons. It's not important that he do so; the humor is evident in everything he preaches.

Humor adds confidence to a speaker. When you step on a podium or approach a lectern, the good speaker projects the image that he or she belongs there. Before one word is uttered, every person in the auditorium can sense that they'd better listen because this speaker has something to say.

You shouldn't have to verbalize this. You don't open your programs by saying, "I belong up here and you belong down there. I'm going to speak and you're going to listen. If you don't, you're losing out because I'm a very good orator." This speaker would be talking to the backs of people's heads as they rushed for the exits.

Self-reliance is an aura that you project. You bring it with you to the platform. If you have to tell people you have it, you don't have it.

A certain style of humor is something that you develop within yourself and that becomes part of everything you say. It's a feeling you have about yourself, your audience, and your subject. *It's an attitude!*

When is this attitude most evident? When good friends gather together. That's when jokes (even insults) and retorts fly all over the place. So if you can see each audience as a group of friends, and treat them that way, you'll never have any trouble bringing just the right amount of good humor to your speech.

Humor Is Work

WHEN I STARTED WRITING comedy, I had the opportunity to study a master of the craft night after night: Sammy Davis. I was working in a nightclub then and watched Sammy perform for two solid weeks. I could easily eavesdrop when people discussed the show on the way out of the club. Since Sammy uses quite a bit of comedy in his act, one comment I often heard was, "That Sammy Davis can really ad-lib, can't he?"

It was true. He did ad-lib well. He ad-libbed the same lines, in the same spot in the show night after night. Don't misunderstand me. That's a compliment to the performer. It shows that the act is well-conceived, well-rehearsed, and well-performed.

It's an ironic reality for writers that when material is written well and expertly performed, no one knows that we exist. But our job is to make the star look natural. The words we put in his mouth should sound as if they were just inspired by the great "Ad-libber in the Sky." Indeed, sometimes we do our job so well that even the performer believes he just thought of them.

Good comedy should look easy. Bing Crosby used to say that the secret of his success was that he sang so effortlessly that everyone thought they sounded like him in the shower. Comedy, done well, is deceptive, too. It looks so easy and natural that it seems as if there is hardly any effort involved in making it happen.

This illusion is often so deceiving that some performers believe it. Television writers and producers have to be wary of that. We want the lines to be written, learned and rehearsed so that we can see what does and what doesn't work. With dependable feedback we can repair most flaws before the show is taped. Occasionally, though, we'll get a comedy performer who believes that comedy really is easy. "Just give me a few props and a basic outline and I'll be brilliant when the cameras are on. Trust me," this person will say.

It's deadly. One percent of the time you'll get brilliance. The other 99 percent of the time you get a comic with egg on his face.

Certainly there are comics who are superb ad-lib artists. Johnny Carson is one. He's unbeatable when he's behind that desk and talking to his TV show guests. The format of his late night show permits that. If you analyzed his shows, you'd see that the humor content is low. That's not a put-down; it's an observation. His is a talk show and doesn't need one laugh following the other. With Carson's skill at orchestrating an interview, the laughs come frequently enough.

However, when Carson is booked into Las Vegas or is in concert, he doesn't depend on his top-of-the-head comedy to carry him through those shows. He has a solid evening of well-written, precisely edited monologue material on hand. He's honed it, polished it, and rehearsed it, so that it will move like clockwork when he gets center stage.

I have a dog at home who was an independent, head-strong puppy. She did what she wanted, when she wanted, and, unfortunately, where she wanted. Her residency in our domicile was very much in jeopardy because of her stubbornness. I finally called in some expert help. A professional trainer showed us what to do to train her and work with her. It was still a contest of wills. But the dog realized, after weeks of workouts, that she might as well give in and do things the way we wanted them done.

Today she's a beautifully behaved creature. She doesn't bolt out the front door. She sits on command. She walks along obediently on her leash. She even retreats to her own special part of the house when told to "place." Guests always comment when they see how well she behaves. "What a good dog," they'll say. They don't understand she's not a "good" dog; she's a well-rehearsed dog.

Perhaps my writer's prejudice against performers prompted that comparison, but it is valid. Effort is always required to achieve the appearance of effortlessness.

You, however, are not trying to become comedians and get your own show on television. (Or are you? If so, I can recommend a great comedy writer.) As speakers, we are only trying to introduce a dash of humor to our speeches or improve the quality of the humor that is already there. Again, as speakers, we don't have to depend on comedy alone for our success. We already have a speech that says what we want to say. Now we want to spice up that talk with wit—make it more palatable. What we're dealing with is "social humor."

There's a two-headed dragon waiting for us. One head says that comedy is easy; there's no need to work at it. Just *sneak* it into a presentation whenever the mood strikes you. The other head says that since we're only adding a dash of humor, there's no need to worry, fret, or even work at it. Both heads are liars.

Comedy is not easy. Read some of Woody Allen's prose or listen to some of his stand-up routines. Listen to recordings of Lenny Bruce's nightclub bits. In all of these you'll discover that the comedy comes out of hard work. Not *any* word can be used for comic value; only the *right* word works.

As speakers, we do have to worry, fret and work at our comedy even though we're only adding a little bit. Comedy is strange. Done well, it's exciting and exhilarating. Done poorly, it's disastrous. Doing comedy is like jumping across a well. You either do it in one jump or you don't do it at all. There's no such thing as jumping across a well in two jumps.

PREPARATION: HUMOR'S ANTI-FREEZE

I love the story that was told at a writer's conference about a man in ancient Rome who was thrown to the lions. This man was noted for his skill at using his wits to escape from dangerous situations. The lions had been deprived of food for some time and were very hungry. Sensing the imminent kill, the crowds cheered as the big cats circled their prey. Then the victim whispered in the ear of one of the lions—the one that seemed to be leading the others. The lion immediately backed away with its tail between its legs, sat in a corner and cowered. While the animal shook with fright, the emperor declared the man free. However, he wanted to know how the man had conquered the beasts. Later, in the emperor's private chambers, the man confessed his secret. He had said to the hungry lion, "You can devour me if you want, but right after you finish eating, they're going to ask you to stand up and say a few words."

It's a traumatic experience to speak in public. You'd be well advised to be prepared before you try it. Since you have to expend the effort on the speech anyway, why not expend just a bit more effort and make that speech better with well prepared humor.

Listed below are some of the areas that will require application:

- gathering your material
- researching your audience
- preparation
- improving your material
- developing your style

GATHERING MATERIAL

Dreams of frustration are common experiences for anyone involved with a particular line of work. Pilots have told me they have recurring nightmares of taking off and immediately encountering obstacles such as trucks parked on the runway, wires that run across the take-off path, high towers, and the like. My writing partner was a drummer and told me of his dreams where he would be on the bandstand for a big show, would get the downbeat, hit the drum and find that it was made of soft dough.

One dream that haunted me for some time was one in which I would be at a party or some prestigious gathering. I would be called to the microphone ready to dazzle everyone with my wit. It was a great emotional charge as I stood up while the audience applauded. The applause would continue while I walked *arrogantly* up to that microphone. Then I would signal for the cheering to quiet down (it always takes quite a while—after all, it is *my* dream). But when I finally had their undivided attention, I couldn't think of a damned thing to say. What a horrifying nightmare to stand there in the spotlight and go completely lamebrained. I don't mean I couldn't think of anything witty to say, or even anything clever. I couldn't think of *anything*, period.

Today that dream still haunts me. Anytime I go to some banquet where there is even a remote chance that I might be called on to "say a few words," I carry a little cheat sheet in my pocket with five or six key words on it. I don't ever want to get caught up there with vacuum of the brain.

Neither do you. If there is one thing that people expect from a speaker, it's for words to come out of his mouth. It's the least we can do for our audiences. So your first task will be gathering material.

(We'll have chapters elaborating on this later. We'll discuss ways and means for you to find humor or create it yourself. For now, just be aware that it must be done.)

What one-liner will emphasize the point you want to make best? Where can you find a story that illustrates your message? Does a poem exist that will amuse your listeners while illustrating your theme? None of this can be left to chance. You can't depend on having an example pop into your brain as you lecture. It doesn't happen that way. In fact, it usually happens that while you're trying to think of something like that you can forget where you were in the speech. All of this has to be done before you step onto the podium.

Jack Benny was once honored with a surprise dinner by his fellow funnymen. Typical of this "roast-type" of banquet, Jack's friends bombarded him with good-natured insults—both funny and devastating. When Jack's turn came, he stepped up to the mike and said, "None of you would have said those things if my writers were here."

RESEARCHING YOUR AUDIENCE

We've discussed many reasons why humor is used in a talk. Each bit of humor, though, has only one purpose—to get laughs from an audience. If that is indeed our purpose, then we should find out what will make a particular audience laugh.

It's pointless to tell a joke in Denver, be greeted with silence and confused stares, and then berate the listeners because that same joke worked last week in Seattle.

You must be aware that there is only *one* audience—the one you're facing right now. You can't get laughs or applause from last week's group. Next week's group hasn't heard you yet. You've got to impress the people sitting out front *right now* and you'd better learn what will make *them* happy. Again, that doesn't mean that a speaker's primary concern is, necessarily, to amuse or cater to the audience. Some facets of your lecture may be meant to irritate them and for good reason. I'm discussing only the humor content of a talk. If you include it at all, you include it to get a certain response from an audience. Therefore (one hopes) *it should get that response.*

The more you can learn about your listeners, the better your humor should work. I always ask the people who book me if there is anything in particular that is being talked about in their organization. If there is, what is it and what is being said about it? I also ask who the people are in the organization who are well known, and so on.

I just spoke to a group in Hawaii and in response to one of my questions, the booker told me that they had a program—I'll call it the "level 20" program—that was disastrous. It didn't work. It never worked. Before it was finally abandoned, it had annoyed almost everyone who worked for the company. I doublechecked to make sure everyone in the audience would understand that point. This gentleman assured me they would. So that became my opening. Here's how I used it:

I took out a speech and apologized for having to read it. Then I said, "I normally don't read a speech, but I had a great talk all prepared for this occasion and then in packing, I made a mistake. I brought my 'level 20' speech instead."

That probably doesn't make any sense to you. It made no sense to me. But it got howls of laughter and a burst of applause from this audience. Nice way to begin a talk.

In doing material for Bob Hope's appearances, we always do some advance work. Are there any famous local sports rivalries? Where is the local "lovers' lane?" What are the good eating places? What are the bad eating places? Are there any nicknames we should be aware of?

We did a show at the Naval Academy at Annapolis once and discovered many facts as well as traditions about the place. One fact we learned was that there is no "lovers' lane" on campus. When Bob talked to guest star Brooke Shields, we had the following exchange:

BROOKE
Last night one of the underclassmen took me to "lovers' lane."
BOB
Wait a minute. There's no "lovers' lane" here at Annapolis.
BROOKE
There is now.

It's not the most inventive gag in the world, but this gang loved it. It was about *them*. It was about *their* campus.

You needn't be as exhaustive in your research as Bob Hope is because he's doing nothing but comedy. Nevertheless, the little bit of humor that you and I add to our talks will be more productive if we take some time to learn more about the people we'll be working to.

PREPARATION

The first time I ever spoke in public was at a retirement banquet for a friend. There was no lectern in the hall, just a stand microphone. I had to read the speech and was as nervous as anyone could be. (Because I knew I'd be scared to death, I rehearsed this performance for about a month, repeating the talk into a mirror several times each evening.)

The talk went beautifully. People complimented me afterward. One remark stands out: "How could your voice sound so good," one co-worker asked, "when your hands were shaking so much?" That's what preparation can do for you. No matter how nervous you may be in front of an audience, at least you'll be able to talk as if you're cool, calm and confident.

Everyone I know who does comedy prepares. It's much too delicate an art form to trust to the inspiration of the moment. The words, the mannerisms, the sentence structures—all are important. All should be practiced and perfected long before your introduction begins.

I once worked with the master innovator, Jonathan Winters. At our first meeting, Jonathan regaled us with several hours of top-of-the-head comedy. He just spoke and spoke and spoke and all of it was funny.

Later, during the course of rehearsals, we'd come upon Winters telling his stories to other people in the cast and crew. They were helpless with laughter just as we were. However, each time I heard the story, it was practically the same. In his own way, Jonathan Winters had mentally "prepared" these stories. Even creative comedians, like Winters, instinctively prepare their material. You should, too.

IMPROVING YOUR MATERIAL

If in retelling one of his stories, Winters comes across a genuine ad-lib that works, you can bet that the next time he tells that tale that gag will be in there in just that exact spot. Any little touch of humor can be improved. It can be lengthened. Usually, however, it's improved by making it shorter. The point is that it should never lie dormant.

Many speakers I know tape all of their appearances and study the tapes. Pieces are removed from slower sections. This enhances the effectiveness of the material that remains.

The greats never stop analyzing their style and content. Early in the radio days of the *Burns and Allen* show, George Burns was concerned about slipping ratings. He analyzed the situation and told the writers that they had fallen into a trap. They were trying too hard to make Gracie funny, instead of simply allowing her character to be unconsciously funny. This was the secret of her real charm and appeal. She should never seem aware that she was saying anything funny. As Burns said, "We've loused up our formula for Gracie."

It must have gotten some good results because the two of them went on for many successful years. Even in later years, George Burns was still improving the quality of the comedy and the show they did together. When their material began to seem stale and the ratings began to slip drastically again, George studied the situation and once more discovered the problem and the solution. By this time George and Gracie had grown older; they had two children. However, they were still doing young boy-and-girl jokes. The audience wouldn't accept it. George said, "You can't do that. You've got to be your age in show business. You can't be any younger than you are supposed to be, nor any older."

They were no longer a young married couple touring in vaudeville. They were middle-aged parents with growing children. Their material had to reflect that.

The humor you inject into your talks may need your constant awareness. Did it work this time? Why? Did it bomb this time? Why? By constant review, the material gets better and better. It'll never get perfect, but damn near it.

DEVELOPING YOUR STYLE

You'll have to experiment to find the comedy style that works best for you and with which you're most comfortable. Don't feel put out by that. Every comedian has had to do it. Jack Benny in vaudeville, though successful, was not the same polished performer he would be years later as a movie, radio and TV star. Jackie Gleason had to search for the characters that worked for him. Lily Tomlin evolved into a great comedic performer. Phyllis Diller cried after her first performance— and quite a few more times after that one. She was always brilliantly funny, but she had to work to find the right vehicle for her brilliance.

No one escapes this. It takes time and experimentation. It will also take a lot of work. However, all the effort put into your humor will pay better dividends.

Developing your comedy style is the key to any success you'll have in using humor. Comedy is not jokes and material. It's also character.

PART TWO: GATHERING HUMOR

A jest's prosperity lies in the
ear of he who hears it, not in
the tongue of him that makes
it.

William Shakespeare

Where Do I Get My Material?

"IN THE BEGINNING WAS THE WORD."

We who are members of the Writers Guild are defensive about the script. We're paranoid about directors who get writing credits for screenplays. We get annoyed by actors who claim that the character they play is their creation. "I created this person," they like to say. But what did the director really direct? Words that were written on paper. The actor "created" his character from the dialogue and descriptive material that didn't exist before a writer wrote it all out for him.

Sometimes in our enthusiasm to protect the writer in this jungle of credit seekers we become the culprit rather than the victim. An article was reprinted in the *Writers Guild Newsletter* on this very problem. It complained of authors who are both neglected and ignored by the industry. At the end the editors gave the readers the name of the magazine that granted permission for the reprint, but nowhere did the newsletter mention the author's name.

All activity does begin with the script—the written word—the material. The designer can't build a set until he reads the description of it in the script. The actor can't emote until he has the words with which to emote. A director can't say "Fade in" until he knows what he's fading in to.

I'm somewhat more liberal than many of my writing colleagues. I sometimes say that I've been writing for 25 years and I've never written anything funny in my life. Most of my associates take that statement at face value. I qualify it. My writing doesn't become funny until someone breathes some life into it. It's all just words until Bob Hope gives it some zing and tops it off with that delightful sneer of his. It's just dialogue until Carol Burnett gets into the goofy costume and funny wig and makes it vibrate. It's only some stage directions until Tim Conway gets that dopey look on his face and pulls laughs from an audience. True comedy is a combination of good writing and skillful performance. You can't have one without the other.

Speakers, though, needn't get involved in this debate. They usually write and deliver their own material. For them, the written text and the performance are generally one and the same. Speakers know what they want to say and they go out and say it.

But I come along now and tell speakers to put humor in their talks. They may say right back to me, "Okay, where do I get my material?" Just like everyone else in show business their first question is, "Where's the script?"

The speaker will probably have to generate his or her own comedy material. Below are several possible sources:

> Listening to others who tell funny stories
> Joke books and services
> Write your own
> Hire a writer

LISTENING TO OTHERS

Before we get into the how-to's as well as the pros and cons of this method, let me discuss the ethics of it. I don't want to be listed in history books as the father of mass plagiarism.

There was a story about several third-rate comics working some minor clubs in New York. While lunching at a deli, one comic asked another if he had seen Jackie Jackson, (we'll call him that) the new talent. The other comic looked up from his pastrami on rye and said, "That jerk! You know what he did? He stole my Lenny Bruce routine."

One thief accusing another thief of stealing something that he already stole? Yet speakers will often do that. They'll read a joke in *Reader's Digest,* or take any old joke and put it in their talk and say, "That's my story."

I maintain that a story belongs to anyone who wants to use it. You don't have to give credit nor do you have to apologize to anyone for using it.

I'm not the complete Jesse James of comedy, though. The basic story—beginning, middle and punch line—may be available to all, but the embellishments usually are not. In other words, if a comic takes an old story and adds something to it, thereby enlarging on it and making it totally his own, then you and I may not have the right to "borrow" those alterations. Those elements should belong to the person who created them.

Likewise, though it might be ethical, it wouldn't be wise to "borrow" a story that has become associated with any one performer. It would only make you look bad. For instance, a very funny humorist I quoted earlier, Charles "Doc" Jarvis, tells something called "the bird story." (It's too long and involved to repeat here; besides, it wouldn't have the same vitality on paper. You just have to hear "Doc" tell it.) Most professional speakers have heard it and know it. It's so familiar to them that it's known simply as "the bird story." Doc didn't create it, but he perfected it. It's now his story. Trying to steal it would be foolhardy. Doc tells it so well that it is the most amusing coming from his lips. If another speaker felt compelled to retell it, full credit should be given to Charlie Jarvis.

Now that I've salved my conscience, let's talk about how you can gather material from listening to other speakers and comedians either in person or from records and tapes. You hear a joke, you like it, and you put it into your routine; and that's okay. However, I implore you that when lifting a joke or a story, that you try to add some of your own flavor to it. Change something about the joke that will make it more your own.

In a later chapter, we'll go further into the "how" of doing that. For now, let me just illustrate what I mean and then move on to other advantages to be found in listening for material.

I once heard a joke that I liked. I had heard it before, but hearing it again reminded me that it might fit into my performance. I think you'll be able to recognize the basic story:

"It's fun to speak to a group like this because I meet many new friends, as I've done today. But I also meet a lot of old friends, too.

Like, last year I was voted Upper Darby's man of the year. (This generally gets some chuckles—the name sounds funny to those who aren't familiar with it.) Now you see, that's one place in this talk where you're not supposed to laugh.

I was voted Upper Darby's Man of the Year, and it's not an easy award to win. The first three bribes I sent them weren't enough.

Upper Darby is my hometown. It's right outside of Philadelphia and they did have this banquet for me. It was very nice. A lot of my friends and relatives were invited.

At this banquet was a woman who taught me in the fifth grade. She was *92* years old. Now I must confess, when she taught me in the fifth grade, she looked 92 then, too.

She was a schoolteacher all her life and had never been married. There was a rumor running around the hall that she had written into her will that she didn't want any men pallbearers at her funeral. Since I was the guest of honor, I took some liberties. I said, "Miss Roan, is it true that you've written in your will that you don't want any men pallbearers?" She said, "Yes, Gene, it is." I took further liberties and said, "Why?" She said, "Gene, the bastards never took me out when I was alive, I'll be damned if they'll do it when I'm dead."

That story always works. In fact, the laughs generally start before I ever complete the punch line. Most of my listeners swear it's true. Why? Because I've surrounded it with true material about myself. I've taken a standard joke and put it into a situation in which it might well have happened. The important point is that the original story was altered and made more "my story."

More on that later. Now let's consider additional reasons for listening to others.

Other people's stories can remind you of some of your own. Have you ever been to a party and couldn't think of a single joke to break the ice? Then someone else told one. That reminded you of a totally different story. This exchange could continue all night. At the end of the evening, you, who couldn't remember a single joke, told 14.

That's what can happen when you listen to another humorist. He tells a story about visiting a doctor. A similar thing happened to you at your dentist's office. It's not the same story, but you would never have recalled it without first listening to the doctor tale.

Their stories may prompt parallel tales of your own. I once heard a story about a man who was refused a room at a hotel. They had overbooked and were sending people with confirmed reservations to a hotel across town. This gentleman adamantly refused and was eventually given a room. Of course, the telling of the tale is more amusing than the plot outline. But while listening to it, I remembered a very similar incident when I was complaining in a department store that a sweeper that I bought should have come with a package of attachments. I argued and fought and got in to see the manager and eventually won my case. Then as I was leaving, smugly enjoying my victory against city hall, I noticed that I had the wrong model number.

These two stories are basically the same, yet audiences would not easily recognize the similarity.

You may be able to convert a story you like to a similar one. Almost any story that you hear can be redone in different circumstances, but with the same beginning, middle, and end. I once read a book about Hollywood in which two writers, Ben Hecht and Charles MacArthur, took a screenplay, *Gunga Din,* to a studio and asked that it be produced. The studio executive read the script and said, "No, I did this story last year. It was called *Front Page.* Both screenplays were by the same authors.

This sounded like a joke to me until I watched both pictures again. (*Gunga Din* did get done after all.) In *Front Page* a reporter is trying to quit his job to get married and go into another business. His editor tries everything to keep him at the paper. In *Gunga Din* a sergeant is trying to leave the service to get married and go into another occupation. The senior sergeant, however, is trying everything possible to keep him in the Army. The plots are basically the same. The settings are different.

On the *Carol Burnett Show*, we used this device often to generate new story ideas. For instance, we did one sketch that was very successful. It involved Tim Conway and Harvey Korman surrounded by enemy soldiers. Harvey decided to act as a decoy to lure the enemy into the open field. On a given signal Tim was to fire the cannon. Well, Tim could never get the cannon to operate. The cannonball was too large— he had no match—nothing worked. Weeks later we tried to do the same sketch in a different setting. Tim and Ken Berry were in a log cabin surrounded by hostile Indians. Ken would lure them into the open, and Tim was to roll a barrel of dynamite down the field to destroy the tribe. The barrel was too big to fit out the window—he couldn't light the wick—and so on.

Same basic idea; two different sketches. (Incidentally, the second one didn't work as well.)

You may get ideas on what to talk about. A friend of mine writes for Johnny Carson. I asked him if that was demanding work since it had to be turned out each day. He said, "It's not the writing that's difficult; it's finding topics to write about."

Listening to other performers might inspire us to do completely different material on similar topics.

For instance, I once heard Rosita Perez, a fine platform performer who combines music with inspirational messages, do a story about how she listened to an expert tell her how to improve her married life. The tale is hilarious. Though I could never borrow that story from her, it made me think that there must be similar occurrences in my own marriage that could be embellished, perhaps enlarged on, and then written into a funny vignette.

You'll learn what others are doing to add humor to their talks. Earlier we talked about different styles and forms of comedy. That was simply a general list. There are many variations of comedy. Only by listening to what others are saying and doing can you expand your awareness of what's happening around you. Each time you think you've got every comedy form classified, you'll discover another variation.

I once heard a business speaker give a sales motivation speech in the way a "fire and brimstone" preacher might deliver it. It got all of the important precepts across to the audience; it was entertaining; and it would be remembered for a long time.

This gave me the idea of lecturing as if I were General Patton talking to his troops. I could also "be" a Marine Corps Drill Instructor. An absent-minded professor might be a great character to use to talk to college kids. These characterization ideas were triggered by listening to that one speaker who turned the idea of delivering a sales talk as a sermon into a successful tactic.

JOKE BOOKS AND SERVICES

There are many joke books available in the libraries and in stores and several newsletters as well that offer comedy material. It would be difficult to try to list them all here. Besides, there's a fringe benefit to tracking down these books for yourself: You'll generally find more and better titles than I could have offered you in the first place.

In upcoming chapters, we'll talk about ways to tailor your material from these joke books and other sources and services. At this time let's touch on the advantages found in using them:

Most joke books are indexed by subject. Therefore, they can be quick references when you need some one-liners or stories to illustrate specific points for specific subjects.

For example, let's suppose I want a joke or story to tell to a group of salespeople. I grab a joke book and turn to the section marked "Salespeople" where I can quickly find gems like these that I might be able to use:

> "A really good salesman is one who can sell two milking machines to a farmer with only one cow—and then take the cow as a down payment."

> "A saleslady in a hat shop gushed, 'That's a darling hat. Really, it makes you look ten years younger.' The customer retorted, 'Then I don't want it. I can't afford to put on ten years every time I take off my hat.' "

I don't know if these are the best jokes on the subject or not. But if you need them in a hurry, you can find them quickly if you've got a joke book or two in your library.

The books and services will give you plenty to choose from. It astounds me how anyone can compile such a bulk of material. But they do it. One book alone boasts 10,000 jokes, toasts, and stories between its covers.

However, such abundance can also be a disadvantage. Most of the material in joke books is not top quality stuff—at least, not for you. It's not the kind of humor that you can usually use in your speech. Consequently, you may have a library of material, but you may not be able to use most of it.

I rarely use joke books. I make my money writing original material for comics. And as I've said, it's almost impossible to turn out fresh jokes if my head is littered with old gags. I would have to lose time trying to clear my mind of old stuff before I could think of new material. That's a writer's common problem.

You'll have a similar problem, though, if you do build up a library of gag books and then find most of the material will be unsuitable. I suggest you begin building up your own private library of really usable jokes. Read through your collection of joke books at your leisure, marking those gags or stories that amuse you or which you think might best apply to your speaking needs. Snip out gags or cartoons from magazines and staple them to an index card or to a loose leaf sheet which can be collected into your own set of books. Make notes of one-liners or stories that might come in handy and file these as well. Now when you need material, the good stuff is not only indexed, but it is readily available to you: You need no longer be bothered with the bad stuff.

None of these gags is carved in stone. Very rarely will you find a piece of material that can be done exactly as it's written in a book. First of all, there's a different style that's used in writing a joke than there is in telling one.

To illustrate, go back and find that second gag we used for salespeople. Read it through again. Would you tell that exactly as it's written? I don't think so. Not too many speakers I know would say, "A saleslady in a hat shop *gushed.*" Gushed? That's what happens when you hit a fireplug with your car.

That joke is intended for the written page. In a speech, it would have to be much more conversational and would need some reason for being told. If I were delivering this story to a group of salespeople, I might do it like this:

"One thing I found out as a salesperson is that you never talk too much. I mean God gave us two ears and one mouth. We should listen twice as much as we talk. Right?

"I found this out when I worked in a department store selling ladies hats. This one customer had one picked out that she just loved. She tried it on and thought she looked beautiful. I practically had the commission in my pocket. Then I talked too much.

"I said, 'That's a darling hat. Really. It makes you look ten years younger.'

"The lady whipped off the hat and said, 'I don't want it.' I said, 'What?'

"She said, 'I don't want it. I can't afford to put on ten years every time I take off my hat.' "

If I ever tell that gag to a sales group, I may find it's a little too long or that I shouldn't break up the punch line with a "What?" Maybe I should even repeat the set-up by saying, "If it makes me ten years younger . . ." Those details will all be polished up in the telling and retelling.

Do play with stories. Transform them from the written page into something that feels comfortable as it passes over your vocal chords. Remember, you paid for the joke book, so you can do whatever you want with it.

WRITE YOUR OWN MATERIAL

Don't be afraid to write your own humor. Attack it with gusto. The first thing you should do is buy my previous book, *How to Write and Sell (Your Sense of) Humor* (Writers Digest Books).

In the next chapter we're going to go through a step-by-step approach to writing. It's a condensation of what is in my last book. (But we go through it fast, so buy the book anyway.)

There are many advantages to creating your own humor. Let's go through them one by one:

It's Organic. All of the material you generate comes from you. It should reflect your style and your attitudes and it should sound *perfect* coming from your mouth. No writer will ever capture all of that for you.

It's Original. You know that it didn't exist until you wrote it out on a legal pad or pushed it through your typewriter. You can face any audience and know that they never heard these gags before. (Although there will always be someone in the auditorium who will say he did.)

It's about You. The material that you generate has to come from your frame of reference. It doesn't come from a book or from a writer. It comes from your mind and your experience.

A fine humorist, Jeannie Robertson, does a brilliant routine about her childhood and her experiences as a Miss America contestant, and what it was like growing up (really growing up) to be a 6 feet, 2 inches-tall teenager. No joke book is going to give her material that applies to her own unique background. That humor has to come from her. Your humor will be better when it comes from you.

It's More Flexible. Material that someone else hands you, or that you may read in a book, is fairly standard stuff. When you can generate your own material, you can tailor it to the situation, the crowd, the place, the time, and so on. You can make it fit where and when you want it to.

It's Gratifying. It's nice to know that you alone can take all the credit when that big laugh comes. You don't have to share your applause with a book, a magazine or another speaker. It's all yours, baby. Eat it up.

In the interest of fairness, I must now confess to some disadvantages in writing your own material. For example—

It Is More Work. Writing comedy is not easy. You'll have to invest more time and mental effort than you would by simply opening a book to the section marked "Salespeople" and copying down a line or two.

It's Risky. Trying out new material is always a gamble. I've worked for comedians who paid me a nice salary to create funny material for them. Sometimes they never used it. They trusted only the tried and truly proven laughgetters.

It takes quite a bit of courage to go out there cold and feel yourself quivering inside until you find out that the audience is really buying it.

Still, for all the disadvantages mentioned, I maintain it's worth the peril and the work.

HIRING A WRITER

If you don't have the time or the courage to try to write your own comedy, what are the pros and cons of hiring someone to do it for you?

Here are examples of some of the advantages:

It's a Steady Supply. You'll always have new ideas coming to you. It's almost like a joke book that is being written for you alone. You'll still have to pick and choose, and probably rewrite, but the ideas will be forthcoming.

You'll Be Getting a Second Opinion. Sometimes we get too close to the material that we're doing. We may love a certain little "bit" in our talk, but the listeners are indifferent to it. A third party may point that out to us. You'll have two minds working on the same problem. If you can't think of a fitting illustration for a talk, your writer may come up with it.

You'll Be Working with a Professional. Presumably, the person you hire will know something about comedy and humor. You'll be getting the benefit of that expertise along with the material.

It's a Time-Saver. While you're working on the serious message or whatever else you need to work on, someone will be sitting at a typewriter doing nothing else but making you sound funny and clever.

That's the good news. Now for the bad:

You Have to Find a Good Writer. We said earlier that a joke book may only have one percent of material that is worthwhile. You may just hire the guy that writes the other 99 percent.

But it's not always easy to find that person who can write *for you*.

We see this constantly in Hollywood. There are many different forms of comedy and writers who excel in those different styles. A person who writes brilliant stuff for Steve Martin may not be able to write for Danny Thomas, and vice versa.

A writer who can't fill your needs is useless to you.

The Writer May Not Understand Your Business. Speakers entertain, but they are not entertainers. That is, their primary function is not to amuse; it's usually to inspire or to educate. Comedy writers deal primarily with entertainment. If they get laughs, they're successful.

However, even the most successful comedy writer may not understand what your function is up on that platform. Even though the material he or she provides is superb, it may not dovetail with what you're trying to accomplish as a speaker.

Writers May Be Too Expensive for Your Needs. Hiring a good comedy writer can be expensive. Since most speakers need only a touch of humor in their presentation you may be better advised to try to provide the humor yourself before spending the money for a writer. However, we'll talk more about hiring writers in Chapter 10.

I've given you several sources for humor material in this chapter. Now, as promised, I'll show you how to work this material into *your* presentation.

How to Write Your Own Material

"I COULDN'T WRITE A LINE," people tell me, "if my life depended on it." Neither can I. Many times in the heat of television production a line is needed "right now." Often Bob Hope will call and we'll try to ad-lib a gem over the phone. It's very difficult. Frequently eight or ten writers will work half a day to generate one line for a sketch and we can't do it. If the professionals have trouble producing quality lines when their jobs depend on it, why should you expect to be able to create them when *your* life depends on it.

Writing good material takes a lot of work. It requires thought and preparation. Writing is considered a lonely profession because it's done best in solitude.

Though it's a challenging and often a lonely chore, I believe that anyone can write comedy. I'll guarantee that you can produce humorous material for your own presentation for two reasons. First of all, it isn't as difficult as everyone makes it out to be. Secondly, the material you write doesn't have to be that good. That last statement is not by way of advocating the use of *bad* material. I'm just saying that the material you write doesn't have to be *that good*. Let me explain.

Recall a party that you attended where you had so much fun your sides would hurt from laughing. Everyone has been in this situation at sometime where not only his sides hurt, his mouth ached from laughing.

Now recall the following day when you tried to tell someone what made you laugh so hard. The fun probably didn't survive the transition very well, did it? That's why the hackneyed phrase, "I guess you had to be there," became hackneyed.

It's the atmosphere, the company, the spirit of the moment, that makes those times funny. I assure you in 99 percent of the cases, it's not the material.

Let me prove that: In any of your laughing fits do you recall any single line that you could sell to *Reader's Digest?* Was there any quote that you thought Mort Sahl should have for his next appearance? Was there any phrase that you would like to have etched in bronze and hung over your desk? Probably not. Was there any funny bit that might even be called "professional quality?" Again, no. *But,* were the lines or the bits funny? Absolutely, positively, unequivocally, *yes.* You don't laugh till your jaws throb, nor hold your sides because you're afraid the giggling might produce a hernia *unless the material is FUNNY.* Now, is it professional quality funny? No. Is it funny? Yes.

At retirement parties, fellow workers give comic gifts to the retiree. The more unpolished they are, the funnier the presentation. When good friends gather, they trade insults and barbs unrestrainedly. They laugh and they have fun. That's not Grade A top-notch comedy material. But it is fun and they have good times together. It is laughter. It is solid humor.

Another facet of the humor that emerges when friends gather or when a party begins to cook, is that everyone tends to join in. Certainly, some people are wittier than others and may get the bulk of the punch lines. But others will try to top them and still others will join in the fun by throwing the straight lines. Very few will withdraw and clam up just because they aren't professional humorists.

There are different forms of humor. There's the good friends/party type; the platform humor; and the professional. Their separate effectiveness is judged by different criteria applied to each. Don't frighten yourself away from writing your own platform humor simply because you feel it can never be professional quality. It doesn't have to be.

I wouldn't give up tennis because I know I'll never be good enough to play in Wimbledon. In fact, I don't want to get too good at tennis. Why? Because were I to become a tournament player (it won't happen) I'd eliminate most of my competition. I couldn't play with the fun guys I lose to now. I'd have to move up to the fiercer, more competitive ranks. So, I'm happy to be a hacker.

Music is another illustration of the different levels of proficiency. Some folks can liven up a party by sitting at a piano or strumming a guitar while everybody else sings along. It's great fun. The people who leave the party hoarse from crooning the old favorites don't turn to one another and say, "I didn't enjoy that because the piano player wasn't concert quality."

It's not that hard to write your own material. We professionals promote that myth because it cuts down the competition.

If you're a skeptic, I'm going to show you before you turn too many more pages that you can write at least one joke. (Let me convince you first, and then backtrack and show you how I did it.)

When the Queen of England visited California in 1983, so did the worst rainstorm we had had in years. President Ronald Reagan wanted to host the Queen at his Santa Barbara ranch. He did so with much difficulty. The royal yacht couldn't sail to Santa Barbara because of rough seas. So, the Royal Party and Mr. and Mrs. Reagan flew to Santa Barbara and then took a treacherous ride in four-wheel-drive vehicles to reach the President's ranch house. Ronald Reagan and the Queen were scheduled to go horseback riding around the 688-acre ranch. But that had to be cancelled because the roads were too wet, too muddy and far too dangerous for the animals.

Forgive the pun, but that is fodder for jokes. Now write a joke line about the cancelled horseback ride after I give you some directions. Pretend this royal visit is still going on. The torrential rains and mudslides continue, but the Queen and the President try to get this horseback ride in anyway. To do this, what sort of horses would they need, or how could they alter the horses to make the ride possible? (Write some ideas of your own before looking at the following samples.)

The Queen is going to take that horseback ride after all. As soon as they can find a horse with webbed feet.

They saddled up the horses. The hardest part was getting the animals to stand still while they put the outboard motors on.

The Queen did manage to ride around the ranch. She was lucky. She found a horse that could do the breast stroke.

I went with ducks, boats, and swimming. Other readers may have gone with scuba gear, fish, four-wheel-drive and hundreds of other ideas.

Some readers may object that it was almost impossible not to come up with some connection since I led you into it. They'll point out that I picked the topic, listed all the background information and even asked some pertinent questions. All anyone had to do was fill in the blanks. Well, that's what comedy writing is.

Even though humor is very subjective, the germs of wit are universal. In other words, the funny idea remains a funny idea no matter how we transfigure it with language. As a person who writes for others for a living, I have had to learn to pick up the rhythm and timing of other performers in order to sell my wares. A joke for Phyllis Diller is different from a joke for Carol Burnett is different from a joke for Bob Hope is different from a joke for Bill Cosby. However, the joke *idea* remains the same; the wording and presentation differ. For instance, in our example about the Queen riding in foul weather, the joke about finding a horse with webbed feet would be expressed by Bob Hope one way, Bill Cosby another, and Phyllis Diller still a third way. In this chapter, therefore, I would like to help you discover how to find that joke *idea*. I'll leave the phrasing and the style for you to supply on your own.

In order to find this joke idea, you have to do exactly what I did for you in the advance work—which is the example I gave you. As I've said before, comedy, humor and wit take preparation and advance thought. I don't deny that there are wonderfully gifted people in this world who can ad-lib anytime, anywhere, anyhow. God bless them, they should cherish their gift. However, I don't think they need bother with this book. The rest of us need some time to prepare our witticisms.

There are three things you'll have to find in order to write your own humor:

- the topic
- the slant
- the comedy connection

THE TOPIC

It's impossible to write a joke without first deciding on a topic. You have to write a joke *about* something. Even if someone were to come to me and say, "Give me a joke about anything," the first thing I would do would be create my own topic. It's like asking someone directions. You say, "Hey, pal, I'm lost. Can you help me?" His first question would be, "Where do you want to go?" No one can help you without that information.

Remember, in my joke writing example I gave a long description of the Queen's visit and the weather conditions. I told you exactly why she couldn't ride around Reagan's ranch. The joke I asked you to write was specifically about the cancelled horseback ride.

THE SLANT

Now that you know what you're going to talk or write *about, how are you going to do it?* That's the slant.

In our example, I forced the slant upon you. A ride through mud and flooding was possible if we did something to the horse.

I recall when Bob Hope asked the writers to do some material about President Ronald Reagan being shot. The President was out of danger by this time but I still found it a difficult subject to joke about. So I asked Mr. Hope, "What's the angle? What can we kid about?" He replied that Reagan was in the hospital doing jokes, so let's kid him about that. From that input, one of the writers came up with this line:

> President Reagan is in the hospital telling one joke after another. The theory is that the bullet passed through Henny Youngman.

I remember hearing one speaker who had pretty much the same slant on every topic. His style was self-deprecatory. The bulk of his humor came from taking obvious points and pretending that was all he knew. For instance, if he were talking about horses, he might say:

> "So I told this guy everything I knew about horses. They were a four-legged animal. One leg in each corner."

Or in talking about computers he might share his wealth of knowledge about those machines with his audience:

> "A computer is a simple machine that has an off-on switch. When you switch it to 'on,' the machine is on. When you switch it to 'off,' the machine is off."

How do you find a slant? By analyzing. By thinking. A man I used to work for had a favorite saying: "Simplicity is the product of thought." Well, the comedy slant is also the product of thought.

Investigate your topic for interesting or peculiar aspects. An example I gave earlier could be found in the irony of a nation concerned about their President, yet he was doing jokes about himself.

To illustrate further, I'd been booked to speak to a group of people who have been through a cardiac rehabilitation program at a hospital near me. I've been through the program myself with many of these people. The cardiac rehabilitation program is a hospital-supervised exercise program to help people recover from heart surgery or to help prevent certain cardiovascular problems. What slant could I take in trying to write a monologue for this group? I'll illustrate with some of the jokes I wrote for this group a little later on but for now let's concentrate *only on the slant*. Examples follow:

- Most of the time we meet, we're all stripped to the waist and attached to heart monitors. That's one angle.
- Another is how hard the nurses there make us work.
- All of us are dealing in some way with doctors, so let's kid them about their bedside manners and their exorbitant bills.
- Most of these people have been in the hospital, so hospital food is fair game.
- And, of course, those troublesome open-back hospital gowns.
- All of the people are supposed to keep accurate records of how much exercise they do on their own at home. We all lie about it, so that's yet another slant.

THE CONNECTION

We know what we're going to talk about and how we're going to approach the subject. Now we need the joke.

A joke is usually a connection of two or more ideas which are related to each other in some amusing way. The relation can be one of similarity, dissimilarity, or complete nonsense.

An example of a similar relationship:

"Anytime you see a man open a car door for his wife, either the car is new or the wife is."

An example of a dissimilar relationship:

"Yesterday was a bad day in Los Angeles. We had floods, torna-
does and earthquakes. And on top of that, my evening paper
wasn't delivered."

An example of a nonsense relationship:

"It is better to have loved and lost than to get your lower lip stuck
under a manhole cover."

Each of these is made up of two ideas which are tied together in a
humorous way. Think of some of your favorite jokes and see if they're
not composed of two or more ideas.

We should already have the topic and the slant, both of which, in
essence, make up the first idea. The connection is the second idea; the
similar, dissimilar or nonsensical element that will blend with our initial
statement.

When you find all this, you've got the joke.

How do we go about searching for this joke connection? In my
earlier book, I suggested writing out a list of items (persons, places,
things, sayings) that are related in some way to your major premise.
Later some of these may even pop out at you when you're searching for a
connection. In this abbreviated study on joke writing, I'll recommend
two methods of stimulating your mind to find that related idea:

1. provide a punch line to a statement
2. ask questions

To provide a punch line to a statement is to make an apt
observation from a list of factual statements about the premise. These
needn't be funny, because whatever caption we come up with will
provide the humor. These are just teasers to challenge us to think. To
illustrate, let's go back to our example about the cardiac rehabilitation
dinner. My statement is, "The nurses in that place really make us
work." Now I search for a caption or a punch line to that verbal set-up.
Some quick examples:

(NAME) came over to me to say hello tonight, and my pulse
jumped to 180.
None of them are RN's; they're all SL's. SL—that stands for Simon
Legree.

They have to shop all over to find white hobnailed boots to go with their nurses' uniforms.

You get the picture?

The second method is to ask questions. Again these are only to stimulate humorous replies or ideas. I used this gimmick in challenging you to write jokes earlier when I said about the Queen's ride, "What sort of horse would she need or how could they alter a horse to make the ride possible?"

When searching for the joke connection, whether by supplying punch lines or asking questions, allow your mind to get a little bizarre. Comedy is not words or jokes or stories. It's a picture in someone's mind. It's like a painting which is not just canvas or pigment. Those are just materials to create the effect; like words used by a humorist.

The real comedy comes when the person sitting in the audience "looks" at a scene in his own mind, finds it funny, and laughs. It's easier for us to *create* mental images if we *think* in mental images.

What makes those images funny are the exaggerations and the distortions that we, as humorists, project. So, when you're in the creative phase of the joke-writing experience, permit your mind to exaggerate, distort, twist, bend, push, pull, until you get the picture that conjures up "funny."

Humor is to the mind what caricature is to the eye. Caricature artists spot outstanding features and put them in a different perspective, sometimes making them almost grotesque. This doesn't destroy the recognition factor. On the contrary, it often enhances it. Sometimes, it's easier to recognize a celebrity from a caricature than from a studio photograph.

Carry your premise to its logical, although bizarre, conclusion. Let's say your son plays a loud electric guitar. In your mind, make it louder and louder, **then louder still.** Make it so loud that he could hit a G^7 chord in Los Angeles and blow out all the hearing aids in Albuquerque, New Mexico. Make it louder than that. Make it worldwide—nay, even into the universe.

People can accept any absurdity. Consider dreaming. When you wake up in the morning after a particularly stimulating dream, you're almost obsessed by it. You want to review it and share it with someone else. Yet when you start to recount it, you discover that there are many flaws of logic in the story: You're in a jungle which suddenly changes into a warehouse. You're flying in a plane which suddenly transforms into a boat. You're with one person who suddenly becomes another. All of this made sense in your dream. You didn't stop the dream or shout "hold the music," and then wake up to correct the obvious errors. You dreamt on.

The same phenomenon happens with comedy exaggeration. It's readily accepted. To illustrate, let me list a few of the hundreds of gags I've done about Phyllis Diller's mythical mother-in-law, a fat lady known affectionately as Moby Dick:

> She wanted to stay at our house, but I put her in a motel. Rooms 314, 315 and 316.
> This lady is so big she has her own zip code.
> One day she wanted to spend a day at the beach. Four passing boats harpooned her.
> My husband, Fang, said, "Does Mom remind you of anyone?" I said, "Yeah, Massachusetts."

Okay, those are the jokes, folks, but forget their comedy value and just analyze their dimensions. This lady grows and shrinks and our minds aren't upset by it at all. She goes from the size of three motel rooms to the size of a state, with several variations in between.

As the writer of your own material, you should capitalize on this phenomenon and use it for comedic value. When painting humorous word pictures, go to extremes. Distort. Exaggerate. Have fun.

When you put all three of these components—the topic, the slant, and the connection—together, you have a joke *idea*. It now needs to be worded properly. (The wording, of course, is the reflection of your comedy style and characterization. Although it's very personalized, some of its precepts are universal.) The wording should maximize the comedy effect. Generally, you accomplish this by surprise.

Sometimes the surprise can come simply by your placement of the joke in your speech. Woody Allen does this masterfully. Many of his gags don't need set-ups at all. They just pop out at you with no warning. That's great. Humor is usually less effective when you see it coming.

I once heard a speaker discussing love, and how easy it was to give it when there were no obstacles. He likened it to seeing a lovely baby and how simple it was to tell the mother that her child was beautiful. "But what," he asked, "do you say when you see a mother with an ugly baby?'' He paused to let the impact settle on the audience, then he said, "Tell her it looks like its father."

The surprise sometimes is created by our wording. We can employ a device not unlike a magician's deliberate misdirection. A sleight-of-hand artist purposely creates a diversion to draw the audience's attention away from his crucial move. It's hard for you to notice a cumbersome manipulation on his part when you're not looking at it. In the same way, humorists try to get your mind going in a direction that leads to a dead end. Then when they've got you trapped, they mentally pull the rug out from under you.

In teaching comedy, I illustrate this with a story about a childhood chum. This kid and I were inseparable in the early grades. This good friend was skilled at getting into trouble and then squirming out of it; more often than not, leaving me to take the blame. We played together, laughed together and cried together. My good pal was the flamboyant, effervescent, courageous one; I was the shy, withdrawn sidekick. But we were friends.

After that narrative, I ask people to describe this person whom they've now pictured in their minds. Generally I get a red-headed freckle-faced guy—kind of a "Huckleberry Finn" character. Then I tell my listeners that her name was Mildred.

That usually gets a laugh. It's a surprise, because although they know I'm leading up to something, no one guesses that it will be a girl. There's nothing in the narrative that says it isn't a girl. Admittedly, however, I've led you to *believe* it's a mischievous *boy*.

Wording should use the tool of manipulation to heighten the element of surprise.

Here's a joke example that demonstrates that device rather well. Notice how it leads you to think I'm going to compliment myself, and then . . .

When my first book came out, I was so thrilled. I even went to the local bookstore and just hung around. I wanted to see if anybody would notice the picture on the back cover and then realize that it was me. Well, sure enough, that first day, 27 people came up to me. Three wanted my autograph and 24 wanted their money back.

SHORTCUTS TO HUMOR

I've compiled a list of ideas which can intensify the comedy in most jokes. Presumptuously, I've named them "shortcuts to humor."

How can they help you? Well, when you sit down with a blank sheet of paper you not only have to write comedy, but your comedy must have a point of view. The following six ideas will suggest a way to go with your writing and will also amplify the response from the listeners. They are:

1. Reflect the truth
2. Relax tension
3. Shock
4. Attack authority
5. Involve the audience
6. Just be funny

REFLECT THE TRUTH:
Have you ever seen a really good impressionist work? She announces, "I'm now going to do Barbra Streisand," then turns away from the crowd, does something or other to her costume and face, turns back, *looking like Streisand*. The audience laughs. What are they laughing at? It's the recognition factor. It's the same reason why people used to laugh at our take-offs on commercials on the *Carol Burnett Show*. When there's a certain amount of recognition, the comedy generally gets a bigger laugh than it often deserves.

Stating the truth has this same effect. You state something in a unique way, the audience recognizes that what you're saying is indeed true and the laugh is amplified.

During one of his radio broadcasts, Jack Benny got a big response from the studio audience when he turned to them and said, "Why am I trying so hard to be funny? You all got in for free." It's not a blockbuster comedy gem, but it was true for every person sitting there. Consequently, it got good results.

When composing your humor, look first for the truth or the reality in your subject. As speakers who work to small, localized audiences, we have a gold mine there. We can hit them right between the eyes, whereas a national comic would have to be more general.

Ronald Reagan used a fantastic line during his campaign. He said, "Recession is when your neighbor loses his job. Depression is when you lose yours. And recovery is when Jimmy Carter loses his."

I don't mean to alienate anyone politically. I'm just analyzing the comedy structure of the line. From Reagan's point of view, the line was a basic truth, stated cleverly.

This also demonstrates that you can play with the truth once you establish it. You can bend it to favor you, so long as it remains recognizable. Jimmy Carter would have seen the point of that line, though he hardly would have agreed with it. But you can also exaggerate the truth. Extend it out to its logical limits. Distort it, bend it, twist it, do anything to it so long as the basic premise still remains discernible. For example:

> I'm not very handy around the house. I once bought a hammer and had to bring it back because it came without instructions.

It's true that I'm not a handyman, but it's an exaggeration to say that I can't use a hammer. Nevertheless, the point is recognized.

Here's another point worth considering. Our culture has many socially accepted prevarications. We've been lying about things this way for so long that often we don't even realize it. For instance, when we leave the gas station, do we *really* care whether the guy that just pumps our gas has a nice day or not? When we leave a boring party, don't we say, "Thanks for a lovely evening?" There's comedy in just pointing some of these things out to an audience.

Here's another example. The workers are ordered to an assembly by their supervisor. The General Manager walks out and begins by saying to them, "Thank you for being here." He'd get laughs (and relax tensions, which we'll talk about shortly) if he added, "Of course, we didn't give you much choice, did we?"

RELAX TENSION:

Nothing eases a tense situation like comedy. That was the dominant theme of the TV series, *M*A*S*H*. Those medical people had grim, but necessary tasks. The suffering was senseless, which made the anguish all the more unbearable. It was their whackiness which helped them survive the rigors of their situation.

In constructing your talk, be aware of those situations that might cause uneasiness in the audience. That's the place for a light-hearted moment. As an example, the General Manager in our former illustration certainly should know that those people called to an emergency assembly are apprehensive. Some means of relaxation at the start wouldn't have hurt.

There are other times when we can create our own tension, cause a little stirring or squirming in the audience. I once spoke at a City Council meeting with the editor of the paper that I wrote for. This was a Republican community and these politicians had asked the editor to have me lighten up on my comic remarks against the Republicans. Since I did a humor column, my position was that I kidded whoever was in power. My jabs weren't partisan; simply topical. Anyway, at the luncheon, I couldn't resist making the following comments:

> I know there is some discrimination exhibited in our paper. It has a few of you upset and I don't blame you. It upsets me, too. (Now at this point the editor was squirming more than anyone. I was afraid he might take the microphone away from me.) I don't think things like this should be hidden, covered over or allowed to fester. I want to address it right now. You all know what I mean. Our paper continually prints pictures of Bar Mitzvah boys, but not once do they publish a photo of a youngster making his First Holy Communion.

The relief was so great that the crowd laughed and applauded. Even my editor would have enjoyed it had he been conscious at the time.

SHOCK:
Shock is the underlying principle that makes people laugh at dirty jokes. They're naughty. They're not supposed to be said in public. They embarrass us and we laugh. Jerry Lewis relies on shock value. On stage he says and does and acts in an uninhibited, zany manner. Most of us would never dare to act like such a buffoon. So we laugh at his antics. Don Rickles shocks when he says things that people ordinarily only *think;* they don't dare say them aloud. He does. We're stunned. We laugh.

Speakers should not be scared away from using this device. It can be utilized in a very dignified way. For example: A respected civic leader was addressing one of his town's service clubs after having been invited to a White House dinner. He spoke about it and said he had been invited to State Dinners seven times. "One more time," he said, "and my silverware set will be complete."

It shocks us to hear a man admit, even in jest, to stealing silverware (and from the White House no less). But the effect is humorous, nonetheless.

Maintain your good taste, but do say things that will get your listeners eyes to pop open and their ears to perk up.

ATTACKING AUTHORITY:

Attacking authority is not as vicious as it sounds. It's like the attack kittens or puppies make when they assault their siblings. It has all the appearance of fury, but it's relatively harmless.

It's also a good gimmick with which to stimulate audience laughter. They love it when you attack that certain "untouchable" person they're not permitted to. Besides the touch of the shock value in this ploy there's also a good deal of revenge. But despite all those ominous sounding words, it remains an essentially inoffensive comedy form.

Authority expects to be attacked. In fact, an attack often helps boost prestige: It's a sign that someone is big enough to be singled out.

Bob Hope uses this device on his military jaunts. When he takes a swipe at the government or the commanding officer, all the enlisted men gleefully line up on his side.

If you can't fight City Hall, you can at least cast a good natured jab at it.

Here are a couple of examples from a "roast" of a supervisor who was *infamous* for smoking cheap and smelly cigars.

> Everybody likes a boss who smokes cheap cigars. You can always tell when he's in the area.
> He's not the only stinking supervisor we have in the plant. He's one of the few with a valid excuse.

Funny lines made funnier because they're against a superior.

This may appear to be a dangerous form of comedy; one that could easily backfire on the speaker. It really isn't. Used tastefully and with careful guidelines, it is very effective.

In a later chapter we'll discuss how to use insult humor without offending.

INVOLVE THE AUDIENCE:

You endear yourself to an audience when you make them a part of your presentation. There are several ways to do this. One is by naming names. If Joe Blow was the program chairman who booked you for this event, tell the audience.

Joe Blow called me three times to do this show. I finally told the operator I *would* accept the charges.

In another instance I spoke before a group in Hawaii. Their chief executive officer—we'll call him Joe Blow, too—had lost 60 pounds since he attended the last convention with this group. I told them:

It's been a rough year for your company. This year, they could only afford to send over *part* of President Joe Blow.

Another way is to talk about their location or their business. They love it when you seem to know as much about their locale as they do. Use places or buzz words, anything that proves to them you know what you're talking about.

Philadelphians, for example, are proud of their "gourmet" luncheon foods—cheese steaks and *hoagies,* for example. A hoagie is like a submarine or a poorboy sandwich, but no real Philadelphian will admit to that. In Philly they're called hoagies and they're better than, and unlike any other sandwich in the world. A speaker might kid Philadelphians about them by saying:

"I had one of your hoagies today. A hoagie? That's heartburn on an Italian roll."

It's possible with some research to find stories that automatically involve your listeners. One example is a joke that Slappy White used to tell that worked beautifully with a nightclub crowd. He would say:

"I just read in *Reader's Digest* where one out of every four people in the United States is mentally unbalanced. Think about that! One out of every four! You don't have to take my word for that. You can prove it to yourself. Here's what you do. Think of three of your best friends . . ."

At this point, people at tables all over the club are chuckling and pointing at one another. They're part of the story already because each table is singling out which of their group of four is unbalanced. Then Slappy continued:

"Do they seem all right to you?"

Big laughs again, because this confirms what each table has been saying: The one they've been pointing at doesn't seem all right to them. Then Slappy gives the *coup de grâce:*

"Because if they do, then you must be the one."

It always played well because the crowd became a part of the joke.

Finally you can get an audience involved physically. Call them onstage or have them do some sort of exercise from their places in the auditorium. It produces great results. Most speakers claim they could never get through a seminar without some type of audience participation.

Earlier I mentioned one of the most refreshing presentations I've ever seen at a National Speakers Association function. It was hosted by Dr. Loretta Malandro from Tempe, Arizona. Her entire program featured audience participation, but one small part will serve as an example here.

Loretta asked all of us to turn to the person next to us, gaze into each other's eyes, and make small talk. However, we were to concentrate on the eyes throughout. After that, she asked from the platform who among us noticed that their partner's pupils were dilated? Many hands were raised. She said, "That's good because dilating pupils indicates sexual attraction."

This got roars from the crowd. Loretta paused and let the laughter continue. She had a great gimmick going for her; everyone in the audience was "writing" his own jokes. Some of them were even shouted out and got more laughter. That's humor. That's a spirit of fun. That's people having a good time.

Here's an interesting addition to all that. Throughout the rest of the day, people in the corridors, at the hotel bar, at the dinner dance that evening, were still doing jokes about dilating pupils as well as other features that Loretta had in her seminar. That's every speaker's dream; to be remembered and talked about hours and days after the presentation is finished. Humor involving audience participation accomplished that for this talented speaker.

JUST BE FUNNY:

This is my escape clause. This last category is simply my admission that the list is obviously not all-inclusive. So if you can think of anything witty to write that doesn't fit into any of the above categories, do write it. Include it in your talk. Have the audience love you. And remember—you heard it here first.

Tailor Your Material to Fit You

A STAFF WRITER ON A SHOW I worked on held up an important writer's meeting because he was waiting for some antiques he had bought to be delivered to his home. The gentleman was a fanatic about old furniture. In my typically narrow-minded manner—I was a little miffed about my precious time being wasted because of this deal— I remarked to the room in general that I could never understand anyone being interested in antiques. "I don't like antiques," I pronounced. The producer said, "Oh really? I've heard your speech."

He was a bit brutal, but accurate. My talk, like the traditional wedding, has something old, something new, something borrowed and something blue. The presentations of most platform humorists share the same elements. George Bernard Shaw was blunt about it. He said, "Good writers borrow. Great writers steal." His quote applies even more to speakers. It applies quadruply to humorists. I have no moral or ethical qualms with this. We did discuss this at some length in Chapter 6, but I'd like to add a further thought here: Good jokes and stories make the rounds because they are just that—*good*. They deserve to be passed on to listeners. Who better to do that than polished speakers?

My outspoken producer was right, I do have some stories in my performance that I got from the Joke Lending Library. I have also spoken to professional speakers who claim that their material is 90 percent original, yet I can almost tell them from what book and what page they got each joke.

Why do we do that? Because these anecdotes are surefire. We know they will get laughs. However, we should remember that in speaking, it's not "laughs" that are most important. Certainly we need them. When we finish telling a funny story, people should laugh. That's what separates the humorous story from the announcement that a train is departing at the depot.

But "funny" you can always get. That's what Chapter 6 was all about. However, good speakers want more than funny. They want a story that will be individualized, a story that not only gets laughs, but gets the biggest and best laughs *only* when *they* tell it. They want a funny tale that is consistent with their image.

We touched on this idea before when we spoke of flip-flopping the material of Joan Rivers and George Burns. By making the comedy inconsistent with the character, we destroyed the humor.

Your humor must reflect your personality, your style and your point of view. Before discussing methods of accomplishing this, let me first add that this rule applies to all of your comedy, whether borrowed or original. I say that because much of the material that we write is "borrowed." Don't ask me how or why it happens, but from experience, I know it does. Perhaps we tend to use jokes or stories that impressed us a long time ago and we stored them in the backs of our minds. When called upon to write something original, we may have gone to that mental warehouse and dusted off something usable from the stockpile.

For example, a writer friend of mine told me about a sight gag he had conceived for a comedy movie. It was a delightful joke even in the telling, and he was rightfully proud of it. Then we saw a series of clips from old Buster Keaton movies and there, in exact detail, was the same sight gag.

Another theory is that joke ideas are floating around in the ether and people can tune their minds in to them in the way we tune our radios in to different frequencies. Some Hollywood writers who subscribe to this theory complain that all the good jokes are floating over Neil Simon's house.

An astounding thing happened to me many years ago which I still can't explain. I was reading the Sunday funnies. (Normal people read the front page. Comedy writers read the funnies.) There was a collection of single cartoons by Barnes entitled "The Better Half." I was dumb-founded. I needed corroboration of this story, so I handed the paper to my wife and asked her to read the jokes, then follow me to the typewriter in my office. There in my typewriter, as part of my uncompleted monologue, were three of the same jokes—identical wording and all.

Before we wander too much further into the *Twilight Zone of Humor,* let's agree that some of the material we think we originate, we don't.

It makes little difference, though. Every anecdote we tell should be indelibly stamped as our own, whether we actually write it ourselves or, as I used to say when I was a kid, "I made that up myself out of a book I read."

The beginning step in tailoring material to you is to select only those stories that reflect your attitudes.

I remember once talking to a well-known comedian who had just seen another popular comedian perform in Las Vegas. I asked what he thought of the show. He said, "It was terrible. He did six vomit jokes." Obviously, this comic had an aversion to this word. (Not that I blame him.) The other comic didn't.

In reading one of Steve Allen's books about comedians, I was fascinated to learn that Allen has an aversion to the word, "ass." It's not prudishness, but simple discomfort with the word itself.

Everyone has feelings of this sort. They needn't be logical or even explicable. If you have them, it's enough to rule out certain stories for you but not necessarily for other speakers.

I had one joke that I particularly liked years ago. I wrote it myself and used it many times. Today I wouldn't use it. I'll relate it here only so that you can see how my attitudes changed.

I was doing a routine about traveling on the Schuylkill Expressway in Philadelphia. One joke was:

I saw a 12-car pile-up there the other day. What happened was a woman signaled for a left hand turn and 11 people believed her.

Today, I am uncomfortable telling that story because I feel that it's unfair to single out women drivers as any less competent than men.

You must always be on the lookout for those stories that *do* reflect your attitudes, your personality and your style. Those are the stories you might want to include.

For example, much of my comedy style consists of inadvertent put-downs of myself. I begin by building myself up and then turning the tables on me. The story about hanging around the bookstore and three people wanting autographs and 24 wanting their money back is an example. However, the story that I opened this chapter with is not true. It's true that our meeting was held up by someone buying antiques. It's also true that my act has some pilfered material in it. On driving home from this meeting, the connection struck me and I created the anecdote.

Now please don't be suspect of other anecdotes in this book. This one is purposely included at this point as an illustration. Everything else in the book is the truth—or very close to it—or might have been the truth if things had been different.

Nevertheless, when this story, in all its apocryphal glory, came to me, *it felt like me*. It had a flavor that I liked. It fit in with my comedy characterization. It had believability when told about me. This is what you should be looking for whether conceiving stories or researching them.

Now that you've selected or written punch lines that reflect a part of you, you'll want to tailor them so that they'll be uniquely yours. Ideally, you'd like these stories to be so individualized that no other speaker can tell them; at least, not the same way (or as well) as you do.

Before getting into the how-to of that, though, let's look again at the nature of comedy. It flows in peaks and valleys. Johnny Carson sometimes kids about those valleys when a monologue is not going over the way he would like. Comedy has to undulate, though. The valleys are necessary so everyone will know where the peaks are. You need set-ups in order to have punchlines. If an entire monologue—from beginning to end—had the same comedic value, it would be monotonous.

Comedy reminds me of watching fireworks. Our community has a display every Fourth of July and the audience reaction is the same each year. The crowd eagerly watches a little speck of light shoot skyward. They *ooh* and *ahh* when the speck explodes into a flash of color. They enjoy the sensation as the embers float back to earth.

These three parts are necessary for the enjoyment of the event. *Anticipation* is part of the fun. (Besides, if you didn't watch the speck of light, you'd miss half the explosions.) That trail of light tells you where to look. The colorful blast is the essence of the display. It's what the people come to enjoy; it's the *thrilling* part of the event, although it's so fleeting. Finally, the *afterglow* extends the enjoyment.

There are also three parts to humor. There's that *buildup* when we know something is coming, but we don't know exactly what or when. Then there's the *flash* (the punch line). Then there's that moment when we *savor* the fun we've just had.

Speakers can use the buildup and the cool-down periods to tailor their material to fit them. If you've done your homework well, you should have a punch line that will deliver the explosion you want. After that happens, you won't have to worry about the success of that story anymore. It will be a solid, surefire, proven, fail-proof story that will have them rolling in the aisles.

Okay, it may not be *that good,* but it's pretty good. When you know you have that blockbuster coming up, you don't have to have great lines leading up to it. You can get smaller laughs and still accomplish your objective: *to make the story your own story.*

Let me give you an illustration of what I mean and then we'll discuss it further. I often use this tale to open my talk:

As you know from the introduction, my profession is to write jokes, but my real love is to stand up here and talk about that. It was kind of predictable that I would go into this field because extemporaneous speaking runs in my family.

A few years ago my daughter came to me and said, "Dad, I have to do a recitation in school. Would you help me with it?" I said, "Sure, honey, but Daddy writes for some pretty famous people. Why don't you let me write something for you, and then when you do it at school it will be funny. It will be different. It will be very much your own." She thought about this for awhile and said, "Well, Dad, it's in front of the whole school. I'd rather it be good."

And I was going to give her the family joke discount and everything.

Anyway, the poem she had you've probably heard. It goes (WITH ONE HAND ON THE HIP AND ONE HAND IN THE AIR): "I'm a little teapot, short and stout. This is my handle this is my spout . . . something, something . . . tip me over, pour me out." I rehearsed her posture, her gestures, her voice inflection. I probably over-rehearsed her.

My wife and I got to the auditorium that night. Our daughter's turn came and she stepped to the microphone like this. (BOTH HANDS ON HIPS) And she began (IN CHILD'S VOICE): "I'm a little teapot short and stout. This is my handle, this is my . . . (NOTICES THAT BOTH HANDS ARE ON HIPS.) I'll be damned, I'm a sugar bowl."

Everyone knew it was *our* daughter because my wife and I were the only ones sitting *under* our seats.

Generally, when I tell this story I point out the person who starred in it. One of my daughters usually travels with me to act as my secretary or to keep me organized, you know. I have three daughters and they're very close in age. They're 19, 20, and 21. One is a blonde; one's a brunette; and one's a redhead and they're all built like showgirls. So if you ever see me with anyone that looks like that, it's my daughter, OK?

This story always works well for me. There are two big punch lines in it: "I'll be damned, I'm a sugar bowl" and ". . . It's my daughter, OK?" I believe the story sounds like me, and also sounds like the truth because I'm talking about being a writer and coaching my daughter in her performance, yet the basic punch line came from a joke book I picked up one day while browsing through a bookstore. Cheapskate that I am, I didn't even buy the book. As I explained before, I don't ordinarily use joke books. This story just popped out at me.

The other punch lines in the story ("I'd rather it be good," and "family joke discount.") are there to make it my story. They're not big laugh producers, but they help the real punch line that's coming because now the story is about *me*. The audience can identify with it. It's not just, "Here's a story I heard about a little girl . . ."

I tried to keep the big laugh going with the follow-up line, "sitting under the seats." One day I kept it going even further and ad-libbed the line about ". . . it's my daughter, OK?" It has since become a very strong punch line on its own.

Listed below are three methods to use to individualize your stories:

1. Surround the story with truth
2. Lead into it with one-liners
3. Localize the story

SURROUND THE STORY WITH TRUTH

Make your tale believable. Remember a large part of humor is surprise. You get your audience thinking in the direction you want them to think, then trick them. When you begin telling a story that has a truthful sound folks are more easily caught off guard.

In my illustration, I'm telling a story about my daughter in kindergarten. That's not a typical set-up for a joke. Most jokes begin, "These two guys walked into a bar . . ."

This also makes the story *mine*. Other speakers may take the punch line, but they can't tell it the same way I do because they're not people who "have written for some pretty famous people."

Other speakers are welcome to the punch line, but they'll have to do just what I'm advising here—work on it to make it their own. This story, as it stands, is mine.

Of course, don't think that the truth means that you're under oath each time you step up to the microphone. Your humor doesn't have to be historically accurate. Your story doesn't even have to be true. But it should be surrounded with truth. At the very least, surround it with something that sounds like the truth.

The story never happened in the illustration I used (and my three daughters will be happy to have documented proof of this now). While I'm in a confessing mood, I want to say that my daughters are close in age and they're all beautiful, but they're all brunettes. Regardless of the facts, both of the punch lines hold up; they sound as if they're true and many people think they are. What counts is—*the story works*.

It's amazing what people will believe. When I was working on the *Carol Burnett Show* a few members of the writing staff would have a drink or two after work. We'd call this a "seat-softener" because it made the seat feel softer during the long ride home. The reason I joined in was that the freeways were so crowded at this time. At 5:30 it might take me an hour and a half to get home. But if I just sat in this bar until about 10:30, all the traffic would let up and I could make it home in 20 minutes. (My wife never quite bought that story, either.)

Anyway, this bar was where the CBS crowd would gather. We'd always meet friends there. One time the owner introduced me to his brother who was visiting from Wisconsin. Since gag writers can't control themselves, I said, "I've only heard of two things that ever came out of Wisconsin, terrible hookers and great football players." Some enormous guy was sitting at the bar and didn't know how we show-biz folk kid around, came over and grabbed me and said, "Hey, my wife is from Wisconsin." I managed to squeak out, "Really? What position does she play?"

You see, that's an old joke that I snuck in there because right up until the punch line, it sounded fairly straight, truthful, and even believable. I also threw in a couple of little jokes to keep the story going. But the biggie—the punch line—is an old one, but because I turned the story into my story, the whole story worked.

Remember that you too can make a story yours by leading into it with some "truthful fiction."

LEAD IN TO IT WITH ONE-LINERS

Perhaps you select a story that begins: "These two guys were playing golf with this gorilla, see . . ." How do you surround that with truth? You don't, unless you're a zoo keeper or a very strange golf pro. Some of the humor that we select is so zany that it is the absolute enemy of truth. Nevertheless, there are ways of sneaking into these stories. One way is to surround them with a spirit of fun. Let me illustrate that with another standard story:

> When I was promoting my first book, I flew all over the country doing interviews. I must have travelled over 50,000 miles, which is not a lot when you consider that my luggage travelled over 100,000.
>
> And this was when there was that big scare about the DC-10s. Everybody was scared. The guy in front of me got up to the ticket counter and said, "Give me two chances to Pittsburgh."
>
> Another writer and I got an offer to do a show in England. And this guy wouldn't fly. I said, "This is a good paying job. You gotta fly." So he called the airline and he said, "What's the chances of a bomb being on a plane?" They said, "Oh, about 1 million to one." He didn't like those odds.
>
> I tried to reason with him and finally he called back the airline. He said, "What's the chances of two bombs being on the same plane?" The lady recognized his voice, chuckled, and said, "Oh, about 400 million to one." Those odds he could live with.
>
> Now he'll fly anywhere. But he always takes one bomb with him.

You don't believe that story. Nobody does. Nobody should. But by leading in to it in a spirit of fun, the audience is willing to tolerate your telling of an unbelievable story. You might use this device if you have a good gorilla/golf story.

Notice that the lines leading in to the "biggie" weren't that believable. They weren't uproarious, either. Again, that's the nice part of this peaks and valleys situation—or as I call it, the "fireworks theory"—the build-up jokes don't have to be powerhouses.

LOCALIZE YOUR STORY

Tell your story as if it actually happened where you are now. People enjoy that because they like to feel a part of the story. I localized my illustration by introducing my daughter, the star of the story that never happened, to the audience. People turned, looked at her and smiled. She smiled back (all my kids are well rehearsed) and now the audience felt they knew the person this anecdote was about. After the speech, they talked to my daughter. They were now old friends.

Some tales can be set in any locale. Good. Set them in the one you're in right now. Instead of, "These two guys came into a bar . . ." try, "After the opening banquet last night, I stopped down at the lounge off the lobby for a nightcap. These two guys were in there talking real loud . . ." and go on to tell what they said.

Here's a story that has made the rounds, but it works on the convention circuit when localized.

> You people really know how to have a good time on a convention. I was in my room last night. I won't give you my room number because I don't want to embarrass anyone here. But the people next door came in after being out partying and they were talking loud. Not real loud, but kind of loud. So I went and got a glass and held it to the wall.
>
> Well, I'd already seen the late show.
>
> And the woman said, "Take off my blouse." So I went and got another glass and held it to the wall.
>
> The one I had got all steamed up for some reason.
>
> Then she said, "Take off my skirt."
>
> Then she said, "Take off my slip." Then she said, "If I ever catch you wearing them again, I'll divorce you."

It generally works well because it's a story about this crowd, this organization and this hotel. Some member of the audience is starring in this story. Not that the audience actually believes it, but they feel as if they are starring in it. It's rather like the thrill celebrities get when Don

Rickles kids them: They're being singled out and spotlighted.

To review: Only use humor that you feel comfortable with and that is compatible with your characterization. Work to make it your own anecdote. Put a little bit of yourself in it so that no one else can tell it with the same credibility that you do. Finally, surprise your audience with your stories. If you have any part of your program that begins, "That reminds me of a story," or "Have you heard the story about . . .?" get rid of it with the three methods we discussed above.

These are not the only three methods, to be sure, but they will get you started and thinking along the right lines. Find your own gimmicks if you must, but be sure that any humor you present to an audience comes from *you*.

Tailor Your Material to Fit Your Audience

COMEDY WRITERS SAY OF A JOKE or a piece of comedy material that "it works" or "it doesn't work." What makes a bit of humor "work?" Audience reaction. Laughter. You can have a joke that you feel is magnificient. You can hire the greatest comedy minds in the world to come in and polish it even further. Call Neil Simon, Woody Allen, and anyone else you want to reword and fine tune the comedy. Hire an acting teacher to hone your delivery. Even get the world's greatest drummer to provide the rim-shot, and if the audience doesn't laugh, you don't have a funny joke. All you've got is an extravagant recipe for egg on your face.

It should be obvious, then, that if our success as humorous speakers depends on an audience's appreciation, then it behooves us to say something that they're going to appreciate. Right?

When I began my speaking and writing career as a draftsman in a Philadelphia industrial plant, I considered the comedy I gave to this audience better than any Bob Hope could give to them. (I don't tell Bob Hope that and if he reads this book, I'll deny I said it.) I make that claim because I worked with those people. I knew them and the day-to-day trials and scandals that hit the plant. If a Xerox machine wasn't working, I knew about it and suffered the same delays as my audience did. I knew exactly which people to kid and about what. I was literally one with the audience. Therefore, I knew what they wanted to hear. So I said it in a funny way.

When you're talking about things that are that specific, the comedy doesn't have to be that fantastic to generate a lot of laughter.

Now that my arm is sore from patting myself on the back, let me make some confessions, too. Feeling like the hotshot King of Comedy after doing a few of these company banquets, I branched out to some local nightclub work. I had a recording company tape my appearance since we all knew this would be the humor sensation of the decade. (If anybody wants it, I have a quality tape of me doing some hilarious material and nobody laughing.) I bombed. Why? Because this was not *my* audience. I didn't know these people as well as I knew my co-workers and I didn't bother to do my homework. These folks weren't interested in what I was saying because I had not found out what *they* were interested in.

As we just discussed in the previous chapter, you have an obliga-tion to yourself and your material to be the best *you* possible. Do your talk in your style, with your attitude and your personality. However, you also have an obligation to your audience. Not that you're doing them a favor; you're doing yourself a favor by saying *what* they want to hear. Or, at least, saying it *in a way* they want to hear it.

An executive can't always say what his people want to hear. I worked my way up in the plant (which I talked about earlier) from apprentice to comedian to executive. (I'm not sure that's the common progression, but it was for me.) One day, by executive order, I had to give a pep talk to my employees. Production and output had to improve, or else.

I delivered the ultimatum, then added, "Now I'm not telling you these things because your jobs are on the line. I'm telling them to you because *my* job is on the line."

They got the message—shape up or ship out. They also realized that I was as much a victim of the threat as they were. We were brothers and sisters in this adversity. Rather than resent me as the authority figure who was demanding slave labor from them, they commiserated with me. I didn't say what they wanted to hear, but I hope I said it in a way they wanted to hear it. (I still believe it was pure coincidence that when I got to the parking lot that evening four of my tires were flat—no, make that five. They got the spare, too.)

You don't have to compromise your beliefs in order to cater to the audience's. In the rare instances where that might be true, drop that bit of humor. Don't do it. It's that simple.

Sometimes, you can even use a joke that goes against the thinking of your audience. It might be an idea that could offend them, but with clever wording, you can use it in front of them with no trouble.

Suppose, for example, I had a joke that was anti-Republican. I'm working in front of a Democratic audience. I tell the joke as is, and they love it.

The following week I'm working before a Republican crowd. The same joke may be used by beginning, "Some of the Democrats say . . ." Now the joke is against the Democrats and the Republicans love it.

The safest procedure, though, is to find out what the audience is thinking about. Find out what they want to hear, and then gear your humor to that. Once you know what the audience expects, your humor can take any form.

As an example, suppose you're working to a college crowd—Filmore University. Their biggest football game of the year was played last weekend against their perennial rival—University of Farnsworth. Filmore won 42 to 0. You can do any joke you want about that game and you'll get screams. In fact, all you have to do is mention the two schools and you'll get a giant reaction. Just say, "Football practice has been cancelled today. They're still sweeping Farnsworth off the field." You'll get roars. Six percent are laughs for the gag and 94 percent are the students still cheering their victory.

However, suppose Farnsworth beat them 42 to 0. Must you then omit the jokes because the students don't want to be reminded of their ignominious defeat? Nonsense. They want revenge. You can provide that verbally. They want to know that next year they'll win. You can reassure them and give them some comedic ideas on how to do it. You can soften the blow of the loss with humor. Tell these students, "Sure Farnsworth won. They were big, hairy, muscular bruisers—and that was just their cheerleaders." They'll love you for it.

The easiest thing to write would be jokes about the hapless team that lost by 42 points. If you stood in front of this crowd and did lines about their football team after such a defeat, you might be booed from the microphone.

Your humor varies depending on the attitude of your listeners. So your homework, then, is to discover what is in the minds of your audience.

It does pay dividends. A few years ago, I was asked to write and direct a short skit to be presented at the local High School Graduation Dinner Dance. At first, I refused because I felt the kids wanted to be left alone to have a good time in their own way. The parents committee assured me that there had been a small show at this event the previous year and the kids were very attentive and appreciative. I agreed, provided that the show would be for the kids and not the parents.

The first thing we did was have an informal meeting with about a dozen members of the senior class. We just talked about what was happening at the school. How were their athletic teams doing this year? Were they proud of them or embarrassed by them? What were some of the big gripes at the school? Which teachers did they like and which couldn't they stand? What was happening with the underclassmen?

At first the students were reticent, but as the meeting wore on, they opened up and told us all the scandals from the teachers on down.

Then we invited several underclassmen and we grilled them about the seniors. We asked them to tell us some of the things about the senior class that they wouldn't tell us themselves.

We got a wealth of material, and it all came from the kids themselves. Six parents acted in the skit and it was a smash. Why? Because every joke hit them right between the eyes. Why? Beause they practically wrote it.

Let me give you an example. At both meetings they giggled about one substitute teacher who, it seemed, was all over the school. She filled in for any regular teacher who was absent. It almost felt as if she could be in two places at once. She had a nickname we'll say was "Jobie." The theme of the dance was the Old West, so we staged a mock gunfight. At one point one of our actors cried out for help.

"Go get the sheriff."

"The sheriff is out of town," another said.

"Well who's taking his place?"

The answer was,

"Jobie."

This line literally knocked some of the kids off their chairs. Because it's a great joke? Not really. Because it was in the mind of every youngster at that dance.

You learn about your audience just the way we did. Ask questions and seek information. In most of the examples I've cited, I knew the audience fairly well. It's amazing, though, how you can sometimes be surprised. So it pays to question anyway, just to be sure.

Bob Hope once asked me to do some material for a police banquet. I did jokes about being double parked, and never seeing these guys except through the rear view mirror, and the like. Then I discovered that the banquet was for Police *Chiefs* across the country. None of the material I did applied.

If you're speaking as an executive to people who work in your company, you can easily do as I did with the high school students. Call an informal meeting with a representative group of employees and discuss topics.

A professional speaker can speak with his contacts. If they're no help, ask if there is anyone else you can talk with before the speech date.

First of all, you'll want to know the make-up of the audience. Who will be there? Will it be top level management or hourly employees? Will it be sales people or engineers? Will spouses attend? In other words get an overall picture of the audience.

Then ask other pertinent questions.

WHAT ARE THEY TALKING ABOUT?

Find out what the scuttlebutt is. In any group there is generally a hot topic being discussed. It's that item they talk about before executive meetings and while gathered around the Xerox machine.

One morning I had to do a newspaper column and I couldn't think of anything to write about that was current. It angered me because I was on my way to play tennis at the club and afterward I wanted to watch the Wimbledon matches on TV. So, I wanted to get this writing out of the way. My family was also going to watch Wimbledon because over breakfast all they talked about was the way John McEnroe was misbehaving at the tournament. Even though they weren't tennis fans, they did want to see if he threw any interesting tantrums.

At the club I had to wait for a court and the clubhouse conversation was all about McEnroe's naughtiness.

I played tennis and came home still without any ideas to write about. So I postponed my writing another day. That night I watched Johnny Carson and most of his opening monologue was about McEnroe's antics at Wimbledon.

Of course, it was. That's what everybody in the country, sports fan or not, was *talking about*. It was so obvious, as my mother used to say,

"If it had teeth, it would bite you."

Anytime you want a hot, current source of humor ask, "What are the people talking about?"

WHAT DO THEY ALL HAVE IN COMMON?

Every assemblage has something in common. Some of your audiences will all work for the same company. Some may work for different companies but be in the same business. They're all in the same place. They have to wait for the same elevators. They're all listening to you at this moment. They're enduring the same weather conditions.

By investigating the common bonds that unite all your listeners, you can mine valuable ideas for humor.

At the opening session of a National Speakers Convention, the first speaker noted that, "we have gathered together in our audience 400 professional speakers. No listeners."

WHAT ARE THEIR COMPLAINTS?

Humor is great for getting something off your chest. I find I always write my funniest material about something that has me steamed. It's my way of getting revenge. Your listeners will love you if you side with them in their gripes. All assemblages have them. The kids in the high school that I wrote the sketch for were upset because the most convenient parking lot had been recently converted to "Faculty Only." The funny lines didn't have to be that funny on this topic. Any mention of this brought roars of laughter tinged with venom.

Had this sketch been written for the faculty, though, the jokes would have taken on a different coloration. The topic would have still been viable, because the teachers knew what was being said, but the lines would have had more of an "I got mine; you get your's" flavor.

People love to laugh at their peeves.

WHAT ARE THEY PROUD OF?

If you're lecturing to students at the University of Georgia, you have to make a mention or two of Herschel Walker. (Or at least you did, before he left school to sign with the New Jersey Generals of the new United States Football League.) Every company or association has something to boast about. They either make the best product, or lead the nation in sales, or their association has the greatest attendance record. There is always something for which they pat themselves on the back. Work that into a touch of humor and they'll follow you anywhere.

Recently I heard a speaker at a convention for one company's employees who earned the trip by completing their projects on time. The speaker noted that, "All of you completed your assigned projects on time. I'm impressed. I never finish anything I start. If you don't believe me, ask my wife."

That gag has several meanings—some naughty, some nice—but the crowd appreciated it because this guest was recognizing their accomplishment.

WHO ARE THEIR RIVALS OR COMPETITORS AND WHAT'S HAPPENING WITH THEM?

As a high school student, I attended a boarding school run by the Christian Brothers, a Catholic teaching order. When our classes broke in summertime, we would make a riotous dash for the swimming pool. I fell into the underbrush laughing one day when during this race one kid screamed out, "Last one in is a Jesuit."

Most groups have that number one rival. General Electric has Westinghouse. McDonald's has Burger King. Army has Navy. Any friendly put-down of the competition gets an amplified response.

WHAT ARE THEY KIDDING THEMSELVES ABOUT?

Earlier we talked about doing jokes after a mythical college team had lost an important game by an embarrassingly lopsided score. We milked the humor by getting revenge on the other team.

Suppose, though, that your contact told you that they've been losing every game by ridiculous scores and that the whole campus is joking about the football team. Then, perhaps, it's all right to do some gags about them. If they're kidding themselves then you can join in.

You have a head start on humor if you can find out what your listeners are already doing comedy about.

WHOM DO THEY KID ABOUT?

You'll often find a group has one patsy. There will be some fun-loving person who seeks out the limelight and does different zany things to remain controversial. Find out who these "zanies" are and what they do and join right in.

Because I have a reputation in comedy, many times, when I speak, people tell me about so-and-so in the group who tells the corniest jokes. I get his name and make sure he doesn't mind being kidded. Then when a joke fails, I say, "That's the last time I ever buy a joke from so-and-so." They love it because they've been telling him his jokes were terrible for years and now the outside world has corroborated it.

GET THE LAY OF THE LAND

This doesn't always apply because your listeners may have travelled in from various locations. At a convention, for instance, the crowd is generally no more familiar with the local geography than you are.

However, many times it will apply, and very well too. For instance, at a college or a commercial location, ask the names of surrounding towns and something about them. Are there any interesting landmarks or traditions? What's the history of this place? Name some of the good and the bad eating places. What's the name of the notorious local lovers' lane?

The above are only a few of the questions that can be asked, and are listed only to prime your creative pump.

When I gather information from my contact I always end our talk with, "Give this a little thought and give me a call if you can think of anything at all that we can kid about or have some fun with."

Should You Hire a Writer?

SOME OF MY BEST FRIENDS are comedy writers. I love the creatures, especially when they tell a joke they're sinfully proud of and I top it. When they top mine, I'm not too fond of them. Once the competition is stilled, we're nice, honest, hardworking (within reason) people. However, we're only human. (For the most part, that is. Some of us are still struggling for that rating.) There are certain things we can't do.

Comedy writing is not an easy assignment. This book should have made the point by now that humor requires preparation, thought, and effort. Making it look effortless requires even more preparation, thought, and effort. Hardly anyone realizes this. Many performers—often, the same ones who get their names in the papers complaining about the quality of the scripts—will visit a writer's office and say, "I have to give a talk tonight. Could you jot down a dozen or so lines during your lunch hour?"

I once received a call from an actress. This was not just any actress, mind you, but one that I had had a teenage crush on. Just hearing her voice over the phone had my heart doing calisthenics. She was producing a show for charity and wanted me to do some emergency writing. The show was on the other side of town, but I would have swam to Europe for this lady.

"I've heard you're a good writer," she said. My heart came dangerously close to breaking a few of my ribs from the inside. "We really need some good writing before the curtain goes up tonight. We've had people working on this for weeks, but if this stuff is funny, then I'm the Queen of Siam. Can you come over to rehearsals and help us out?" Does Superman come to the aid of innocent victims? Does Mighty Mouse rush singing to the aid of the oppressed? Of course, I could help her out. I'd simply change into my writer's leotards and cape and fly right over there.

I got into my car and drove a couple of blocks, then said to myself, "Wait a minute. Some of my colleagues worked diligently over this script and this lady dismissed all that effort with sarcasm." I would probably rush over there, work under impossible conditions, then have my efforts greeted with snide asides after the affair. I turned around and came home again. Let her impugn my reliability; not my comedy.

I'm always amused by performers who pick up 120 pages of script that was created from nothing and then berate it because it's not worthy of their talents. Their talent, incidentally, consists of reading the words that others slaved over. It's rather like chastising Thomas Edison for not inventing a light bulb that wouldn't burn out.

Fred Allen became a hero of mine when I read about him coming into the radio studio to find some performer ranting about how substandard the script was. Allen said, "Where were you when the pages were blank?"

Forgive my tangential journey into self-indulgence, but I just want you, the buyer of comedy material, to realize some of the reality. Not everything the writer puts on paper is brilliant. (Nor is every acting performance of superior craftsmanship, either.) If you, the speaker, are going to enter into a working relationship with a writer, it would be nice to know up front what a writer *can't* do for you.

The writer probably won't be able to hand you a finished piece of magnificent humor. There are several reasons for this. The writer is working on something that you want; not something he wants. The inspiration and the excitement may not be there for this particular topic. Suppose an executive comes to me and says our tri-level circuit breaker project is failing and it's destroying morale. Give me some cute material that will lift the spirits of our H-16 welding team. I might not be all that thrilled about the assignment. As much as I love welding (it's a hobby of mine, naturally), this job simply might not motivate me.

You may not be communicating your desires properly. I once did a show for a well-known comic who insisted that there be no insult material in the routine. I tried to follow instructions, but slipped a few in. He objected. We had a meeting and he took them out, so I rewrote the piece. Then the producer saw the rewrite and claimed it wasn't funny. She was right. It wasn't funny, but it was what the comedian had wanted and asked for.

The night of the show, the comic ad-libbed lines that were in terrible taste. Worse than I would ever have dared to write. Someone wasn't communicating.

There's also a difference between an idea and its execution. Once I gave a seminar to a group of screenwriters. Each of them had in his briefcase an outline for a film script that was dynamite. Yet they couldn't sell them to the studios. They wanted to know why, if all these know-it-alls were turning down their brilliant story ideas, there were so many lousy films being made.

The answer is that some brilliant, salable ideas make terrible scripts. They're not written well, or they can't be written well. These people had story lines in outline form. They might well find that when they try to add dialogue, it won't translate so easily.

I have fought with producers many times over a particular idea that I liked. They argued against it. Sometimes I won and often I wished I hadn't. On those occasions, when I sat behind my typewriter, I discovered they were right; the story didn't go anywhere.

You'll discover this as the buyer, too. You'll have a concept that you know is stupendous. Yet the written material isn't. Sometimes it's because the concept has flaws hidden in it.

I've had this happen to me a few times as a sit-com producer. I would work out a story line with writers and then assign them the script. When they brought back the first draft, it was disappointing. A note session and a second draft would generate no improvements. To save the script, I would attack it myself and discover, as the other writers did before me, that it wouldn't work.

The concept and the execution are two different things. Sometimes the concept is valid, but the writer doesn't deliver what you had envisioned.

Even with a writer, you will have to do much of the work yourself. Bob Hope has had as many as 12 writers working for him at one time, yet he still "writes" his own monologues. He edits the material that is provided for him and assembles it. The raw material comes from the writers, but the finished product is his.

The reader might wonder, if he or she has to go through all this, why hire a writer? For most speakers who just want to add a dash of humor to their presentations, a writer is probably more trouble than benefit. Your own research and creativity, as we discussed in Chapters 6 and 7, will probably be easier, cheaper, and better.

Writers can be useful, though, when you need

- special material for one occasion
- different material for each speech
- a steady supply of fresh material
- a lot of material

You'll notice that someone like Bob Hope fits all those categories, so he hires writers.

If you're a speaker who has decided that you'll need someone else to help generate your humor, you'll be interested in:

- How to find a writer
- How to select *your* writer
- How to work with a writer
- How to treat a writer
- How to keep a writer

Let's now go through all of the above one by one.

HOW TO FIND A WRITER

'Taint easy. Comedy writers, outside of New York and Los Angeles, can't even find one another. There are associations for almost every conceivable occupation, but there's no group of comedy writers. That's why I began my newsletter for humorists. It's called "ROUND TABLE, A gathering place for comedy writers and humorists." It's supposed to be an exchange of ideas among humorists so the woman who was lost in Dearborn could communicate with another writer hidden away in Albuquerque. I mention the newsletter here because it does showcase writers. Each monthly issue has a page or two devoted to our subscribers. Several comedians have already contacted some of those writers for assignments. You might find someone in there who suits your style of humor. (Also we want you as a subscriber. ROUND TABLE, P.O. Box 13, King of Prussia, PA 19406)

You might discover a writer by reading books, magazine articles, or short fillers that appeal to you. You can contact the author through the publishers or the national syndicate.

There are several national writers clubs. They might recommend writers with specific specialties. I'm not sure how many comedy writers are in these clubs, but there may be a few.

ASSOCIATED BUSINESS WRITERS OF AMERICA
Suite 620
1450 S. Havana
Aurora, CO 80012
(303) 751-7844

THE AUTHORS GUILD, INC.
234 W. 44th St.
New York, NY 10036
(212) 398-0838

INTERNATIONAL WOMEN'S WRITING GUILD
Box 810
Gracie Station
New York, NY 10028
(212) 737-7536

NATIONAL WRITERS CLUB
Suite 620
1450 S. Havana
Aurora, CO 80012
(303) 751-7844

Most professional comedy writers will belong to the Writers Guild of America; either the east coast or the west coast branch. They will put you in touch with a given writer's agent.

WRITERS GUILD OF AMERICA, EAST
555 West 57th St.
New York, NY 10019
(212) 245-6180

WRITERS GUILD OF AMERICA, WEST
8955 Beverly Blvd.
Los Angeles, CA 90048
(212) 274-8601

You might try coaxing humorists out of the woodwork with advertising. A small classified ad is inexpensive and somehow or other, we find anything in the paper that has to do with comedy.

Lastly, you might pioneer in the field; that is, find your own writer. Keep an eye out for people who have an outstanding sense of humor and who do some creative humor as a hobby. That's how I began my career. An executive came to me and asked me to give a presentation at a company function. It went well. I was hooked, and stayed with comedy.

HOW TO SELECT *YOUR* WRITER

You may uncover many closet humor writers through any or all of the above, but you want *your* writer. Comic Kelly Monteith used to do a routine on how we personalize professional people. "I went to see *my* doctor" . . . *"My* lawyer advised me" . . . "I just had a meeting with *my* accountant." We don't *own* these people. They just work for us, but it's strange how we claim them as our own property. As Kelly goes on, "It's funny. I was just talking about this the other day with *my* hooker."

You will want a writer, though, who is suited to your style. The material the writer delivers should "feel" like your material. You should be comfortable with it. A writer who can't deliver this is useless to you.

In investigating writers, ask for a page or two of material on a topic of your choice. If you don't select the topic, you may get material from "the trunk." That's material that has been sitting around for sometime. It may be on yellowed paper with the corners crumbling. It'll be good because only a fool would send you his bad stuff as a showpiece. Yet, it doesn't show you what the writer can do on topics that you select nor how fast he can generate material for you.

If you ask for some samples on a current event, something that just made the papers this morning, and your writer comes back with page after page of brilliant, funny material, perfectly suited to you, lock that writer in the closet and swallow the key. From time to time, pass some food and blank pages under the door. This person is valuable.

Some writers may object to writing audition material. The objections may be justified. If they've got a good reputation, you should know enough about them from that. Perhaps you should know what they do from the people they work for. If a person has been writing comedy material for 15 years for Rodney Dangerfield, you can safely assume that writer knows his way around a joke.

Nevertheless, you're not Rodney Dangerfield. You still are not certain this writer can produce material you'll be happy with.

There are two ways around this (probably more, but two I'll suggest). First, pay the writer for the audition material. It may be wasted money, but it's cheaper than signing a long term contract with someone who can't help you. Second, you might arrange a short term contract with a reputable writer. If he can't produce the material you expect, the financial damage won't be that severe.

HOW TO WORK WITH A WRITER

I don't recommend buying just one piece of material. You'll very rarely be happy with it. A piece of material needs breaking in. You'll have to add that little touch of you, which may change the writing drastically. You may try it out and find that certain parts don't work, and thus destroy everything else in the piece that depends on them.

If you contract for just one piece of material, the writer naturally will feel that once it's done, he's done with it. You'll get a rewrite (if that was part of your agreement), but it will probably be halfhearted. The writer has no equity in the piece.

I suggest, rather, that your relationship with *your* writer be an ongoing one. (We writers hate one-night stands if a typewriter is involved.) You can build your material gradually while working along with a writer.

The first thing you'll want to do with your scribe is decide what you're going to work on. This can be your choice, his choice, or the combination of both.

Edit the submission and decide what you like and what you don't. Be forthright; it only helps the writer do a good job for you. That's what you want and what he wants, too. (Later, we'll talk about the care and handling of writers.) Ask for more material, better material, or both.

Try the material out. If it's at all possible, have the writer there to experience the audience reaction and to monitor your delivery.

Discuss the good and bad features of the material. What's working? Get more of that stuff. What's not working? Improve it or cut it. In other words, get a well-directed rewrite.

Repeat this process as often as necessary until you have a piece of material that is working well for you and that you're happy with.

Start all over again with the next chunk.

If you only need a few gags to spice up an important talk, then, yes, you can buy just that from a writer. But do overbuy. If you need five gags, don't just contract for five. Ask for 20 or 30. That way, you'll get the best five. If you don't get five out of 30, then you should go back and reread the section on selecting a writer.

HOW TO TREAT A WRITER

When my daughter brought our first grandson home from the hospital, I was a bit out of practice with infants. I was afraid to hold the youngster for fear I'd do something wrong or drop him, or whatever. Of course, one can't resist holding his first grandson. I took him and discovered that these little people are much more resilient than you think. Writers aren't.

They require special care and feeding and are more delicate than tropical fish.

In dealing with them, start with a budget. Writers enjoy getting paid, despite the popular opinion to the contrary. Everyone, from the emcee of the Rotary Dinner Dance to the headliners at the MGM Grand in Las Vegas, think that comedy writers turn out endless reams of material and it's all to be donated to the needy. I have had millionaire entertainers pop into my room, ask for three or four pages of material that they can use when they're asked to say a few words before the President of the United States and his wife that evening at a $1000 a plate dinner, and then never even offer to buy me lunch in exchange.

It's simply a show business custom. An entertainer who was working a small nightclub where he got paid $25 a night asked me to come see his act. I did. Between shows he asked what I could do to help him with material. We stood at the bar and discussed different ideas. Each time we ordered a round of drinks this man disappeared. I don't know where he vanished to, but I had to buy the drinks. Then he'd return. We'd talk, then the bartender would come back to attend to our empty glasses. The refills would arrive and my comic friend would evaporate.

Writers get the same song and dance all the time: "Write me something, and I'll pay you a few bucks when I start working better clubs." Did they tell that to the guy who sold them the grey tuxedo with the fancy piping on the lapels? Did they tell that to the guy that sold them the patent leather shoes? Did they tell that to the guy who collects the greens fees at the country club? (They all play golf for a hobby.)

If you don't have a budget, write your own stuff.

Let me list some arrangements that you can have with your writer. (Throughout the rest of this chapter, I'll give my opinion on the advantages and disadvantages of each.)

> PER JOKE: Here the writer would submit many lines and you would select those you want at a predetermined fee.
>
> PER ROUTINE: You would agree on a set fee for a complete routine of so many gags or of a given time length. For instance, you could buy a 30-gag routine or a bit that will run six minutes. Generally, since this is a finished piece, the writer will agree to at least one rewrite.
>
> PERCENTAGE: In this instance, a writer would agree to provide comedy material to you at a predetermined rate of so many gags a week or a certain amount of stage time a week in exchange for a percentage of your speaking fee. I recommend this method in working with new writers because it gives them an incentive to increase your earning power through good, solid comedy. It also has a fairness element to it.
>
> RETAINER: The speaker would pay a certain fee, regularly, for a regular supply of comedy material.

I haven't mentioned any fee ranges because this can vary from practically nothing to very expensive professional fees. This is up to the individual speaker and the writer he or she can find. Ideally, the arrangement should be beneficial to both parties.

Be definite and coherent in your requests. Writers are providing a service and can't do it well unless they know what you want. It's your act. They'll write anything you want as long as there is a stipend involved. You have to know why you hired writers in the first place and just what you expect from them.

Give them lots of strokes. Writers are an insecure lot. They pretend not to be, but they are. Comedy originates as a cover for some feeling of inferiority. Anyone who devotes his life to the creation of comedy must have massive inferiority complexes in there somewhere. So be gentle.

The writer's feelings aside, though, it's just good business. You want product, and you'll get more, if you're tactful.

When I was a beginning writer, most of my contact with the comics I worked for was through the mails or by phone. I would send my material out and then wait to see if they liked it or not.

One comic called up and complained. "I can't use half of the stuff you sent me," he argued. "I want you to send the same amount of stuff right away—no charge." I said, "You got what you paid for. I gave you just what we agreed to in our deal." I sent him 30 lines and he was angry because he didn't like 15 of them. If I were to rewrite on that basis, I'd only get one paycheck for my entire life.

Another comic called and was ecstatic. "Two of those lines you sent me were blockbusters. Get me some more stuff like those." I sat down and cranked out some more brilliant "blockbusters" and got it in the mail immediately.

Notice: one comic liked two lines; the other liked 15. But one concentrated on the two that worked and then got lots more inspired material. The other centered on the 15 that didn't and got an angry writer who couldn't work for that comic anymore. Who benefited the most? (Some of my friends claim the guy who got rid of me did.)

In building a piece of material, the only thing that's important is what you put into it, not what you throw away. Concentrate on the positive.

HOW TO KEEP A WRITER

This is an extension of the last point. Pay your writer a fair price. Don't hassle over the quality of the material by holding up his salary or trying to reduce it. You selected the writer and you agreed to terms. Pay him. If the writer isn't producing, don't renew the contract.

No writer will stay with you if everytime he has a bad batch of gags you want a reduction in price. When you give a talk that's not up to par, do you give part of the money back to your employer?

I work on a retainer basis with one comedian and will occasionally turn in some material that's not consistently hilarious. He'll read it and say, "You had a bad day, didn't you?" That's it. There's no ranting and raving and claiming that I'm trying to destroy a career. I just had a bad day. He knows it and I know it. I've also had a lot of good days and that's why I'm well into my second decade of working with this entertainer.

Give generous recognition. It strokes the writer, but it's also good business. You get more and better material when the writer feels appreciated. Mention the writer's name from the platform. Have him take a bow. I remember being in a gorgeous nightclub one opening night with many celebrities. The comic I was working for introduced them all, and then introduced me from the stage. I stood up, elated, and waved to the adoring crowd. Then I reached over and shook hands with one of the entertainers. I said, "It's a pleasure to meet you." He replied, "That's the longest bow I've ever seen in my life." (I may have gotten carried away with the celebrity recognition.)

Introduce your writer when you can to other opportunities. Some folks won't do this for fear of losing a good writer. Again, it's poor business practice. You can't keep an enthusiastic person static for too long. If the writer stays too long with nothing else happening, he'll tire of that and the writing will suffer.

You've found this one great writer. You'll find another.

I just want to take a moment here to remind you that most speakers won't need much outside material. There may be rare cases when you or your company may occasionally want to hire a professional writer. Sometimes it's because a speaker wants to be a pure humorist. But for the most part you can add humor to your talks without the expense of hiring a pro.

Timing and Pacing

COMEDY IS HARDLY EVER discussed without timing being mentioned. What does it mean? I don't know, and I've never seen a definition. Jack Benny was a master of timing. He also had great stage presence, delivery, and material. How do we isolate the timing? Are there any successful comics who don't have timing? Is a performer funny because she has good timing or does her good timing make her funny? It's a mystery.

Timing's definition may be elusive, but the phenomenon is real. Monologue artists can hardly work without audience feedback. Even though their material remains unchanged and their delivery is unaffected, their timing is off. When we had to shoot the Carol Burnett Show without a studio audience, the performances weren't as sharp.

Follow me for a few steps, and then I'll hazard my own explanation of "timing."

Some researchers propose that laughter is basically a shout of victory. When a life-or-death struggle was resolved, the victorious caveman would laugh. There must be come validity to the theory because we still see it today. When boxers sense victory, they smile or even laugh. In films, the baddie who gets the drop on the goodie laughs.

Sometimes, though, we see the loser laugh nervously. It's the same principle: the laugh then is an indication of a mock victory. It's an attempt to convince an opponent that we're not really helpless. We also see that many times in boxing. One fighter is staggered by a vicious punch and he smiles at his opponent. He's saying, "You may think you hurt me, but you didn't," while he's trying to discover which way is up.

A comedian is in a duel of wits with his audience. He tosses out a straight line and challenges them to come up with a punch line. They try for a fraction of a second, then the comic tops them. He's defeated them, and they laugh.

Timing is that ability to sense what is going on in the mind of the listeners. It's knowing just how long to make the pauses for each audience. It's sensing how loudly to speak and how quickly. When to be flippant and when to be dramatic. It's tuning into the psychology of your listeners. It's challenging them—and then topping them at the precise moment.

That sort of timing is intuitive. I doubt if rules can be formulated for it. It's like trying to teach charisma. If it can be learned at all, it must be self-taught with experience being the coteacher.

You'll have to learn timing the same way the masters did—by trial and error. (Jack Benny may have been a master of timing because he'd been learning it for three quarters of a century.)

I will say one thing about timing: humor is like economics in that people expect value consistent with their investment. As Shakespeare said, "Brevity is the soul of wit."

That doesn't mean that all gags have to be short. It does mean that the more time you spend building to a punch line, the better that payoff has to be. A speaker can throw off a quick one liner, and if it doesn't get a big laugh, he can just continue his talk as if nothing happened. However, if a speaker invests three solid minutes building up to one punch line that's a dud, it's hard to hide it.

Try to get a feel for how much each punch line can support. You may be able to reinforce some longer stories with shorter, less hilarious one liners along the way. Then the audience doesn't feel as if they've invested the time for nothing. They've had fun along the way. But don't be misled. This won't cover up for a weak punch line.

Let me give you an illustration that shows how this phenomenon can help a joke that's top-heavy. (That's a story that requires too much set-up to justify the punch line.) I once did a retirement party for a guy whom we used to kid about his drinking. Actually, he didn't drink excessively, but he did like to brag about his prowess at the bar. When he was having a good time at a party, he would take his spectacles off and tuck them safely into his jacket pocket. Here's the joke I did at his party.

> Everybody knows that when Bill's had one or two too many he takes his glasses off. I was talking to his wife of 25 years right before the dinner tonight. I said, "It must be easy for you to tell when Bill's been drinking anytime he comes home without his glasses on." She said, "What glasses?"

This is a funny joke. (You'll have to trust me on that.) In my estimation, though, the buildup is much too long. It is necessary, however. We must know that Bill takes his glasses off when he drinks a tad too much, and we must know he's been married for 25 years. The following rewrite has a little fun along the way. See what you think.

> You all know that Bill has been married to the same woman for 25 years. Although she says that after 25 years with him, she's not quite the same woman.
>
> And you know that he takes his glasses off anytime he drinks too much. I don't know why. I guess he just doesn't like to see himself in that condition.
>
> I was talking to his wife about that tonight. I said, "I guess it's easy for you to tell Bill's been drinking anytime he comes home without his glasses." She said, "What glasses?"

It's the same joke and although it's actually longer, the one punch line we're talking about now feels shorter. The set-up is not burdened with so much exposition.

If you have a good story with a powerful punch line that just hasn't been working for you, take the advice of me and Bill Shakespeare, and break it into smaller pieces. "Brevity is the soul of wit."

Pacing is different from timing. Pacing is the amount of humor you include in your talk and the intensity and positioning of it throughout your presentation.

We'll be talking, throughout the book, about speakers who are primarily delivering a message, but who want to use humor to fortify it and to keep their audience attentive and alert. Pure humorists, too, must be aware of pacing. We spoke earlier of the peaks and valleys of comedy. Some jokes have to be funnier than others. The trick is to space the "biggies" throughout the performance. The peaks must occur with some regularity. Otherwise, one long valley can kill you with your listeners.

You can take the same comedic material, rearrange it, and wind up with two totally different speeches. One will be dynamite and the other will put an audience to sleep. The difference is the pacing.

This skill is also necessary for informational and inspirational speakers. Beginning with a few jokes and ending with one doesn't help the body of the speech. Humor must be used throughout the speech to keep the audience alert.

Let's recall some of the reasons for using humor in a speech to discover how to keep our presentation well-paced.

AT THE START

It's important to use humor at the beginning of a talk. Remember: We said earlier that humor is not necessarily joke-telling. You can establish your sense of humor without a long story. It might be done with a glance or with a word or two, but it should be done early because there's usually some tension present in an audience at the beginning of a speech. This audience doesn't know if you're going to be any good. They don't know if they'll like you. They don't know if they'll agree with what you say. Perhaps you may say something that will cause them to have to work harder. It's similar to the tension that exists between youngsters who move into a new neighborhood and the children who already live there. The audience is leery of any unknown. Therefore, any joke at the start will get a magnified response because you've broken through their defenses and reduced the tension.

You'll also serve notice to your listeners that you're a nice human being. Most people like a person who has a sense of humor.

Any benefits can be reversed, though, if you open with a clinker. This doesn't mean your opening has to be the biggest laugh of your presentation. It just has to be good, as in "not bad."

You want to open smart. If you open with an old, "I heard it before" groaner, the tension is going to increase; not be relieved.

Your opener should—

1. be light and easy

2. sum up the situation
3. apply as directly to the audience as possible

It should be light and easy because you don't want to strain too hard here for laughs. You're not trying to wow them with your funny bone, you're simply trying to make friends and relax your listeners. You want them to recognize that you have a sense of humor and you're not taking yourself or this talk *too* seriously.

Summing up the situation conveys to the audience that you know what you're talking about. You're a sharp lecturer who knows as much about what's going on as they do. They'll pick this up.

As an example, I was recently at an awards banquet where each recipient gave a tedious acceptance speech. As it drew closer to midnight, the audience grew more restless. One speaker accepted his honor and opened with this line that summed up the situation:

"I'd like to give an eloquent thank you speech, but I'm not going to. I'm a firm believer that every banquet should end the same day it starts on."

Saying something that applies to your listeners will perk up their ears. You're not only speaking to them; you're speaking *about* them. It's hard for people to resist that. Many people who don't believe in astrology still read their horoscope every day because it's about them.

Here are some examples of good, utilitarian opening lines. This first one was delivered by a person who had recently had heart bypass surgery to an audience of 200 people who had also had heart bypass surgery that same year:

"It's nice to be here tonight. Considering what we've been through this year, it's nice to be anywhere, isn't it?"

The second was delivered at the opening ceremonies of a National Speakers Convention by the president, Don Thoren:

"We have 400 speakers here this year. I hope we have a few listeners, too."

Then there's a line that Bob Hope used to open the Academy Awards when they were held around Easter:

"Welcome to the Academy Awards, or as they call it around my house, Passover."

If you must open with a longer story, make it a goodie. You don't get a second chance to make a first impression. Keep in mind the economics of humor: the payoff has to justify the time the audience invests in the set-up.

Following are three guidelines that you might use to pace the humor in your talk.

HUMOR SPACED THROUGHOUT YOUR SPEECH

This is to keep your audience alert and eager to listen. The mind can fall into a rhythm which lulls it to sleep. Your wit can be a splash of cold water that keeps your audience listening. Any message, no matter how significant, can get boring. A serious talk needs splashes of light-heartedness.

The simplest way to space humor is mathematically. Insert a goodie in your presentation, let's say, every 10 minutes or so. Now you may change that number based on your own experiences. It may be every six or seven minutes. Fine.

This needn't be timed with a stopwatch. You obviously wouldn't want to interrupt an important flow of information merely because your 10 minutes are up and it's time for a "funny." Search through your talk for natural breaking points.

This humor doesn't have to be a lengthy story, unless that's the style you're most comfortable with. I'll emphasize again that humor is not necessarily telling jokes. It's anything lighthearted that snaps your audience out of the rhythmical monotony.

Let's suppose, for illustration, that you've just completed a section of your talk which is a railing against some political proposal. Your point in this segment is that we don't have to buy all the propaganda just because the politicians tell us to. You've been very forceful and serious about this point. You might now say (if this is your comedy style):

> "Politicans can make mistakes, too. They vote for themselves, don't they?"

Or if you prefer longer stories, you can show that when politicians talk, it's not imperative that anyone listen. You can tell the story about the Senator who, years ago, visited a small town and was invited to a public hanging. It was an honor to have such a dignitary at an affair like this, so the mayor of the town asked the condemned man if it would be all right if the Senator said a few words. "It's all right with me," the prisoner responded, "but could you hang me first? I've already heard him talk."

We speakers sometimes get so intent about our oratory that we don't listen to ourselves. We're delivering a message that we believe in and we assume everyone else shares our enthusiasm. They don't. At least, not all of them, all of the time.

This lesson hit me between the eyes when I was traveling around the nation promoting my first book. I had been visiting two and three cities a day for two weeks and my last appearance was on a phone-in radio show at two o'clock in the morning. When I got on I talked about comedy writing and answered all of the questions with as much enthusiasm as I could muster.

Then a woman called in and asked me, "Are you ever funny around the house or with your family?" I said, "It depends on the time and the place, but yes, I generally fool around and am funny." She said, "Well, why don't you start doing it on this program?" I had been so intent on talking about comedy writing that I forgot to entertain.

When I give seminars to writers, I have the same tendency. My message is so important to me that I think the audience is sitting on the edge of their chairs just waiting for my wisdom. They're not. As the speaker, I have to pull attentiveness out of them.

It's a good idea to have someone monitor the audience while you concentrate on your message. Have someone else gather information about your listeners. Are people putting their heads down and not watching you? Are they reading their own literature while you're performing? Do they start whispered conversations as you speak? These are all signs that their attention is dwindling.

Those are the spots where you should add a little surprise for them; something or other that will snap them back to attention. It's not even necessary that they hear your *bon mot*. The sound of others laughing will bring them back. They'll say, "Something happened and I missed it. I'd better listen from now on."

TO SET A POINT IN THE MIND OF YOUR AUDIENCE

Humor can help your audience understand the prominent points of your speech and to remember them better and longer.

If your talk is well constructed, it will have these important moments well spaced throughout. Highlighting each of them with a lighthearted illustration will then assure that your humor is well paced.

Make your point. Illustrate it with some wit. Make your point again, and move on to the next.

My speaking friend, Cavett Robert, tells a story that illustrates this about a manager who once gave a ripsnorting, fire-and-brimstone oration on the importance of improving employee productivity. Raises would be given fairly, and when deserved, he promised, but only on merit. He said:

"I want to put a raise voucher in every one of your pay envelopes next week, but with one important stipulation written on it . . . the raise is to become effective when you do."

It's hard to ignore so graphic a reminder.

USE HUMOR AS A REWARD FOR LISTENING

You've given your audience some solid information and they've absorbed it. You're working hard to educate or inspire them, and they're striving diligently to digest it. Okay, take a recess.

Give the audience a reward and make it clear that's what it is. Tell them that you're getting away from the lessons for a beat. Just relax now and listen to this story. Let your mind sit back and slip off its shoes for a while because what's coming is fun and you won't have to learn it or remember it. In fact, if you don't want, you don't even have to listen to it. We'll get back to work in a minute, but right now, we're taking a break.

Audiences are very easy. They'll accept bonuses and bribes. They almost expect them. After all, they're working harder than you are. You know the subject you're talking about. They're still learning.

These excursions are easy to get into because you admit up front that they have nothing to do with your talk. Something that happened just reminded you of an incident you want to share with them.

In my speeches, I generally end with a question and answer period. It's fun and informal and each question generally reminds me of a story. So sometimes I'll use it as a bonus, by saying, after the question is asked, "Okay, I'll answer that, but first I gotta tell you something that happened to me yesterday . . " Now the audience not only wants to hear the story that I can no longer put off, but they'll also be more intent on the answer to the original question. Somehow setting it aside like that builds the anticipation.

One question that's generally asked is, "How do writers in television generally get paid?" My reply then might be:

How do we get paid? Okay, I'll answer that question for you, but first I have to tell you a funny thing that another writer did to me. You have to understand that you never believe anybody in show business when they tell you how much money they make. We all lie about it. I'd be a happy man if I made as much money as I tell my friends I make. Anyway, a while back a writing friend of mine called and said, "Hey, how are you doing?" I said, "How am I doing? I got offers for several pilot deals. Right now I'm negotiating with two different shows and they both want me. I think the movie is going to sell very soon. And the books are selling like crazy. The publisher wants another. I'm doing terrific." My friend said, "Look, how about if I call you back when you're alone," and hung up.

Then I answer the question and move on to the next one.

Review your talk with pacing in mind. Use a combination of the three guidelines to help position the humor in your speech. One final word of caution: since we're not trying to convert all speakers to comedians, add the humor sparingly. You don't want to add so much that it becomes clumsy. Add just a dash; then if you study and decide you need more, add it in.

Humor to Avoid

IT'S IMPORTANT TO REMEMBER that we're discussing speakers who use humor, as opposed to professional comedians. The comic's goal is to get laughs; therefore, it's okay to get them anyway he wants.

You, as a speaker, though, are using humor as a tool, a means to an end. Your overall goal is not to get laughs. You want to convey a message and comedy helps you do that.

We know that the reasons for employing humor from the platform are to get people to listen better, to retain what they hear, and to respect us as speakers. *We want them to like us.*

That final item is most important. First, all of us want to be liked or respected. It's just more fun that way.

Secondly, people pay more attention to us if they like us. Since speakers are communicators, this is tremendously important.

Humor is one of the tools that can get folks to like you. You must be selective, however. Some humor is delicate and dangerous, and is best left to professional entertainers. Which kinds? Well, let's get away from the stage and the podium for a while and just look at human nature.

We all know people that we like to be around. They don't even have to be friends, just interesting acquaintances. There are some folks I love to play tennis with. They are fun on the court and they're a joy to sit around and talk with in the clubhouse after the match. Some parties I enjoy more if I know So-and-So is going to be there. Some friends I relish going to dinner with because they're always delightful.

Everyone knows people like these. Think of a few of them and try to analyze just why you enjoy being around them.

In my own analysis I've discovered that I enjoy people who are fun. They're the ones that brighten up a room when they enter.

I also enjoy being with people who make me feel welcome. This is a glorious virtue. Perhaps, like me, you've been to parties where you don't know many people. A person who can pull you into the inner circle and immediately make you feel as if you always belonged is a Godsend.

Finally, I've noticed that I like being with people who make me feel good about myself.

These things you enjoy in other people are exactly what you want to bring to the podium with you. Any humor that helps you accomplish that is acceptable.

Now let's investigate the flip side. You and I also know people we'd rather not associate with. Think about why.

I don't like to be with people who are dull. Dinner is no fun when So-and-So continually talks about some subject that interests only him.

I don't savor second-class citizenship. Some people do have the ability to always make me seem inferior. Don't get me wrong; I am in many ways and in many areas, but there are things I enjoy more than having this pointed out to me.

One particular person pops to mind who epitomizes both of the above. My wife and I attended a dinner and sat with this gentleman and his wife. I listened to how many miles he ran each morning. It was his way of staying in the excellent shape he was in when he won the High School Cross Country Championship, and then went on to excel in several sports in College. I pretended interest when he told me how difficult it was to run since he was now so successful in business. He had difficulty finding the time for his strenuous physical fitness program. He also talked money, of which he had plenty.

I was champing at the bit. I wanted to wow this guy with my show business accomplishments. I'd written for big stars and won Emmys and everything.

Finally, somewhere well into dessert, he deigned to ask, "What do you do?" My heart jumped so much it almost knocked my tie pin off. With all the humility I could muster I said, "I'm a television writer." "I don't watch television," he said.

Since there was no point in continuing my story, I simply excused myself to go to the men's room, and went out to the parking lot and let the air out of his tires.

People who are rude and obnoxious don't win my heart, either.

You will have your own dislikes which will not be a part of the humor style that you design for yourself. My personal list can be capsulized as follows:

1. dull
2. superior
3. rude

Some one liners can be delightful; others can be offensive. Whatever style you've chosen for yourself, make sure it will make an audience like, not dislike, you.

Now let's take my list of "don'ts" and discuss them individually.

DULL

It's frightening to be at a microphone and to read boredom on the faces gazing up at you. Dullness is the one unforgivable sin of speakers and performers. You can be untalented, untrained, uninformative, but for heaven's sake don't be uninteresting.

Each year, the Academy Awards telecast has to explain the voting rules. No one really cares about it, but apparently it's obligatory. So each year they try to invent some innovative way of making the explanation entertaining. Recently they were overwhelmingly successful. They had a Marine Corps Drill Instructor read these rules to his charges. It was very authentic, done just as if he were explaining how to care for an M-1 rifle. It was so entertaining that a few days later, Johnny Carson had the Marine Corps Drill Instructor who did the bit as a guest on his show.

Even the dullest of topics can be enlivened with humor.

SUPERIOR HUMOR

This is an attitude where the performer says to the listeners in so many words, "I'm hip and you're square;" "I'm smart and you're dumb;" "I'm rich and you're poor;" "I'm the boss and you're the workers;" or "I'm in and you're out." The performer stands at the mike and pronounces that he's glad he's so much better than those poor slobs who are listening to him.

It's put-down humor that is designed to feed the ego of the performer. It alienates an audience and no speaker wants that.

I once had cocktails with another writer and he ordered some drink, whatever was in at the time, and I ordered a Manhattan (I like the cherries). He laughed derisively and said, "Who orders a Manhattan nowadays?" I said, "Probably the people who want them." (I do like the cherries.)

Perhaps my order was square, but it was crass to point that out to me.

We have to be careful that this attitude doesn't creep into our programs. It's insidious.

I used to do a joke that I've since dropped for this reason. At most of my talks, I'm the "Hollywood Writer" talking to a group of businessmen. To illustrate this I would say, "I'm happy to be here. I've never been in a room with this many ties before." First of all, I dropped it because it's a lousy joke. But even if it were a gem, I wouldn't use it anymore because I designed it to show the difference in our lifestyles. It never came off that way. It was more of a put-down of the official dress of the businessman. This line could have been roughly translated as saying, "Aren't you guys fools to dress up in uniforms and go to an office every day, while I sit casually by my swimming pool in the glamorous city of Hollywood and have a grand time?"

There are other ways of saying that our lifestyles are different that will kid me rather than put down my audience. Things like:

> We dress casually in my work. In fact, "casually" is a nice word for it. I have one writer friend who would give you the shirt off his back—for spite.
>
> They kid me about the way I dress at the office. One day, since our expenses are tax deductible, I wrote down lunch with a friend on my desk calendar. It came to $20.78. Another writer looked at it and said, "What'd you do? Buy a new suit?"

Do you read the difference? One puts down my audience. The other makes them feel good about themselves. They're proud that they dress nicely and not like me and my colleagues. Both, though, point up the difference in our lifestyles.

Here's another more blatant example. A Hollywood star had made a film in a foreign country. At the completion of shooting the government threw a farewell party for the film company. There were officials of the country there as well as representatives of the U.S. government. The star made a short farewell speech. He said:

"The only way I'll ever come back to this country is if my doctor tells me I only have a month to live. Then I'll come back, because time passes more slowly here than any other place in the world."

When Bob Hope travels on his USO tours, he is given grand receptions everywhere. Dignitaries and officers at each location dine with him and entertain him. Yet his humor is always of the enlisted man. He becomes one with the guys sitting out there watching his show. He may boast of meeting the brass or dining with them, but it always comes back to "sabotage" him. For example:

Your commanding officer ordered a 21-gun salute when I arrived. Next time I wish he'd wait till the plane lands.

The General came out in this terrible heat to meet me when I got off the plane. I said, "Don't salute, General. You've got terrible sweat stains on your shirt." He said, "I'm not wearing a shirt."

I like to make myself appear superior and then destroy myself with lines like:

I'm glad I dress so much nicer than most of the people here. The girls are all after me because of it. In fact, when I walked in the door tonight, one girl nudged the other and said, "Get him."

My book is in its fifth printing. The first four came out blurry.

Even my aunt and uncle who still live out on the old farm enjoyed my book. They said the pages were very soft.

One of the best ways to recognize the difference between good humor and this "holier than thou" superior type is to watch how Johnny Carson and David Letterman operate. Periodically, they will both have zanies on their shows. Someone or another who has just won the hog calling contest of Stinky River. Carson has fun with these folks and their hog calling skill, but he doesn't ridicule or embarrass them. Carson almost gives you the impression that he's bewildered by what they do and how they do it, but he might like to learn it sometime. Letterman gives the impression that he's glad he has never been associated with this before and hopes never to be in the future.

Corporate speakers have to be especially careful of this superior attitude because in most cases they are the superior. Any humor that highlights that and makes the employees feel inferior because of it can be counterproductive. Try to place yourself in your audience and hear your words from their point of view. If there's a chance it might offend you, drop the bit, or rework it. Almost any point you want to make can be made without offending.

Each time you prepare to perform, practice being your own audience, too.

RUDE

Again, that single word looks shocking sitting there all alone. It's just as jarring from the platform. Racial, ethnic, sexist and off-color gags fall into this category. Now, mind you, I'm not prudishly banning all of these, simply cautioning you to be wary of them. Some of the above may fit into your program nicely, but study them first so that you don't come off offending your listeners with them.

At a St. Paddy's day affair in Los Angeles, the late Pat O'Brien said, "It's a good thing God created whiskey. It kept the Irish from ruling the world." But then who better to deliver an Irish joke than Pat O'Brien?

Some slightly naughty jokes may be perfect for your routine. However, if there is a chance that they might alienate a reasonable percentage of the crowd, drop them. At least first check with someone who should know. A representative of the group you're addressing may be able to give you some standards. If there is still any doubt, do without the questionable routine.

Notice that we haven't banned insult jokes. Used properly these don't irritate listeners. In fact, they have the opposite effect; they bring the people into the festivities. It used to be a celebrity-status thing to be insulted by Don Rickles. When good buddies get together, the insults fly. Admittedly, it is an area where care has to be exercised, but we'll go into a full discussion of using insult humor safely and effectively in a later chapter.

To capsulize, professionals can and do get away with some material that you and I shouldn't attempt. They are using humor as an end; we are using it as a tool. We don't want to risk destroying the main objective of our speech with humor that irritates our audience. Review any humor you use from the audience's point of view. If any material is doubtful, replace it.

Once again, treat your audience as old friends and you should have no problem. You wouldn't do anything to irritate your old chums, likewise, you won't offend your listeners.

How to Break Material In

As I've said before, the only real judge of comedy is the audience. The rest of us are only guessing. "Breaking material in" means trying it out in front of an audience so you can see what parts they enjoy, which are slow, which need improvement, and which sections you want to lock away in a vault.

Some professional comics will play smaller dates in local clubs or visit comedy clubs to break in new material. It's a more informal atmosphere and there's not the same pressure on their career as when they're opening in high-priced rooms.

It's the proverbial chicken and the egg dilemma. You want your material to be letter perfect before you face an audience, but you can't get that precision without first facing an audience. It seems like an unsolvable puzzle, but there are ways around it.

Someone once asked Dr. Charles Jarvis how to try out new material safely. He said he never used new material. However, Dr. Jarvis updates his act constantly and there are new gags in there almost every time he makes an appearance. But what he meant by his statement was that there is no such thing as "new" material—it's all been tried out hundreds of times before.

Each speaker should try out his humorous material before including it in his program. We'll discuss ways of doing that.

THE FIRST PERSON YOU HAVE TO CONVINCE IS YOURSELF

This may appear obvious, but it's often neglected. Earlier we said that people complain, "I can't do comedy." What they really mean is, "I can't do *other people's* comedy." If you read or hear a joke that gets great audience response, that doesn't mean it will work for you. *You* have to break it in. *You* have to try it out. *You* must

1. Like and believe in the piece of material
2. Be able to *do* the material
3. Be convinced that you can do it well

Let's take a look at these three points, one at a time.

1. LIKE AND BELIEVE IN THE MATERIAL

What's the difference whether a speaker likes a humorous bit or not, so long as the audience enjoys it? If a piece of material is funny, and we recite it word for word, won't it always be funny?

I learned a great lesson from Jack Benny once by writing a bad piece of material for him. Notice I'm not confessing to writing bad comedy material. It was a bad piece of material *for Jack Benny*. There's a difference.

Jack had agreed to appear as a special guest on the opening show of Carol Burnett's tenth season on television. I wrote a short bit for him to do at the opening.

Jack called and said he liked the piece but would like a short meeting with the writers. I went to his office to discuss the material with him. He soothed my anxiety by reiterating that he thought the piece was funny, "but . . ." (comedy writers learn to dread that word, but . . .). The "but" in this case was that Jack, regardless of whether he genuinely thought it was funny or was just being tactful, didn't believe the piece. He was supposed to walk out on stage after the announcement instead of Carol Burnett. He wanted to know why he would do that. I suggested that he was buying a piece of candy and got lost. He objected that he wouldn't walk onto a lighted stage. We kept discussing and changing, and finally one of Jack's associates suggested that it was only a small piece at the top of the show. Perhaps Jack could suspend belief this once. Mr. Benny got a little peeved and said, "How many times do I have to tell you? When I'm doing a joke about my Stradivarius, I *have to be holding my Stradivarius*."

Jack Benny couldn't go out there and ask an audience to have faith in a routine that he didn't have faith in. It wasn't anything that the audience had to do or not do. It was simply that he felt a reponsibility to the listeners. He couldn't convince them of something he didn't swallow himself.

If even Jack Benny didn't think he could put over material he didn't believe in, the rest of us had better have faith in our routines. Any doubts you have about humorous material is detected by your listeners.

Why? Because we can't hide our feelings. They escape whether we want them to or not. Albert Mehrabian in his book *Silent Messages,* did a study of communication. There are, first of all, the words. That is what we say. Then there are the vocal characteristics. These could be the pitch of the voice, the tone, the emphasis, and so on. Last there are the nonverbal signals. This has nothing to do with words or voice, but rather what we're doing while we're making the statement. Some of these are: our physical appearance, our demeanor, physical expression, gestures, touch, and so on.

Those of us who write scripts are aware of these nuances because sometimes the words aren't enough. For instance, suppose our hero, Ivan, has to say to our heroine, Myrtle, "Myrtle, I love you." That alone doesn't tell us much, does it? So, we give our actor stage directions to help him. (Only where necessary, though. They get angry when we do too much of their performing for them.) We may write the same words and get three different readings, as follows:

IVAN

(TO MYRTLE, PASSIONATELY)
Myrtle, I love you.
Or this way:

IVAN

(BORED, AS IF TRYING TO DISMISS HER)
Myrtle, I love you.
Or even like this:

IVAN

(TAUNTING HER, LAUGHING DERISIVELY)
Myrtle, I love you?

One of my favorite examples of nonverbal communication was in the film "Klute." Jane Fonda played a part-time prostitute. In one scene she was embracing a lover and telling him she loved him. She said it was fervent passion. The whole time, though, she was checking her watch to see just how much more time her customer was allotted.

Mehrabian analyzed the importance of each of these three phases—verbal, vocal characterisics, and nonverbal. Take a guess yourself. On a percentage basis, just how important do you feel the words are in conveying your message? What percentage of your meaning is conveyed by the vocal characteristics? Is what you say more important than how you say it, or vice versa? Then estimate what percentage of your meaning is transmitted by the nonverbal signals. Stop for a moment and jot down your estimates.

Here are the percentages that Albert Mehrabian discovered through his research.

Verbal	7%
Vocal Characteristics	38%
Nonverbal	55%

Over half of what we're transmitting to others has nothing to do with what we say or how we say it. It has to do with our nonverbal signs. Most of those signs have to do with how we feel about what we're saying. Therefore, if we don't like a piece of material or don't believe in it, we will be telling the audience just that; not necessarily with our vocabularly, but with our demeanor. It can be more eloquent than our prose.

Remember, too, that this discomfort with a piece of material can be for reasons other than someone not being convinced it's funny. It can be a belief that you don't subscribe to. Racial and ethnic humor may fall into this category. Some people can't tell off-color jokes. It can be political or religious humor. It can be anything that makes *you* feel uneasy and it will translate itself to the crowd.

2. YOU MUST BE ABLE TO DO THE MATERIAL

You don't know that for sure until you try it. I remember writing a sight gag for *The Tim Conway Show*. As we were shooting this particular page, Tim kept changing the joke trying to get something new to work. It was a joke that had something to do with an Indian and a Cavalry officer making a peace treaty. Conway had a large spear and in trying to symbolically break it over his knee he would injure the Cavalry officer, starting the war all over again. I was convinced the joke, as written, was funny, so I told Tim to try it that way. He stepped out of the way, handed me the spear, and said, "Show me." When I tried to demonstrate, I found out why Tim was changing the joke. It was physically impossible to do. On paper it looked great, but none of us writers knew that it wouldn't work because we never tried it. The only true test is a trial run.

Danny Kaye has done some hilarious novelty songs over the years. He does double-talk, patter, and phony foreign dialects superbly. He also makes them sound easy. But give them a try yourself and see how different it is.

Red Skelton does entertaining pantomimes as the "Old Man," the "Little Kid," and whatever other characters his creative mind invents. His mime skills are so extraordinary that you can almost see his age change. He seems to grow or shrink at will. It doesn't look that difficult, but stand before a mirror and see if you can do it.

Don Rickles does an act that seems simple. It's only insults and attacking humor. Pick out someone in the audience, do a couple of lines about how they're dressed, how terrible the wife looks, some remarks about their ethnic background, and you're a smash. Right? Wrong! Copy down a small segment of Rickle's act sometime and try doing it convincingly. It's not easy.

So don't trust a mental visualization of yourself performing a piece of material or telling a joke. Break it in. Recite it *aloud*. You'll be surprised at what a difference it makes. Do it full out, also. You want to get a feel of the act just the way you'll eventually do it before an audience. You may find that you can't do it.

I once saw a policeman teaching a self-defense class to women. One of the first tactics he taught was to scream as loud as possible when attacked. This might frighten the attacker or attract help. Many of the students noted that and mentally tucked it into their bag of tricks. However, the instructor then pointed out that a good percentage of people *can't* scream. They think they can, but they've never tried it. We don't get much chance to practice it. Most of us honestly don't know if we can let out a convincing yell or not. If you doubt me, close the book, close the door, and try one. (Please warn the family first.)

This, of course, is just one example of things you think you can do, but perhaps can't. There are hundreds of others, and they differ for each person. You'll never know until you try them—out loud and full out.

Remember, too, that no joke or piece of business is carved in stone. They can all be changed or altered to suit your own style. As you try out material, you'll discover the delivery that is most comfortable to you.

3. BE CONVINCED THAT YOU CAN DO IT WELL

This is slightly different from point No. 2. You tested material there to be sure that you could *do it at all*. A child doing wonders with a hula hoop makes the procedure look easy. You attempt it, and it's around your ankles. Here, we're talking about something that you not only can do, but you also want to try it to see how *well* you do it. A musician summed up the phenomenon in talking about the popularity of guitars. He said something to the effect that it's the easiest instrument to learn to play and the most difficult instrument to learn to play well.

Speakers have to break in material to discover which pieces they can do well. Comedians and humorists learned this a long time ago. I know and work with some legendary performers who won't do "he says-she says" jokes. By that, I mean jokes with dialogue going back and forth. Some very versatile performers refuse to do one liners. They've learned that they don't handle that form very well.

I remember sitting backstage at the London Palladium as Bob Hope was rehearsing his monologue for that evening's performance—the Command Performance to celebrate the 25th anniversary of Queen Elizabeth's Coronation. The individual gags had already been written on cue cards and Hope was going through them to hear how they sounded. He was uncomfortable with one gag and lifted it from the routine. It happened to be my joke. I complained, "That's a good joke. The Queen will like that." Hope said, "Will she? Really?" I said, "Certainly." He said, "Then you get out there and do it."

The line was said and taken in good-natured fun, but the point remains that Bob Hope tested the material aloud, found this particular joke uncomfortable, for whatever reason (it needn't be logical), and discarded it.

Try to test all your material and make sure it's something you definitely want to take to the podium with you.

TRY NEW STUFF OUT ON FRIENDS, RELATIVES, AND SMALL GROUPS

Now that you're sold on the stuff, you have to find out if others share your confidence. The only way you can find out is to plunge in, throw the stuff at them, and read the response. Naturally, you won't get the explosion of laughter and applause that you'll get in a crowded auditorium, but you should be able to judge the sincerity of their reactions.

Sometimes, it seems nothing is more obvious than a forced or phony laugh. However, there are a few guidelines to follow when trying your material out on others:

DON'T ANNOUNCE THAT YOU'RE TESTING MATERIAL

That's like trying to be amusing after someone says to you, "Say something funny." It puts an unfair burden on you and on the group. Just sneak it in.

EXPERIMENT WITH YOUR MATERIAL

While breaking in new material, try it in different ways. Phrase the punch line differently. Use different gestures or facial expressions. The one that you don't feel completely confident about may be the one that gets the best results.

Advertisers do this constantly. They split their advertising to gauge effectiveness. One mailing may go out with red brochures, another with blue. Then they measure the results. They'll try a certain slogan in one part of the country and a paraphrase of it in another area to see which draws the most response.

Since we all admit that we're only guessing about humor until we get that audience feedback, why not guess with measurable reaction?

Some speakers break material in when they are doing free speeches or giving speeches at a discounted rate. I can't recommend that practice, because each time you perform you're an advertisement for yourself. There are potential buyers in each assembly. It's dangerous to risk material that you're not absolutely sure about in front of potential customers. My belief is: When you're good, you'll get paid. Don't be good only when you're getting paid.

INSERT IT INTO YOUR PROGRAM

You're now comfortable with your routine and you feel reasonably certain that others will appreciate it also. Now it's ready for public scrutiny. Understand that it's still not perfect yet. It still has to be honed and polished with the help of the audience's critical eye (and ear). Your material is now ready for the unavoidable Baptism by fire.

Don't introduce too much new material at once. Change your talk gradually. One or two experimental chunks in an otherwise powerful speech won't hurt your reputation on the platform. Stay with those pieces until you're satisfied that they can work. They they become a part of your impressive talk and that makes room for new pieces to be broken in.

It might be wise to try out the material right before a strong segment of your speech, whether it's humor, drama, or pathos. It helps your confidence to know that regardless of what happens with the new material, you've got the biggie coming up to help you recover. Should your experiment be successful, then you've got two strong pieces back-to-back. Quite impressive.

Again, for your confidence, you might prepare a "saver" for yourself. A saver is a line that saves you from the embarrassment of having a bit of humor that fails. Don't use this device indiscriminately, though. Use it only when you absolutely have to.

As an illustration, you might keep a line like this ready for use after you blow one:

> I always include at least one story that doesn't work real well. It makes the other ones look better by comparison.

Continue reviewing your new material until it finally gets that lustre and polish that makes it worthy of your speech. Study rewording or repositioning. Especially investigate shortening the entire routine.

Try to avoid the temptation to blame the audience if things don't go well. That's much too easy an escape. Put all the blame squarely on either your material or your delivery. Experiment with both until you and your audience are content with it.

If the material continues to disappoint, don't abandon it, but shelve it for a while. File it somewhere where you can recall it. The solution may not be apparent to you at the moment, but it may jump out at you sometime later. At that time, it will be nice to have the original which you can then rewrite and salvage.

PART THREE:
DELIVERING HUMOR

Good Humor is one of the best
articles of dress one can wear
in society.
William Makepeace Thackeray

Establish a Spirit of Fun

WHAT IS A SPIRIT OF FUN? It's too complex to define in one or two sentences. It's like trying to characterize personality. I'll try to illustrate what I mean by it with a story.

Several years ago my nephew visited our family on the West Coast. I had seen him quite often when he was a youngster, but not much after he became a young adult. My family hardly knew him at all.

My youngsters relished any guests, but especially family. Nevertheless, there was that awkward moment when he first arrived. After the standard, "How was your flight?" "Can I get you something to drink?" "How's your family doing?" we all had to create some more original conversation.

The kids naturally took up the slack when the adults faltered. They wanted to show Tommy all of the things they were most proud of. Most of these things were alive. Our family dog, in her exuberance, promptly knocked over a cocktail glass and slobbered all over our guest's trousers. Then my daughter introduced her cousin to her three cats. Trampe (pronounced Tramp-ee) was the mother of the brood. After she gave birth to six illegitimate kittens, the name took on added meaning. Over my protestations, we also kept two of the kittens—Mismatch, so named because he had totally different markings from the rest of the litter, and Freckles, because she had freckles.

My other daughter chaperoned Tommy to her room to see her tropical fish and their new babies. She explained all the care that had to be taken after their birth, and as they swam around, she'd point to each one and tell Tommy what its name was and why it was so christened.

My son then proudly brought out his boa constrictor named "Corny," short for Cornelius. He encouraged my nephew to hold the animal because "it's very clean and very tame." My wife and I, aside from having run out of conversation, felt we had to apologize for this road company of "Zoo Parade." Mercifully, the coffee was brewed and we retreated to the kitchen. A bothersome fly was flitting around. We made the usual protestations like "Where did he come from?" and "There's always one in the kitchen." The fly then landed in our visitor's cake. He smiled down at it and then looked up at my wife and me and said, "What's its name?"

I burned my nose from falling in my coffee laughing. But from that moment on, all anxiety about being gracious hosts disappeared. We no longer had a guest in our house whom we had to entertain. We now had a friend, a relative, a part of the family. *That's what a spirit of fun is.*

Initial awkwardness often exists between a speaker and listeners, too. A spirit of fun, right from the start, dissolves that awkward feeling so that you can feel comfortable with the crowd and they can feel comfortable with you.

A spirit of fun is not necessarily jokes, or opening with your best story, or getting a big audience response. It is establishing an attitude. The visitor in my story did open with a good joke, but the attitude behind the joke was what was important. My nephew was saying, "I'm a guest in your house and I feel very comfortable being here. The children don't bother me. The parade of pets doesn't annoy me. We're all trying very hard to do what is socially acceptable, and that's fine, but now let's relax and enjoy one another."

Through some means or another—that's how we should all begin our talks.

We'll get into the how-to of the spirit of fun later in this chapter. Right now let's see what it can do for you and for your audience.

A SPIRIT OF FUN PREPARES THE AUDIENCE FOR HUMOR

It's important to prepare your audience for humor. It makes the humor that you use more effective. I know firsthand because some people take my brand of humor seriously. One icebreaker that I use sometimes is a complaining kind of humor. No matter what happens I'll find fault with it. If someone graciously offers me the front passenger seat of the car, I'll say "Oh sure, make me sit up where I have to listen to the driver while you folks in the back can have a really fun conversation." When we go out to dinner I'll check with my wife on what is being cooked by our hosts. If it's chicken, I'll say, "I'm looking forward to dinner. The doctor says I'm allowed to have anything but chicken, you know." I use it to get a spirit of fun going, but there are some folks who believe what I say and later won't believe I was only kidding. I've had entirely different meals cooked for me. So it pays to prepare your audience that along with your message, you're going to have a little fun.

You really don't want to surprise your listeners. The punch line should always have some astonishment connected with it, but not the fact that you're introducing humor. As an example, take a great Rodney Dangerfield joke.

I never get no respect. For Christmas my father bought me a bat.

We haven't gotten to the punch line yet, so don't look for the comedy up there. Let's just stop and see what's going through our minds. Knowing Rodney Dangerfield, we're eager to hear the rest of this line. We're anticipating the fun. So far this sounds like an ordinary statement. A lot of kids get bats as gifts. We know, though, that something is coming and we listen intently for it. Then Dangerfield hits us with the line.

First time I tried to play with it, it flew away.

We laugh. In our minds we say, "Oh, he wasn't talking about a baseball bat at all. He was talking about a bat that sleeps upside down in a cave. He's a funny guy."

Perhaps our minds don't talk as squarely as that, but we say something to that effect. However, if some person were giving a boring lecture on the effects of gamma rays, and suddenly threw that in, we might not see the double *entendre*. If this person had etched in our minds that everything he said was technically accurate and precise, then the term "bat," with the connotation of baseball bat that's necessary for the joke, would be accepted as a baseball bat. Now when he says, "it flew away," we're confused. Baseball bats don't fly. *Maybe it slipped out of his hand? Oh, I get it. He wasn't talking about a baseball bat, but about a bat that lives in a cave. Then why did he lead us to believe it was a baseball bat?* The confusion weakened the joke. We eventually got it, but it was no fun anymore. It came too late. We should have been prepared for it.

You do want the joke to surprise, but you want them to know that a joke is coming.

I once stopped in a crowded bar on my way home from a writing assignment. The poor bartender was scurrying like crazy and it took him some time to get around to me. I wanted to make him feel that I didn't mind the wait, and I thought I would do that with a joke. I really was in no hurry, and didn't mind the delay. When he finally slapped a napkin on the bar and asked what I would have, I said, "You got here just before I died of thirst." It was the wrong joke.

He had never met me before and didn't know I was kidding. It came off as a sarcastic complaint and he didn't care for it at all. I had one drink and left before I got my nose broken.

He should have been prepared—by me—for the humor. Perhaps an opening joke like, "I'm glad I stopped in here on a day when you weren't too busy," might have shown that I was sympathetic to his problems. Possibly we would have talked a bit about how active the place was and why, then I could have said, "Well, before I die of thirst give me a gin and tonic." That might have made us buddies—or he may have punched me in the nose. The point is that folks accept humor better when they see it coming. Not the punch line, mind you, just the fun.

A SPIRIT OF FUN PUTS YOU IN COMMAND

Some of the greatest thrills in my life were seeing great entertainers perform in clubs. There's such a feeling of being in the presence of greatness when they make that stage entrance. From the time Sinatra first comes out of the wings everyone knows that stage belongs to him. Bobby Darin used to take over a theatre and there was never any doubt that you were going to see a tireless performance. Jack Benny had that sprightly walk that exuded confidence. Even Johnny Carson's march from the curtains to his camera spot each night is powerful.

All of the greats have it. It signals the crowd that they know what they're doing and they're good at it.

Their charisma is the end result of years of hard work and success.

They're known and respected. The speaker has to extract that respect from an audience in a short time. A spirit of fun can help do that.

I once saw Pete Rose give a baseball clinic for some youngsters. He went through the baseball swing in slow motion, explaining it all the way. Suddenly he seemed transfixed by what he had just done and said, "I don't know whether you know it or not, but you've just seen a perfect baseball swing." He was building himself up, but with a sense of humor.

I'll sometimes talk about my writing and inadvertently put myself down. I might say that I sent Carol Burnett an autographed copy of my book and she was thrilled. She said, "I'm so glad my copy is auto-graphed. It's the only good writing in there." That's putting myself down, but with a sense of humor.

I once saw Liberace's stage performance and he said to the audience, "People wonder if I've heard the rumors about me. Sure I have. I started them." He's kidding himself with a sense of humor.

All of these examples show a self-assurance. They're saying to an audience that the performer has an image of himself that he likes. Pete Rose can kid about what a good ball player he is because he knows he is a good ball player. Whatever else this audience thinks is not going to change that. I can put my book down because I'm proud of it and this crowd's opinion of my writing is not going to change my opinion of my writing. Liberace can kid about his image because that image is making millions for him.

All of the performers are serving notice to this crowd that, "I'm not depending on you for my well being."

Bobby Darin could walk on stage with such confidence that it could be considered arrogance. He approached the mike one time and a patron shouted, "Boy, Bobby, you'd better be good." Darin said, "Sir, you don't have to tell me to be good. I've been backstage for a half-hour in front of a mirror telling myself the same thing." He knew every time he went before the public he had to be good.

A spirit of fun comes from self-confidence. You approach the podium saying to yourself, but directing it to your listeners, "I know what I'm doing up here. It would serve you well to listen. I'll be the teacher and you'll be the students. I'm going to make it as painless as possible for both of us, so let's relax and enjoy one another."

Like Bobby Darin, you'll know that there is nothing this audience can say or do to you that you haven't prepared for.

I hope you've gathered by now that this spirit of fun is primarily an attitude. It's a combination of the self-image and sense of humor that you have within you as you step to the lectern. It's the beliefs that you hold about yourself, your topic, and your audience.

Since it is an attitude, you're the only one who can control it. I was outlining this chapter in my head as I was having my teeth cleaned at the dentist. I discovered a phenomenon that day that applies here. Dental work, even the painless kind, falls into my bottom 10 of favorite things. I lie there very calmly at the start. Then they start working on my teeth and gradually I tense up. My hands push against the arms of the chair, my shoulders hunch, and so on. There is no real discomfort; I'm just preparing my body in case there should be some. When I realize what I'm doing, I relax and start the process all over again. The important thing is that I relax simply by saying to myself, "Relax." You can probably accomplish the same, as far as self-image goes, before approaching the platform.

With a healthy self-image, you'll be more relaxed. If you're relaxed, your natural sense of humor will emerge. Again, we're not talking jokes or stories, but a sense of humor, a sense of fun. The audience will feel it too, and you'll be brighter and more creative.

Following are some ways that you might give yourself this spirit of fun.

DON'T TAKE YOURSELF, YOUR AUDIENCE, OR YOUR SUBJECT TOO SERIOUSLY

You, your audience, and your subject should each be placed in its proper perspective. Remember when we first talked about a sense of humor, we discussed that it was seeing, recognizing, and accepting things as they are. That's all we ask you to do now.

Let's look at you first of all. Don't believe your press clippings, your retouched photograph, or especially your introduction. We both know they're all true, but they all glorify you. Suppose for a moment that a new rule was written into the universe whereby every speaker had to be introduced by a recital of everything he or she had ever done. It would be like an epitomization of the last judgment. Along with all the good points would be the faults you have. Not too many people would ever stand up and give a speech.

Despite your wishes to the contrary, this is the person who is going to address this assembly; it's not only the person in the introduction, but the one who has done everything the intro says, and has also done many things that you would never allow to be mentioned in public. Be grateful that they're only listing your good points, but remember the others too. Don't take yourself too seriously.

Your audience shouldn't overwhelm you, either. When I used to teach gag writing at an evening school, I was disappointed that the students didn't take my subject as seriously as I did. They neglected assignments. They ignored points that I highlighted as especially important. The awful truth was that none of them had the same fervor for comedy writing as I did. To me, it was a way of life. To them it was a diversion.

Regardless of how select your listeners are, they will never have the devotion to your subject that you have.

You should not permit this to reflect on you as a speaker. The fact that people don't want the information you're giving is not proof that you're not giving good information or teaching as well as you know how.

To quote Bill Gove again, you should be responsible *to* your audience, but not *for* your audience. By that he explains that you should be responsible for being there on time with a speech that is well thought through and well prepared. You should deliver it with all the skill at your command. You can't be responsible for your audience liking or even accepting it.

Most speakers will find it hard to believe that their subject is not as important as they think it is. Sales people will argue that everyone sells; either themselves or a product. Motivational speakers argue that if you can motivate a person, he or she can succeed in any business. I love humor, and we humorists feel everyone else's subject is unimportant; only humor works all the time. But—none of us is right.

Your subject is important and it should be heard, but keep it in perspective. When I was a youngster, I was a bit hotheaded, especially when it came to sports. It was my way of proving to the world that I was worth something.

In one softball game between my classmates and the faculty, the faculty was tormenting us with good-natured cheating. I was playing first base when one of my teachers got on base on an illegal single. He hit a foul ball and then bribed the umpire, also a faculty member, to call it fair. It was really funny, but I was blinded with rage.

I kept complaining about it until the teacher who was on first base with me suggested that I lighten up. I said, "That hit could mean the game." He said, "Will it matter 100 years from now?"

Will what you're saying today matter 100 years from now? Probably not.

REVIEW YOUR ASSETS

Speaking is a terrifying experience, especially right before your introduction when you haven't even said anything yet. You sit there or pace the back of the hall mentally envisioning everything that can go wrong. That can destroy confidence.

Just as when I sat in the dentist's chair and relaxed simply by realizing that I should, so you can regain your confidence by realizing that's what you have to do.

Review your assets. Remember the good things about yourself that got you here in the first place. They didn't invite you by picking your name out of a phone book. You deserve to be there and speak on *your* subject. Recall the many successes you've had with this same speech or at least the same topic in the past.

Right before show time, as the good song says, accentuate the positive and eliminate the negative.

FANTASIZE AND VISUALIZE

An interesting thing happens in dramatic arts. The shy girl playing the Queen walks with a regal grace. The cowardly boy playing a tough detective shows no fear. We act the way we think. If these youngsters thought better of themselves originally, they would carry themselves better.

We can use this phenomenon to give us a confident stage presence. Before going on, visualize the person you wish you were. I know one performer who paces and hums, "Thanks for the Memories," and on cue walks on stage with the confidence of Bob Hope.

It also helps to dress the part. One speaker told me that he paid an exorbitant fee for a beautiful suit. I said, "It looks great, but no one is going to know that it costs that much." He said, *"I'll* know."

Years later, I did the same thing. I went to the finest tailor in town and picked out a material that I loved. That suit cost a fortune, but when I was in it, I felt like a million. I took the kids with me to pick up this luxury and weakened even more. I had to have ties that complemented this suit. The tailor selected two ties which were $20 apiece. That was exorbitant at the time, but I had to have them to go with a suit like this. Two of my children were with me when I bought the ties, so I said, "Let's keep this our little secret. Don't tell Mommy." First thing they said when they got home was, "Daddy paid $20 for his ties." My wife raised my own past objection: "No one will know that those ties cost that much." I said, "I'll know."

The money was not for the suit or for the ties. It was for the feeling I had when I wore them.

MINIMIZE THE IMPORTANCE OF RESULTS AND MAXIMIZE THE IMPORTANCE OF PERFORMANCE

One of the most debilitating thoughts that can cross your mind before a speech is that *they* won't like you. It spreads terror throughout your innards. It prevents you from giving your best performance.

Think of a board that is three feet wide and 10 feet long suspended between two chairs. Could you walk it? Certainly. Anyone can. Now take the same board and suspend it between two buildings 20 stories high. Could you walk it? You'd have your doubts. Most of us wouldn't dare to, but if anyone did, he wouldn't walk it with the same ease that he did when it was between two chairs. The terror has robbed some coordination from his body. We create our own negatives.

As speakers we take that board and put it 20 stories high with our own imagination.

John Wooden, the legendary basketball coach of UCLA, never mentioned the word "win" to his student-athletes. He encouraged them only to do their best. His philosophy was that if you do your best and you're more skilled than your opponent, you'll win. If you do your best and the opponent beats you, he deserved to win all along. There was nothing you could do about it. However, if you worry about winning, it invariably will prevent you from doing your best. Then an unworthy adversary may well beat you.

Speakers, too, should adopt that attitude. Prepare well and do your best, but leave the audience's work to the audience.

Should you find yourself intimidated by any group, try one of these two methods to eliminate the fear.

First, analyze the facts logically and realistically to see just how important this group is to you. Will one unsuccessful performance affect your career that much? If they love your presentation, how much can they do for you?

I remember nursing one speaker through this fear right before a showcase performance. This was a chance to really do well and get some speaking engagements. He was terrified that they wouldn't like him.

Together we dissected the audience. Most of the people sitting there were other speakers who had performed in the showcase. Then there were a bunch of people who were looking for free speakers. There were only about six in the audience who would hire this particular man. If he did great he would get six jobs; if he did terribly he would lose six dates. Big deal.

A second method I've heard suggested is to exaggerate your fears. If you're afraid of doing bad, fantasize about doing not just bad, but horrendously bad. Imagine the audience starting to heckle, then they start throwing things, then they approach the stage with a bushel of feathers and a barrel of hot tar. You may see the idiocy of the power you've given this group. Even if you don't see all this as idiotic, when you do get out there, whatever happens to you has got to be less traumatic than what you prophesied.

In summary, try to relax and have fun with whomever is there to hear you. Treat every audience as old friends and you should have no problems being personable and delightfully humorous.

Humor Comes from the Audience

THERE'S A METAPHYSICAL POSER that asks, "If a tree falls in the forest and there's no one around to hear it, does it make any sound?" I don't know the answer, if indeed there is one. The reply I like best came from the coach on the television show *Cheers*. He said, "If there's nobody around, how do you know the tree fell?"

If you tell a joke and no one in the audience laughs, you haven't told a joke. In any humor, the most important element is neither the set-up nor the punch line. It's what follows them—gales of laughter. Sometimes we'll settle for a chuckle, or in a really tight situation, a snigger. Nothing at all, though, means you haven't told a joke.

You can control the set-up, the timing, and the punch line, but not people's reaction. You're at the mercy of a crowd of strangers.

Speakers are not the most important people in the room. We get the glorious introduction, which, 96 percent of the time, we write ourselves. We have the spotlight trained on our well-groomed countenance. The microphone is aimed in our direction. Our retouched photo, usually 10 years too young, is in the program. Nevertheless, we're not the most significant people in the room. The folks listening to us out front are.

If you doubt it, test it. Picture yourself as a program chairman saying to you, the speaker, "We're not going to have any attendees at the afternoon session. We think you'd be the perfect speaker for it." Or this:

"Nobody is coming to the convention this year. We'll give you $1,500 to be the keynote speaker." It's absurd.

The audience is like photographic film. They absorb whatever information you allow to reach them. You may set up a great photograph with creative lighting, a well-designed layout and pose, and extraordinary composition. All that is for nothing if you have no film in the camera.

So the most fundamental suggestion one can offer to a lecturer about to use some humor is, "Don't forget your audience."

The film is obviously important, but so is the photographer. No role of Kodachrome has ever leapt off the drugstore shelf and developed itself. The film will not bring home vacation snapshots without a photographer, yet no photographer can do it without the proper film. The ideal orator-audience relationship is mutual respect.

A speaker and an audience should not be adversaries. Certainly at the podium you exercise a certain amount of control, but it must be tempered with respect. You need them as much as they need you.

Realizing that the audience has the last laugh (indeed, the only laugh) with any humor that you attempt should generate a healthy respect for their power over you. It's a power that a good speaker should be able to harness and turn to benefit.

Most of the conversion of the audience energy is accomplished in advance. It's utilized in the planning and the writing of the speech as we discussed in Chapter 9. We try to find out as much about them as possible: who they are, what they're saying, what they're thinking, and so on. Nevertheless, there are still some tricks you can use from the podium.

Let's investigate some ways to use your audience to make your humor more impressive.

GET TO KNOW YOUR AUDIENCE

In addition to the research we discussed in Chapter 9, you should physically meet your audience whenever possible. Any method that will enable you to feel comfortable with a crowd while you gather some information and ammunition to use in your humor is valuable.

You'll want to get to know these people to build your own confidence. Almost every speaker or performer experiences some stage fright. Regardless of how many successful talks you've given before, there is always the fear that this is the audience that will destroy you. Rodeo performers say, "There's never been a horse that hasn't been rode, and never been a man that hasn't be throwed." All of us have that fear that this may be the audience that might "throw" us. Getting to know them and to see that they're not a collection of two-headed ogres might relax you.

You can get to know them to any degree that will accomplish this for you. Some speakers insist on meeting the attendees individually, shaking their hands and greeting them pleasantly as they file in. I don't like this because to me it steals some of the thunder from my appearance. I don't mean this to sound egotistical, but in some ways this is like meeting the star of a nightclub show before the curtain goes up. In Vegas, when the announcer brings on Sinatra, the orchestra hits their chord and the Chairman of the Board walks out and chills run up the spine of every fan in the theater. That effect would be destroyed if Mr. Sinatra stood by the doorway and greeted the customers as they entered.

I prefer to socialize at the cocktail party (if there is one) the evening before the event. Meeting people in a social context makes it easier for me.

At the very least, I like to be in the auditorium to watch the crowd's acceptance of some other speaker. In my frenetic state, I may be fantasizing that these folks are loud, raucous, rude, boisterous, and armed with overripe fruit to toss at the stage or the dais. Seeing them sitting there like well-behaved adults, listening attentively to someone else and even laughing at the right places when the other speaker cracks a joke, settles the butterflies in my stomach.

Use any method that will convince you that these are nice folks who are not out to get you. They're friends and should be treated as such.

The other reason for getting to know your audience is to gather information about them as ammunition that you can use in your humor. That's why I prefer the social meeting. In a relaxed atmosphere, I can ask people about their work. It's genuinely interesting to me, but it also gives me fodder for my ad-libs and my references. The more I know about these folks, the more I can relate to them.

I'll sometimes gather information by asking questions during the luncheon or dinner. One occasion pops to mind. I was appearing at a Personnel Management Convention. My hostess was discussing some business with an association officer during the meal. She said, "We'll run a reference check on him," and they both chuckled. Since I overheard it, I asked what it meant. She explained that it was a standard investigation they ran before hiring anyone. As my opening remark I said, pointing to my hostess, "Miss Wilson asked if I could speak at this banquet and I told her I would be happy to. She said, 'We'll get back to you as soon as we run a reference check.' " The remark got laughter and applause and I hardly know what I said. It was just the result of getting to know the audience.

It's a way of establishing friendship between you and your audience. My good buddy, Bill Gove, has a nice phrase in his introduction. I hope he'll forgive me if I paraphrase it, but it goes something like this, "We asked Bill Gove to give a speech today, but Bill said he doesn't give speeches. However, he would like to visit with us for awhile."

Image is very important to a speaker or performer. I visited a comedian client of mine as he was interviewing a new secretary. One of the secretary's duties, he explained, would be to act as the heavy in keeping fans away. He said, "You have to arrange for me to get to my car without anyone stopping me, and you have to make it appear as though I would prefer to stop and chat and sign autographs. But even if we're in a hurry and someone reaches me, I have to stop and be polite. I can't blow my image."

This celebrity might have been stopped by everyone and his schedule wouldn't allow that. He sincerely didn't want to offend anyone, nor did he want to alienate any of his fans by appearing rude.

SPEAK FROM THE AUDIENCE'S FRAME OF REFERENCE, NOT YOURS

Speakers are like teachers. A teacher knows what he's talking about, but the students don't. If they did, there would be no point to the education. The listeners are the ones who have to learn. Therefore, it makes sense to speak in a language they understand.

In show business, we have inside jokes. These are delightful stories that only show folk would appreciate. Musicians have great stories, but many of them go right over my head. Every industry has them.

Obviously, there's no point telling a story that no one will understand. It's like speaking in a foreign language. The opposite applies, also. A humorous idea is enhanced if it's related in a language with which the listeners are familiar.

Each year I do several talks at the local grade school, the junior high school, and the high school. We talk about creative writing. I gave a talk during the day and then spoke in the evening to executives from several savings and loan companies. I would hope that I brought my same sense of humor to each of the talks, yet you can appreciate how different the content must have been. With the youngsters, I would take their side against the teacher. I would kid about homework. I could even be somewhat sophomoric with the kind of humor that I used. I would appear imbecilic if I did any of the same jokes or even used the same style with the businessmen.

You must learn to think like your audience thinks and speak like your audience speaks. I don't mean to offend McDonald's fast food chain. Their food is fine and my youngsters and I grab several meals there. However, I once spoke for a rival company. At the talk I said:

> I used to eat quite a bit at McDonald's. You've heard of them, haven't you?

This brought boos and hisses from the crowd because it was a friendly rivalry and they wanted me to know it. I went on:

> Their sign always said they served over 100 million. They knew it was over 100 million because they'd already gone through their third pound of meat.

This got cheers and applause. I added:

> I just said that because I wanted to get on your good side.

It wasn't a mean swipe at McDonald's, because everyone knew this rivalry existed and I was just speaking from the frame of reference of my audience.

I've also spoken to the Catholic fraternal organization, the Knights of Columbus. I did a similar gag with them.

> You all know who the Knights of Columbus are. That's a group of men that gets together once a month and prays that it rains for the Masons' picnic.

Do everything you can to capture the frame of reference of your listeners and then use it to your advantage.

EXPERIMENT WITH YOUR AUDIENCE

I pride myself on being the best baby entertainer in the world. No, I take that back; my older brother is. However, I'm a close second. A baby entertainer is someone who can make faces or silly sounds and get infants to giggle. You need a huge repertoire of silly moves and ridiculous sounds and then you use the hit-or-miss system, trial-and-error. You start by rubbing your head in the babies' bellies while making neighing sounds with your lips. This generally gets them. If that fails, you try the surprised look and double take. Should that fail, hit them with the flying hand through the air while saying, "Booga-booga-booga-booga-booga." I won't bore you with more because these are much better done live and to someone under the age of one. The point is, though, that we Masters try everything until we get the Almighty Giggle.

Sometimes you have to use the same method with audiences. (For heaven's sake, I don't mean to use the same material.) I mean you have to experiment. Try different things, but find out what they want and expect, and give it to them.

This is where the items we discussed about getting to know your audience also apply. When you get to know the people you'll be working to, you may get some clues as to what type of material and humor they would appreciate. See what type of humor they're using among themselves. Notice which type they appreciate most. Then apply that in your speech.

It doesn't require that much flexibility because, remember, your humor content is probably only a small portion of your talk.

Some of you may be able to adjust from the platform after analyzing your audience. It's a rare and valuable skill. Many professional comics do just that. They feel out their audience and then use the type of material that will go over best. If you can do that, fine, but it is very tricky.

WORK TO A FRIENDLY FACE

Again the devices we discussed in getting to know your audience will come in handy. By meeting several people, you may find one or two who are genuinely charmed by your wit. They'll find all of your *bon mots* amusing. AHA! Save those people.

When you begin using your humor in your talk, you'll need all the friendly assistance you can get. Turn to these allies when you need them. Obviously, you can't stand up there and talk directly to them. You can, however, use any method you want to take in the whole audience. Some recommend switching eye contact from person to person around the room. Others suggest working to the back of the hall. There are those who propose that you look over the heads of the audience. Any of these are fine. But when you come to the punch line, you may want to turn to the pushover. At the critical moment, it's a tremendous confidence builder to be staring at a face that you know is going to laugh like crazy.

If you're really lucky, you may discover a few others while you're speaking. Great. Alternate among them.

We said earlier that cooperation was required between you and the listeners for your humor to be effective. It's give and take—like a good marriage. Even good marriages, though, have their rough times. You and your listeners will, too. Let's look into a couple of them.

As hard as you search for that friendly face we just spoke of, you may be distracted by the "sourpuss" in the audience. If you catch that face glaring defiantly at you, it can disrupt any concentration you have.

I did a show not too long ago where one man kept staring at me with that "Okay, wise guy, make me laugh" look. It threw me totally, and I found myself, after each punch line, looking to him for approval; I got nothing but a smug look of disdain.

Finally, I hit my audience with my biggie. It got screams. Now I smugly looked to this guy as if to say, "Okay, wise guy, what did you think of that?" What happened then, astounded me even more.

My antagonist, as if reading my mind, sat there still not laughing. He just nodded slightly and winked at me.

I must admit that I seem to find a face like this in every crowd and it still disrupts my concentration. My advice, though, is to dismiss it quickly. No comic will ever please everyone in the hall. Your goal is to amuse *most* of them. Forget this challenging smirk and remember that there are many people out there who are enjoying you.

One humorist told his audience, "If I can just get one laugh tonight; if I can just make one person out there smile; if I can get just one chuckle, then I'll know that my act stinks."

Don't let one person throw you. You're working to the whole audience.

However, we do have to face reality. The audience does have a power over you. There will be those nights when, collectively, they may not appreciate your humor. It may happen. Certainly, you want to cut down the number of times that it does, but it may happen every once in a while.

It's not the end of the world. Some other audience next week will love your material. Keep in mind Bill Gove's admonition: "Be responsible *to* your audience, but not *for* your audience." You do what you have to do. Do it as well as you can. After that, if they don't like you, that's their problem.

Don't be too quick to blame the audience, though. Look to your own performance, first. If it's something that can be changed or corrected, act on it.

Don't surrender to the audience's authority without a struggle, either. If they're not laughing or finding you amusing, that's when you have to work harder. The tendency is to speed up, give in, and get out of there. Don't do that. Instead, sell your material even harder. If they still don't like you, there's not much more you can do about it, but at least go down with a fight.

Involve the Audience

MOST OF US CAN ONLY LAUGH at someone we like and when we like someone we laugh more readily with him. People used to say to me, "I don't think Jackie Gleason is funny." I'd ask why and they'd say, "He's too loud." He's what they consider a rude, boisterous, loudmouth. They can't laugh at him. Some folks have the same problem with Don Rickles. "I don't see anything funny about him," they say. What they're really saying is that they think his insult humor is crude and regardless of how hilarious it might be, they refuse even to chuckle.

I'm more guilty of this than anyone. I've had favorite funny people that I've roared at. Then I worked with them, disliked them, and found everything they did after that uproariously unfunny. It's almost impossible to laugh with someone you dislike.

You can dislike singers and musicians all you want and still enjoy their music. But comedy, more than any other entertainment form, requires a commitment. You almost have to become a partner with the performer, and that's difficult unless you like the person.

When I was newly married at the tender age of 21, I was privileged to be invited to go drinking with my father-in-law and one of his boozing buddies. This was quite an honor because my wife's father prided himself on his drinking and fighting. The invitation to join in was my unofficial welcome into their "men's" world.

It was almost a ceremonious occasion. I weighed about 135 pounds at the time. My father-in-law was a tough hombre who could lift a refrigerator by himself. His friend, Sam, could lift them both. At the corner bar, they kept ordering rounds of drinks and my money was no good. This was my induction into their world and everything was on the house. Sam would announce it each time he ordered drinks. He'd say, "One for me, one for the kid, and one for the . . ." and would refer to my father-in-law by an ethnic nickname.

We did a lot of loud talking, laughing, and drinking. One patron got caught up in our festivities and bought a drink for us. He also shouted to the bartender, "I want to buy a round. One for my friend here, one for the kid, and one for the . . ." He also used the ethnic reference. In an instant, Sam picked our benefactor up and threw him over the bar, a fight broke out, and my introduction to their world ended up with a sore, swollen lip and a black eye.

I asked Sam what the hell got him so angry. He said, "Nobody calls your Pappy that name except me."

It's hard to laugh along with people unless you genuinely like them.

The gentleman who ended up behind the bar in a sea of broken glass should have become our buddy before he started doing our brand of humor. (And I should have stayed home with my wife.) As a speaker who is going to use humor, you should become a buddy to each audience. You do that by joining in their fun and inviting them to join in yours.

I learned this secret of showmanship from Phyllis Diller. Let me tell you a couple of stories to show how important the pros consider this precept, then we'll discuss ways that you can apply it.

Phyllis and her producers hired me for my first honest-to-goodness television writing job. They wanted me to work on her upcoming NBC production, *The Beautiful Phyllis Diller Show*. Naturally, I was delighted, but also a bit frightened. Was I ready? Could I do it? Would the producers like my work? Phyllis was making an appearance at an exhibition of some of her paintings in Baltimore, Maryland. It wasn't too far from my house, so I motored there to talk with her, ask her advice, and get some reassurance.

Phyllis was at the peak of her career and her appearance brought out many fans and lots of media coverage. I was kind of lost in the crowd. I did manage to get to Phyllis and we exchanged pleasantries, but that wasn't enough for me. I had so many questions to ask about the upcoming show and my part in it. I blurted out a couple quickly, and Phyllis said, "Gene, not now. The white light is on."

Her meaning was immediately clear, and she was right. She was performing. All of her concentration, energy, and charm at that moment had to go out to her audience. She and I could meet later and talk business, but right now the crowd was the star.

I stood back and watched. She was gracious and entertaining and I loved her for it. I've never stopped loving her.

I wrote for her show and must have done something right because her producers got me a full-time staff writing job in Hollywood the following year. I was like a kid in a candy shop, working on a hit variety show and meeting a different celebrity every week. I was also making more money than I'd ever dreamed of making and it was glorious.

At the end of that first season, I was going to take a trip back to my hometown to visit my family. When I told Phyllis, she was delighted and offered this advice: "You're in a glamorous profession and your friends will want to know all about it. *Share it with them.*"

She was admonishing me to be generous with the good fortune that I had enjoyed that past year.

Both of these incidents taught me the respect that Phyllis Diller has for her audience. Notice that both stories focus on the listeners. In the first, she was telling me that the people who came to meet her or to interview her had to get their fair share, before she and I could concentrate on our business. This was *their* time.

In the second, she was more concerned with the enjoyment of my friends and relatives than with my vacation. Naturally, she knew about my tendencies to make a fool of myself and was warning against that. But, again, the audience was the object of the most consideration.

As a speaker, you have to acquire this healthy respect and consideration for your audience; especially if you're going to use humor.

Much of this has been considered in the preparation and writing of your speech. However, the following are some strategies that you can use from the stage.

MAKE YOUR AUDIENCE FEEL WELCOME
Any time someone gets up to talk there is some tension generated. The audience asks, "Will I like her?" "Will he do well?" "Will it be worth

my time to listen?'' There are many other unresolved questions that might ramble through their minds.

You are in the driver's seat—or you should be. You have the microphone, the spotlight, and the attention. In effect, you're the host of this affair. It's up to you to make the guests feel at ease and to assure them that you're very comfortable in their presence.

Like any good host, don't leave your guests in limbo for too long. Welcome them into your presentation. You do this first of all with your stage presence. Your demeanor should convey confidence and comfort. In an earlier chapter we discussed many ways of creating that attitude. Use any one of them, but be sure it's the first signal you send out to your audience.

Secondly, you give your listeners permission to feel comfortable themselves. This is probably best accomplished with nonverbal communication. A gathering will generally welcome a speaker with a sign of acceptance, such as applause. You can reflect that welcome back to them with a smile, a nod, or a glance at them. Anything that says, ''I accept your welcome and extend it back to you.''

Then, as I recommended previously, an opening remark that is incisive and that includes the audience, shows this crowd that you know them and their problems and you're on their side.

I notice this especially when I meet people for the first time. After the introduction we exchange hackneyed greetings: ''How are you?'' ''It's so nice to meet you.'' These serve a social purpose, but they really have no meaning. How nice it is to be greeted by someone who has a personal remark, something that applies to me alone.

For instance, if someone shakes my hand and says—''I read your book and agreed with everything except the chapter on writing situation comedies''—I might stay with that person all evening. It's refreshing, too, to have someone say, ''Nice to meet you. That's a very unusual tie and it goes so beautifully with that jacket.''

That's what a speaker can accomplish with a sharp, humorous opening line. Instead of the cliche, ''It's nice to be here,'' the speaker will say, in effect, ''It's nice to be here *with you.*''

BECOME ONE WITH YOUR AUDIENCE

If you want to have fun with a crowd, join in their fun. The man in the bar earlier in this chapter would have had a lot less healing to do if he had become our buddy before presuming too much.

I've seen many speakers who come on like bitter, irascible, old teachers. They march to the stage almost brandishing their switches. You can almost hear them begin with, "My name is Mr. Dudley. I'll tolerate no talking in class. Any homework that is not handed in on time will not be graded. Anyone late for class will be marked absent. Are there any questions? Turn to page 10 in your geography books."

Some are obsessed with establishing authority. It's hardly necessary. They have the microphone, the flip chart, the lectern, and all the chairs are arranged facing them. How much more reassurance do they need?

There's a line in the play, *Death of a Salesman,* that always impressed me. It's germane here. Willie Loman is chatting with an old friend when the friend's son enters. The son had gone to school with Loman's own sons, so they talk for a beat or two, then the son hustles out. Willie says, "Why did he rush off like that? I would have liked to talk." The boy's father says, "He has to rush off. He's pleading a case before the Supreme Court." Willie is astounded and says, "The Supreme Court? Why didn't he say something?" The father replies, "He didn't have to. He's doing it."

If you're up on the platform and all eyes are gazing at you and all ears are listening to you, you needn't tell these folks that you deserve to be up there. Just tell them what you came to tell them and they'll decide whether you really belong there or not.

What's the phrase you hear most when people meet famous people? "Boy, she's a nice lady, very down to earth." That means this celebrity didn't spend the entire time saying, "I'm better than you." No, she joined in with her fans and became one with them.

Frank Sinatra doesn't walk on stage and say, "Before we begin I want you all to understand that I'm a big star. I will sing the songs I like and when I'm done, I would like your applause. At the very end, I'd even like you to stand and applaud. But that's optional." He wouldn't do that. He doesn't have to.

You don't have to, either. You're standing center stage and everything about you should pronounce that you belong there.

Your humor will be more effective if you become one with your audience rather than try to establish a sense of superiority. The best example I can think of to illustrate this involves Bob Hope's military tours. Mr. Hope receives a hero's welcome every place he stops on these tours. The highest ranking officials meet and entertain him. During these tours he has met and dined with cardinals, generals, chiefs or staff, senators, congressmen, even presidents. When he walks on stage, though, he complains about the same things that the GIs complain about. All of his jokes say, "Hey, ain't you and I got it tough?"

ENCOMPASS ALL OF YOUR AUDIENCE

I can speak on this point with "firsthand wounds." I was ignored in one of the smallest audiences on record. For two years I produced a show with my partner for a certain star. As producers/head writers, we had many meetings with the top man. It began to dawn on me several months into the second year that during these meetings the star never looked at me. Once I became aware of it, it was obsessive. I knew that I worked to a certain portion of the room (more on that later) when I spoke, so I gave him the benefit of the doubt. When we came into his office for meetings, I purposely took the chair that my partner traditionally sat in. That did no good. The star now turned in the other direction and spoke only to my partner.

Understand, there was no outward animosity between us. I think he respected me as a writer, although I'm not at all sure. For whatever reason, he simply neglected to acknowledge me.

I toyed with solutions. Should I just stand up and leave in the middle of a discussion? That was decisive but risky. What if none of the two who remained missed me? Should I remain behind and ask the question point-blank? "Why do you ignore me totally?" Risky also. What if he just walked past me without answering the question? Then I wondered, "Maybe I'm dead and don't realize it."

I struggled with my alternatives, but the show was mercifully cancelled and the meetings ceased. Finally, we all ignored one another.

I do know, though, that it is infuriating to be overlooked so obviously. In my more forgiving moments, I allow that the gentleman was not even aware that he was doing it. After all, I wasn't aware that he was doing it for many months.

In fact, I must confess that I do it. For some inexplicable reason, when I talk I favor my left side. I stand at a microphone and naturally glance to my left. Lord knows how many years I've done it, but I only became aware of it recently.

I would do shows where friends came to watch. They would sit on the right side and after the talk, I would notice that not once during the presentation did I notice their reaction. It was because I never looked at them.

Now I force myself to turn in that direction. However, it still feels awkward.

People in my audiences must have felt the same abandonment that I felt at our meetings: "Why is he not talking to me?" The solution, of course, is to become aware of the problem. I recommend selecting different people at different times throughout your talk—preferably in different areas of the room—and speaking directly to them. There's obviously no way that you can work to each individual in the room, but you can at least cover all areas of the room.

I suspect that we avoid certain areas because of a basic insecurity. As good as we get, deep inside all of us there probably remains some fear of public speaking. This may be the manifestation of it. That's only a guess because I honestly don't know why I'm more comfortable facing left. I have to struggle against it, though it still baffles me.

Previously, I suggested a confidence builder when doing important parts of a humorous presentation: turn to a friendly face. This still obtains. It doesn't contradict what is contained in this section. If you are careful to gear most of your talk to the entire room, then turning to your ally only at significant moments won't be noticeable to the crowd.

One caution: It's deadly, and very offensive, to work to one friend, one group, or one table.

Some of us at National Speakers Association affairs will fall into this trap. The more prominent members might all be seated at one table and we speakers will try so hard to impress them and be friendly to them that we work only to them. It's terribly rude to the rest of the audience. I sometimes feel like I'm back to being a nobody at my meetings if I'm in one of those "neglected" audiences.

I've also been to nightclubs where the celebrated performer will have a few friends at ringside. Here I'm not only offended, but angered. I feel as if I'm paying exorbitant prices for this crowd to have a private party.

Each time you step to a podium, you're working to the entire assemblage. As much as reasonably possible, give each person there your full consideration. It's demeaning not to. I know. I worked for a year and a half for a star who never looked at me.

BE AWARE OF FEEDBACK

When you're speaking to a group, the communication is not one-way. They're also speaking to you. Their nonverbal communication is probably more eloquent than your oratory.

However, just as your message is lost if no one is listening, so is the audience's message wasted if you're not attuned to it.

While you're at the lectern be aware of what your audience is saying to you. Respond to it. Comedians do this all the time. It's practically inconceivable for a stand-up comedian to do a worthwhile routine without a live audience. The timing isn't there. A joke, as I've said before, is a contest of wits. The performer has to lead the minds of his listeners in a certain direction, then judge just when they're ready to be surprised. If there is no one out there, there is no way of knowing when to surprise them.

I have a facility for taking a fairly simple concept and complicating it beyond human comprehension. I can circumlocute with the best of them. In my efforts to simplify everything, I confuse it past all recognition. Sometimes, after going through one of these long-winded, circuitous discourses, I glance out at my students and see nothing but blank stares. I say, "I think I botched that up. Let's start from the beginning." Or I'll ask, "Did anyone in the room understand what I just said? If you did, would you kindly explain it to me?"

My audience tells me that they didn't understand a word I said. Your audience will tell you when you're getting boring and they'll tell you when they're interested and when they're appreciative. Listen to them.

A lecture is actually a dialogue. You're addressing a crowd, but they're communicating with you, too. Any good stage performer will tell you that. Tune in to your audience. Involve them in your presentation. Forget yourself from time to time and concentrate on them.

ACTIVELY INVOLVE PEOPLE

You don't have to be the only one who speaks or moves in your presentation. Some speakers are accomplished at also bringing audience members into their program. If you're comfortable working with people and it helps your presentation, then use it. If you're not comfortable, don't use it. Remember humor has to be you.

Following are several methods I've seen used effectively. I've tried some of them myself.

Bring People on Stage. Dr. Loretta Malandro, whose presentation I've referred to several times (because it was so terribly good), has a steady parade of people to and from the stage. She hints at some concept, then invites participants on stage to act out a part, then she will quiz the audience on their conclusions. After some opinions are offered and there is some discussion, she will reinforce the point she wanted to make.

It's very entertaining; it involves everyone there, and it's very educational.

When I did some entertaining I had a nice gimmick that I would use when there were children in the audience. I would call one of them up on stage and tell him a story that involved a good deal of double-talk. The story was fun to listen to, but it was also fun for the audience to watch the look on the youngster's face because I wanted him to repeat the story after me. The tale was simply this:

There were these two skunks, In and Out. One day Out went out to play and the mother skunk called In and said "Where's Out?" In said, "Out went out." The mama skunk said to In, "You go out and get Out and bring Out in." So In went out. In looked all over for Out to bring Out in, but In couldn't find Out. So In came in. Mama said, "Where's Out?" In said, "Still out." Mama said, "You go out and get Out and don't come in without Out, In." So In went out again. Now, while In was out, Out came in. Mama skunk said, "Where's In?" Out said, "Out." Mama skunk said, "Out, go out and find In and bring In in." So Out went out. Out got In and brought In in. The mama skunk now said, "Out, how come when I sent In out to bring Out in, In couldn't find Out? But when I sent Out out to bring In in, Out got In and brought In in?" Out said, "It was easy . . . In stinked."

Then I'd ask the little fellows to tell the story just the way I did. The youngsters never got too far without getting lost. I'd have the audience applaud them, give them a dollar bill, and always got a warm round of applause.

You Can Ask Questions. People who speak on sales motivation do this well. They ask people in their audiences questions that can have only one answer: "Don't you want to improve your income?"— "If I guaranteed that listening to this tape could double your sales, wouldn't you buy it?"—"Doesn't what I'm saying make sense?' Those, of course, are general questions to the entire audience and are almost rhetorical in that no real response is needed.

You can get discussions going with real questions, though. When I speak to the youngsters on creative writing, I always ask what it means to create and then take individual answers. It gets the kids thinking about what I'm talking about and they enjoy giving the right answers.

I've heard seminar leaders say there would be no way of getting through a half-day seminar without questions and responses from the audience.

Humor can employ the audience participation and audience questioning devices, too. I've heard a few speakers ask the audience to fold their hands comfortably. Then they ask them to notice if the right thumb crosses over the left or vice versa. If the right crosses over the left, you're sexy. If the left crosses over the right, you're sneaky. Each of these gets a laugh. Then the speaker will announce that if the thumbs were just side by side, those people are sneaky about their sex. That generally gets the biggest laugh.

You can ask questions and have a joke reply for whichever response you get. You might ask a simple, rhetorical question and get only a mild response from your audience. Then say, "Are these questions too tough for you?"

Answer Questions from the Audience. I have fun with this and most audiences enjoy it. In fact, I once considered dropping it because some speakers said it appeared too contrived. They felt that— "If you're a speaker, speak. Don't have the audience do half your work for you." Then I gave a talk to the Northern California Chapter of NSA and the evaluation cards overwhelmingly urged me to keep it in.

I have fun during the question and answer period for several reasons. First: The burden of doing prepared material is off me. Now I can suprise myself with some of the replies. Second: Each question reminds me of an anecdote, so we're still having fun even as we're continuing the dialogue. Third: By this time, I know my audience pretty well and I can kid them. They also know me pretty well and can kid me right back. Some of my questioners have gotten giant laughs after topping one of my wise-guy lines to them. It's great fun.

Name names. This is a device that some speakers use effectively and it astounded me at first. A speaker would be talking to the assemblage and then he would isolate one person and talk just to her. The whole time he is talking he is calling this person by her first name, as if he's known her all his life. The speaker would go around the room calling each person he addressed casually by first name. I was amazed.

Then it hit me. At most gatherings people, nowadays, wear name-tags. With just a glance, anyone can know their first name. Yet it's very effective.

I'm not really good at using this method because I don't wander up and down the aisle as these speakers do. But I know it can be a powerful device in using humor. If you do a good bald joke and then pause and turn to a gentleman with no hair and say simply, "Do you know what I mean, Tom?" you've got a guaranteed second laugh. Tell people that, in show business, you don't get a gold watch after 25 years the way you do in industry. In entertainment and nightclubs, if you do real well, they name a room after you. "Everybody knows what a thrill it is to have a room named after you." Turn to a guy whose name tag you spotted earlier and say, "Isn't that right, John?" It'll work.

All of the above methods are optional. Use them only if you're comfortable with them. The important principle to remember, though, is that your audience is important to you. Respect them and be considerate of them. Any chance you get, welcome them to your presentation and make them feel happy to be a part of it.

Let Them Know Where the Jokes Are

WHEN YOU DO COMEDY, you're playing cat-and-mouse with your listeners. You're trying to fool them. It's not unlike the deception of a magician. Few of us believe that any illusionists are really blessed with mystical powers. We watch them knowing that they're going to trick us and we enjoy it. They make fools of us and we applaud.

You deceive an audience with humor, also. Earlier we discussed how you manipulate the minds of your listeners. You get them thinking in one direction and then spring your surprise on them.

Sometimes, though, you might fool them too well. Your misdirection may be so skillfully executed that they don't realize that you've done a joke.

This is a dilemma. Does it imply that you should be less accomplished in setting up your joke? No. Although, the set-up, sometimes, is the problem. You can lead your audience so far away from the punch line that it loses all relevance when you finally get to it. Generally, though, this is not a problem with delivery so much as with the writing. You've made your punch line too obscure.

We're talking more about a well-written piece of humor that can fail because your set-up is *too good*.

Let me give an example, not from the platform, but from my mischievous adventures on the tennis court. Every so often at the club, there will be three of us trying to get a fourth for a game of doubles. I may see the fourth player, let's call him Charlie Wilson, approaching. Without giving any indication that I've seen him, I'll say to the others, when Charlie just gets within hearing, "I'll play with anybody except Charlie Wilson. I don't know what it is. He's a nice guy and all, but I can't play with him . . ." Then I'll look startled when he gets there.

That's a dangerous ad-lib and could someday get me a Prince Graphite racquet buried behind my left ear. I'm doing this nonsense full out. Everything that I'm saying to the other tennis players sounds real. So how do I avoid getting cold-cocked? I have to let Charlie Wilson know at exactly the right time that I'm kidding.

We'll get into the how's and why's of saving my skull in this example later. The point here is that my attempted humor had to seem real. I can't do this joke if I'm going to tell Charlie Wilson that I'm going to do it. It destroys the effect. But somewhere I have to let him know that it is a gag.

The reader might take a moment now and consider different ways of getting that moment across to the poor victim. We will discuss it later, but it might be more beneficial to think it through yourself and then have your findings corroborated by the upcoming text.

I realize when I do this type of humor that I have to orchestrate the entire episode. I have to notice who is coming without their noticing that I noticed. I have to do the ad-lib lines as if I really didn't want to play with Charlie Wilson. Finally, I have to know when to stop and tell Charlie this is all a put-on.

You have the same responsibility in presenting humor. It's your duty to let them know where the jokes are. It's an obligation that you can't take lightly because if you do, audiences will surprise you. Every humorist can probably tell of times when they were setting up for a big laugh and the crowd laughed too early. It sounds like a bonus, an extra laugh. It's not. It throws you. Instead of concentrating on the big punch line you have coming up, your mind begins to try to figure out what just happened. You can easily blow your big laugh wondering why you got a small laugh where there wasn't supposed to be any laugh at all.

You have to tell your listeners where the jokes are. The irony here is that you can't do it at the joke. The punch line is too important to be sending out signals while you're doing it.

This is a tremendously important point that many people miss in presenting humor. Humor, for the most part, cannot be presented humorously. Most humor must have a motivation behind it. You're not just saying a line—you're saying a line for a reason. The line is funny, but the reason may not necessarily be. You, as a performer, must be true to the reason rather than to the comedy.

In other words, if a line must be said with anger, say it with anger. If with confusion, be confused. If stupidity is a prerequisite for your line to get laughs, act stupid. Don't act funny.

To illustrate, there was a great line during an argument in the play, "The Odd Couple." Oscar is as furious at Felix as a person can get. He chases him around the apartment, finally verbalizing all the complaints he's had about his roommate. His anger builds and climaxes with the line, ". . . and I hate those silly notes you keep leaving me around the apartment signed 'F.U.' It took me two months to figure out that F.U. meant Felix Unger."

The audience is doubled with laughter at this moment, but there is nothing at all amusing to either Oscar or Felix. One is furious and the other is frightened. If they were otherwise, the line wouldn't be funny.

We once did a sketch on the Carol Burnett Show where for some reason or another Carol and Harvey Korman, as husband and wife, begin listing one another's faults. Naturally, they each get angry and defensive and we have a fierce family argument. Then, in making up, Harvey says that he didn't mean all the things he said. However, he goes one too many. He mentions a fault that *wasn't* in the original discussion. the line was, ". . . and I really don't think you have a turkey neck."

You'll have to take my word for it, since the line is out of context, but it broke the studio audience up. Nevertheless, while hundreds of people were laughing, Carol just smoldered in shock and anger, and Harvey looked like he wanted to bend over and kick himself for being so careless. They said something humorous, but they didn't say it humorously.

In one of my talks, I mention that my message is that we should attack all of our goals with a sense of humor. Most of the conventioneers listening to me have previously heard learned speeches on management, or business conditions, or the economy, and I come along with humor. I tell them, "I'm sometimes embarrassed about my message. I told my wife, 'I'm going to travel a great distance; I'm going to work very hard and no one's going to learn anything. I don't think I can do it.' She says, 'Yes, you can. Remember our honeymoon?' "

I say that line as if it has great import, then I look a bit confused when it suddenly dawns on me what it *really* means. It triggers the laugh.

Now I have done that same line hundreds of times, but each time I must realize, for the first time, what my wife *really* said. I can enjoy the humor of my story because I didn't understand it until just this moment. That's the role I'm playing. Of course, after the laughter dies down, then I join in and laugh, saying to the audience in so many words, "I just played a joke on you."

An incident highlighted the importance of this point to me. I was producing a variety show and one cast member kept ad-libbing during the shooting. He would make references to the audience, the stage-hands, the scenery, anything at all. Not only did it generally not get laughs, but it destroyed the believability of the sketch we were shooting. I had a talk with him.

He objected that he was simply trying to keep everyone relaxed and promote a spirit of fun on the show. That was commendable, but it was harming the finished product. Then he said, "You're always telling me how Harvey Korman did this so well on the Carol Burnett Show. How come he didn't ruin the finished product?"

Then I saw the difference. Harvey Korman did ad-lib, and brilliant-ly, but Harvey always ad-libbed in character. If he were playing a pirate captain and a stagehand knocked something over, Harvey would not ad-lib as Harvey. He would say whatever a captain of a pirate ship might say. He would never stop a performance to ad-lib; he would do it in the context of the play.

That's the way your platform humor should be done—in character.

We haven't chased the dilemma, yet. We've said that you have to tell the audience where the jokes are, but you can't do it at the joke. The gag has to be true to the motivation and delivered in character. We only have two other choices:

1. Let them know a joke *is coming*.
2. Let them know you *just did a joke*.

Actually, there's a third alternative, which is both of the above.

A JOKE IS COMING
Don't let me mislead you. This doesn't mean that you should telegraph the punch line. That should always remain a surprise. It simply means

that by your nonverbal or verbal signals you tell your audience to get ready because a reward is on its way.

This also doesn't mean that you should employ this with every bit of humor you do. Some gags are best presented as pure surprises with no forewarning. My ad-lib on the tennis court would be worthless if I clued Charlie Wilson in any way. It *had* to be delivered as if I had not seen him and had no indication that he was listening.

Some jokes, though, need a preamble and others are simply more effective with one. Let's investigate some ways of telling your listeners that some fun is on its way.

WITH YOUR FORM OF COMEDY

Often the form of a joke is its own announcement of the punch line to follow. For instance, a limerick has a rhythm that we're all familiar with. It has four lines of set-up and the last line is the punch line. Certain gags have punch lines that come at a predictable time. For instance:

HE: What's black and white and red all over?
SHE: A newspaper?
HE: No, a wounded zebra.

Everyone knows that the answer to the question is the place for the joke.

Certain comedians have developed a form that is so recognizable, that you know when the gag is going to be delivered. Johnny Carson says, "It was cold today." The audience gets into the rhythm of the gag and supplies the straight line in unison; "How cold was it?" The entire nation knows the joke is coming now! "It was so cold today that in New York the Statue of Liberty was holding the torch *under* her dress."

Bob Hope has a form that predicts the punch line. He makes a statement and you know the next one is going to be a punch line based on that fact.

Gandhi got the best picture award because it presented something different in movies. (That's the statement of fact. The punch line is coming next.)
. . . A sheet with only one person under it.

I write a newspaper column that is a series of about a dozen jokes on some current topic. The form is so predictable, that when I call my column into the editor, she hears the straight line and says things like, "Oh boy, this is gonna be a good one." She's anticipating the joke that I've got coming on the set-up I just read. It's not a bad idea to get that same eagerness from your audience.

WITH WORDS

Many times we can tell an audience that a joke is coming by actually telling them a joke is coming. It's not that unusual. We do it conversationally all the time. We add some emphasis to some point or another we want to make by preparing our listener for it: "Wait'll you hear what he said to me."—"You'll never guess what she did then."—"This one'll kill you."

The psychology is obvious. We have something important to say, but we want the listener to know how important it is without first hearing it. We don't trust their judgment of what is and isn't important, so we tell them.

Phyllis Diller does it occasionally. Here's an example:

You'll never guess how I fix my hair. *Are you ready for this?* I chew on a grenade.

If you have a punch line that is deserving of a forewarning, use any handle you want to let them know it's coming.

WITH FACIAL EXPRESSIONS

This one I particularly love because it's very precious. Johnny Carson is a great practitioner of this. Watch during his monologue some night and you'll often see it happening: He'll be so thrilled with the joke that is upcoming, that he'll have to stifle a laugh himself. He'll get a mischievous grin on his face, look to Ed McMahon, who will certainly be laughing because he laughs at even Carson's straight lines, he'll rub his finger under his nose which is a polite way of saying, "I don't want you to see me laughing at my own jokes," compose himself somewhat—and deliver the punch line.

None of the above is derogatory because all humorists do it. More often than not it precedes a line that is a bit hokey. It's the humorist's way of saying, "I'm a little embarrassed by this line that's coming next, but

I'll do it anyway because I'm pretty sure it's going to get a laugh."

I use it in my act when I tell a joke that has a false punch line to it. That is, I tell a story and then do a punch line. The folks laugh. I laugh with them, but I know I have a line coming up which is about four times as funny as the one I just did. So I signal that it is coming by trying to stifle my own laughter, and hold up my hand as if to say, "I know you think that was a funny line, but wait till you hear this one."

And incidentally, there is nothing wrong, provided it's your style, with laughing at your own jokes. Red Skelton did it for years and he's not regarded as a bad comic.

WITH PAUSES AND EMPHASIS

Silence can be comedy's greatest friend sometimes. If you have a great line coming up and you know it is great, *make them wait for it*. Tactfully done, it will pay dividends.

Milton Berle is one of the most compulsive comics. He can't let a straight line go by without a topper. But there were times when someone would insult Uncle Miltie and all the world knew that Berle had a funny comeback. But he would just look at the audience and savor the moment. In effect, he was saying, "I know I'm going to top this bozo, and you know I'm going to top him, and I know that you know that I'm going to get back at him, but I'm going to wait until you can't stand it any longer, because then it will be funnier."

Possibly the greatest example of the long pause is the fantastic radio joke that I mentioned earlier: Jack Benny being mugged by someone who said, "Your money or your life." The long pause got the big laugh. Everyone knew Benny would have an answer, but the pause was hilarious.

Verbal emphasis will also let your audience know that something special is coming. For example, you do a dialogue joke and without using a specific example it goes something like this:

He said, "something, something, something." Then she said, "Oh yeah, something, something something."
Then he said, "Something, something, something."
Then *she said.*

Here the speech gets slower and the emphasis is obvious. Everyone knows when the speaker highlights that statement so much, it has to be the punch line.

There is almost an unwritten code about how some joke forms are delivered verbally, where the emphasis is, and so on. Jack Benny had a great story about guesting on another comedian's radio show. Jack claimed that the other comedian, since he was paying the writers, got all the punch lines. Jack said, "I had only one punch line in the entire script. Out of force of habit, I read it as a question."

YOU JUST DID A JOKE

Remember the pathetic plea of the failing comic? "These are the jokes, folks." He's trying to tell his audience that he just did the funnies, and is begging for laughs.

You needn't resort to that, but you may have to let the audience know that a punch line just appeared.

Let's refer to my ad-lib example on the tennis court. (I do a lot of comedy on the tennis court. Most of it while the ball's in play.) To save a friendship and prevent a headache, I had to let my buddy know that I was kidding him. It couldn't come before or during the joke for the reasons we've already discussed. It had to come afterwards.

The way I did it was to sense just when the joke had gone far enough, smile at Charlie Wilson, shake hands, and welcome him to the court. Naturally, while he was shaking hands, he came back at me with some sort of insult or another.

The way I signalled to good old Charlie Wilson that I was kidding is one method you can use with your listeners.

FACIAL EXPRESSION OR NONVERBAL COMMUNICATION

Just as we discussed this method as a warning of an upcoming punch line, so it can be a signal that you just did one.

Probably the greatest example of this was Jack Benny. When someone hit Jack with a great put-down line, he would turn and stare at the audience. It was a most eloquent and effective stare. It was a glance that could be interpreted in many different ways, which was probably why it was so valuable. It might have said, "Did you hear that? Aren't you going to help me?" Or: "I'm going to ignore that remark. I hope you folks do, too." I'm not even sure it needs a literal translation because it got results. It brought out the laughs, and it milked the laughter.

When the laughs from the stare would begin dwindling, Jack would change it. He would gracefully bring his hand to his cheek, and just let the little finger play at the corner of his mouth. It would resurrect the laughter.

Benny was such a master of this technique that his reaction would get bigger laughs than the punch line. He had a rule on his show that no one was to continue until he turned back and faced them. He wanted to milk that glance for all it was worth.

There are times, too, when the audience needs some coaching from you. Some of your statements are ambiguous until explained by your reaction to them. I know there's at least one moment in a story I tell that needs a nonverbal explanation. I tell the folks that I did a benefit for a certain group each year for 10 years and never received a dime.

Finally, at the tenth year, they gave me a little laminated plastic card that made me an honorary member of their association. Now, as you read this, what are you thinking? Should you be glad for me? Should you laught at that gift? I doubt if you would applaud.

But exactly what should you think? The answer is, you honestly don't know. I haven't given you enough information. Is it an honor to be made an honorary member of this group? There are some associations in which honorary membership is coveted and actively sought. My audience is confused at this moment. So after I tell them, I wait a slight beat, then shrug my shoulders as if to say, "Big deal." Now they are free to laugh along with me. I just told them that getting this award for 10 years of service was a joke. (The big joke comes later, but this illustrates the point.)

Sometimes you may have a good line, but it's a bit subtle. It's so delicate that it could easily slide by most of the crowd without them ever realizing it's a joke. Your nonverbal signal will trigger the laugh.

Woody Allen, in his stand-up routines, has many jokes like this. Allen doesn't use the standard Hope-like set-up and then joke. He often has a punch line just appear. Obviously the danger in that is that without warning, it may sometimes slip past us. So Woody has a punch line signal. He nods his head up and down as if saying "Yes." What he's really saying in a sophisticated way is, "These are the jokes, folks."

Watch the comedians and you'll discover that most of them have it. George Burns does a trick with his cigar. Groucho had a nod like Woody Allen's and then a gesture right at the audience. You wouldn't dare miss his punch line. Joan Rivers points the finger around the room, sort of an adaptation of Woody Allen's nodding head. Phyllis Diller has the disgusted look or the raucous laugh. Most of them have some nonverbal mannerism to signify punch line.

WAIT FOR YOUR LAUGHS

One piece of advice I give all comedy writers has nothing to do with writing comedy, but, boy, is it important. I recommend that they separate their jokes physically on the page. Don't put several jokes in one paragraph. Make each joke a separate paragraph. Even when I have a topper—a line which is not really a complete sentence—if it is another laugh, it's another paragraph.

Why is this important? Because the writer has spent tough hours creating these jokes, he or she doesn't want a single one of them missed. Sometimes in the haste to read a piece, we'll read right over good jokes. Separating them makes the reader pause. He may be confused and not recognize that there is a joke, but he'll wonder why it's a separate paragraph. He'll go back and search until he sees the humor.

You may have noticed this also when you read an occasional cartoon that doesn't seem to have any point. Rather than dismiss it, it almost becomes obsessive to find out what the cartoonist had in mind. Generally, you'll find something that you overlooked. Now you may not decide that the joke is a masterpiece, but at least you searched it out.

Speakers must do the same thing. The tendency is, if the laugh doesn't come immediately after the punch line, to speed up. We want to get out of there as quickly as possible before our audience realizes we tried to do a joke and failed. The opposite will serve you better. Challenge the audience. Wait for your laugh.

Listen to this advice:

> I learned a lot about getting laughs and about ways of handling jokes of different types at the Stratford. I'd lead off with a subtle joke and after telling it, I'd say to the audience, "Go ahead. Figure it out." Then I'd wait till they got it.
>
> One of the things I learned was to have enough courage to wait. I'd stand there waiting for them to get it for a long time. Longer than any other comedian has enough guts to wait. My idea was to let them know who was running things.

That's not bad advice and it came from a gentleman who profited nicely from putting these lessons to work for him—Bob Hope.

It takes some courage to stand up and give a speech. It takes even more backbone to use humor. However, if you're going to do it, do it. Present your humor full force, and don't be afraid to tell the folks where the humor is. Don't be afraid to wait for your laughs, too. You had the fearlessness to present this audience some humor. You deserve your laughs. Get them.

How to Use Insult Humor Safely

PICTURE YOURSELF IN THE CENTER of a large hotel lobby in any big city. It's arrival day for a national convention of businessmen.

As they straggle into the hotel, you eavesdrop on a couple of conversations. The first is between Mr. Lawrence Hawkins and Mr. Richard Sage.

HAWKINS
Dick . . . Dick Sage. How are you?

SAGE
I'm fine, Mr. Hawkins, and how are you?

HAWKINS
Couldn't be better. I see that business has been picking up in your district.

SAGE
We may be up for District of the Year.

HAWKINS
You must be quite proud. Is the family here with you?

SAGE
They wouldn't miss it for the world. Except for my son, Jim, who couldn't get time off from work.

HAWKINS
That's a pity. I'll see you at the cocktail party tonight. Give my love to your wife.

SAGE

Will do, and you do the same.

That's the end of that little playlet. It's kind of dull, but very civil and friendly in its own way.

Now we overhear the greetings of Mr. Donald Van and Mr. James Evering.

VAN

Jimmy Evering, is that you? I thought I recognized that potbelly.

EVERING

Well, if it isn't Donald Van. You haven't changed since the last convention . . . not even your suit.

VAN

Well, at least I have two suits to change into. The way your department is going, I'm surprised you can afford trousers.

EVERING

Ah, you're a funny guy, Van. I know, I've seen your sales reports.

VAN

Talk to me at the end of the convention. You know I'm up for an award this year.

EVERING

For what, "Drinker of the Year?"

VAN

Look who's talking. I heard your plane had to stop twice along the way to pick
    up more of those little bottles.

Well, we've listened to enough from these two jokesters. The questions is this: Which of these two pairs do you think were better buddies? I would certainly guess it was the second pair. The more quickly people get around to fiendly put-downs, the closer they are.

Do you feel that there is any dialogue in the second playlet that is offensive? I doubt it.

Were I to continue with the scenarios, Hawkins and Sage probably wouldn't meet each other for dinner that evening, nor seek each other out at the cocktail party. Evering and Van probably would.

Insult humor can be a symbol of friendship. For the speaker this can be invaluable, because you certainly want to be liked by your listeners.

Also, one of the quickest ways to bring a person into an intimate circle is to include him in friendly banter. Picture a group of eight or nine people, all of whom know one another, and an outsider who may know only one of the others. It's conceivable that the interloper would feel uncomfortable for a while. The conversation, most likely, would skirt him. Some harmless put-downs aimed in his direction could welcome him into the inner sanctum and could make him feel more a part of the group.

One of a speaker's first duties is to do just that—to pull all these strangers out there listening to you into your circle of friends. Don't overlook the power of good insult humor to accomplish that.

Whether or not to use insult humor is up to each individual speaker. Again, I remind you that comedy must be your own. If you are uncomfortable with abrasive humor, then avoid it. I find Don Rickles hilarious. His mind is lightning-quick, his humor is funny, and to me he's not offensive. Nevertheless, I couldn't use his material. It's a touch too aggressive for my platform personality. I would do it badly.

Your platform personality may shy away from even the mildest put-downs. Then don't use them.

I do, however, want to make two points.

First, that insult humor should not be summarily dismissed as too arrogant and offensive for platform use. Actually, it is a warm and friendly form of humor *when used properly.*

Second, if you are a speaker who chooses to use this form of humor, use it wisely. It's a powerful aid for a speaker, but it can be dangerous. It's like fire or electricity. They can warm our homes and cook our meals; they can also burn your house down. Their awesome power must be respected.

How then can you use insult humor safely? By following these rules. I'll list them here then discuss them singly:

1. Kid about things that are fabricated or obviously untrue
2. Kid about things that the audience kids themselves about
3. Kid about things that are of no consequence

If you analyze these rules, you'll notice that they are all designed to take the "hurt" out of the insult.

As a child, I remember seeing a stage performance by a gentleman who was expert with a bullwhip. He did some incredible stunts. He snapped cigarettes right out of an assistant's mouth, ripped paper that was held by audience members into shreds, and finally ended by binding two audience members together by encircling them with fierce cracks of his whip.

He was unbelievable. But I applauded more the courage of the stooges. How could they stand there and be lashed by a whip that cracked like a gunshot? Then my Dad explained it to me. The loud crack of the whip was at the very tip of the weapon. The tricks were done with the other part of the whip long before the report sounded.

Insult humor, skillfully employed, is just as harmless. We lash out furiously, but the sting is removed.

Now let's study the rules individually.

KID ABOUT THINGS THAT ARE FABRICATED OR OBVIOUSLY UNTRUE

Avoid coming too close to a nerve. That kind of insult, regardless of how funny, is lethal. It not only offends the victim, but it makes everyone else in the room uncomfortable. When a comedian berates a heckler, even when the person deserves the performer's attack, it still causes an uneasy feeling in the theatre.

It's very difficult to keep the audience on your side after using insult humor with any venom in it.

When I did my after-dinner stints at 25-year and retirement parties, I made one group of my fellow workers infamous. At each party, since they were generally present, I'd do gags about their drinking prowess. I'd do things like:

> They stop at every bar along the West Chester Pike. I mean, I call it the West Chester Pike. They call it the Chug-a-lug Trail.

> I'll give you an idea how many bars they stop at. Harry's car is only six months old and already he's gone through three sets of door handles.

> They were late for this party tonight, so they had to drive right by Devine's (that was a bar directly across from work). Mr. Devine was so surprised he immediately went out and bought a new deodorant.

Practically anytime I needed someone to kid, I picked on this notorious gang of drinkers. Yes, they did stop for one quick drink after the day's work, but the rest was entirely manufactured. None of these men had a drinking problem and everyone in the audience knew that. These gentlemen were promoted at the same rate as anyone else. Management attended these parties, also, and knew that the "drinkers' reputation" was fantasy. In fact, these guys were probably initially considered for any promotions because their reputations were such that their names popped into everyone's head first.

It would have been impossible to do any such lines if any one of them had a problem with alcohol.

Many of my emceeing chores were for people I didn't know that well. In order to gather relevant material, I would meet with several friends and close coworkers of the person to be honored. However, after writing monologue, I would always take it to one of the honored guest's closest friends and have it checked to make sure that none of the gags would be offensive. If there was doubt, the joke would be dropped.

KID ABOUT THINGS THE AUDIENCE KIDS THEMSELVES ABOUT

I recently did a show for a national company. Most of the employees were from Texas. At the cocktail party the night before my speech, a group of four Oklahomans got up and sang "Okie from Muskogee" just to put it to the Texans. The group was terrible and the band had their hands full constantly trying to find their key. Of course, the worse they were, the funnier it was. The rest of the night, everyone kidded these poor guys and they loved it.

The following morning, at the opening of my talk, I thanked the group for welcoming me into their midst and inviting me to the party. I said, "It really was very gracious of you although it did have its bad points. Up until last night, 'Okie from Muskogee' was my favorite song."

It got a great reception because it was a safe insult. When people kid themselves, the hurt has long since been removed.

Of course, some care must be exercised. I remember at one of the parties that I emceed, the workers were all kidding about a blueprint machine that never seemed to work right. It was the big office joke. I jumped right on that topic and did about 15 gags on the thing at the next party.

It was a mistake. The supervisor of that department talked to me later and was not so much angry as hurt. He was disappointed in me.

The problem was that they did kid about this machine at work, but always among themselves. I did it with the executives present. I had undermined his competence as a manager. He was right; my material was inconsiderate.

This is an example of material that violated all three rules. It hurt my friend and it hurt me.

KID ABOUT THINGS THAT ARE OF NO CONSEQUENCE

Why did my example about the recalcitrant blueprint machine hurt so much? Because I was hitting this man right where he made his living. All of us want to do a good job, impress the boss, and get a raise or a promotion. This friend of mine did, too. Then I came along and with a few wise-cracking gags, I made him look bad as an office manager. That's wrong.

Now suppose instead I had kidded him about the cheap cigars he smoked. The lines could have been much funnier and more devastating, but he would not have been offended. He might have been truly honored and even sent me a box of cigars the next week as his way of getting even.

Do you see the difference? (I often wish I had.) The one series of jokes were about something that was vital to this man—his livelihood. The other would have been meaningless. The fact that a man smokes smelly cigars doesn't mean he's a bad manager.

We had a consultant who worked in our office and he had the loudest voice in the world. It seemed to get even louder when he got on the telephone, as if he didn't trust those little wires to carry his message safely. I kidded him mercilessly about it with lines like the following:

> I feel sorry for Harry. He has to call Theodore (the loud voice guy) 20 times a day. You all know Harry. He's the guy whose right ear is three times bigger than his left.
> Theodore has the loudest telephone voice in the company. He's the only guy that you can hang up on without losing volume.

There's no way any reader can tell from those lines whether Theodore is a good consultant or a bad one. Will any executives in the audience consider him for a raise, or will they want to demote him? Neither, because none of the gags has any real consequence. Having a loud or a soft telephone voice doesn't make a person a good or bad consultant. It has absolutely no bearing.

The only way those lines could be offensive were if Theodore was sensitive about his booming voice. Then, of course, the lines shouldn't be done.

Perhaps there should have been a fourth rule: don't kid about things that people don't want to be kidded about. However, that's too broad a statement. It also takes the control away from the humorist.

Some humor, any humor, will offend some people. We have done some bizarre sketches on television shows that were totally nonsensical and unbelievable. Yet we got letters from associations that complained, say, that we were undermining the egg industry. I doubt if anyone thought twice about our reference to eggs. If a few did, I doubt that it would have made an entire nation stop buying eggs. These people objected to any joke that had the word "egg" in it.

I single out the egg industry here, but I've received similar letters from many other people. If we listened to all of them, we could never again do another line about anything at all. An awful lot of laughter then would be missing from the world.

That is too much authority to give to anyone outside of the humorist. My three rules will help you do insult humor harmlessly. You'll use them because you don't want to irritate anyone. You are your own best censor.

Tips on Ad-Libbing

WHILE I WAS DRIVING to a speaking engagement, I was making notes on this chapter. I dictate my random thoughts into a voice-activated recorder, then transcribe them and arrange them later. This chapter was particularly challenging, though. Ad-libbing is an illusive art and the notes weren't flowing freely.

The scheduled talk was before about 60 members of a suburban woman's club. I arrived a bit early and enjoyed some lunch while they completed their business meeting. There were reports by committee members and some bickering over how and when to collect certain fees. The club president kept motioning to me that it wouldn't be much longer. I was relaxed. I had a good meal before me and some delicious hot coffee. Take as long as you like.

Awards that several members had won at the recent convention were presented and the members applauded. Then the President said to me, "Just one more brief announcement, then we'll bring you on." I nodded an okay. Then she addressed the assembly:

"I'm going to make this last announcement before we introduce our speaker. I don't want any objections to this, and I don't want any oohs and ahhs."

I sensed trouble. She went on:

"In fact, I'm going to read this because I don't think I can do it otherwise.''

She took out a document and read:

"Dear fellow members of the Woman's Club: I have enjoyed serving you as President. It has been for me both a duty and a privilege." On "privilege" her voice started to waver. She backed away from the microphone and whispered to the lady next to her at the head table, "I don't think I can do this." Then she began again.

"It has been for me both a duty and a privilege. However, due to family pressures and . . ." Now she broke down in tears. I went for more hot coffee because I knew I had to follow this act with jokes and lighthearted banter.

The other official at the head table stood up and hugged the President who was openly bawling. "I'll read it for you, honey," she said. The President thanked her with a simultaneous nod of the head and blow of the nose into a tissue. Her stand-in read the rest of the letter which was, of course, a resignation. Now the membership started to cry. Someone tearfully moved that this resignation be regretfully accepted. It took some time before someone could stop sniffling long enough to second the motion. A voice vote unanimously allowed the President, for health reasons, to abdicate.

The President, still chairing this meeting, sniffled her way through my introduction. As she did, all of the ladies at the head table, scurried away. It was like a signal was given to man the battle stations. What they were doing was coming out front so they could see me talk from a better angle. But it frightened me a bit. Also, I should mention that the woman who hired me for this appearance had to leave town and couldn't be at this meeting.

I walked to the microphone to polite applause, muffled somewhat because every person in the audience had at least one tissue in her hand.

My opening remark was:

"I want to give you an idea how good this talk is going to be. Mrs. McNulty hired me for this speech, and she left town. The head table abandoned ship. And your President quit."

It's interesting to note that when I got back to the writing staff—I was working on "Mama's Family" at the time—and told this story about the tearful resignation, the first question was, "How long did it take you to get them back?" In other words these show business people knew that this episode distracted my audience. They wanted to know what I did to get them interested in my talk, and how long it took.

That's one value of the ad-lib. When something takes your audience's minds away from your lecture, you *have to* recapture them. Since you can't know in advance what is going to divert them, you can't preplan what to do to counteract it. You have to improvise. You're forced to ad-lib.

What is an ad-lib? The word comes from the latin, "ad libitum," which translates to "at your pleasure." It means to improvise, to extemporize, or, in our case, to come up with a funny line on the spur of the moment.

This chapter is called *tips* on ad-libbing because there are no iron-clad rules. It's not the kind of a science that you can list steps, one-two-three, and guide a student to skillful improvisation. It's an art that can't be capsulized that easily. Reducing the ad-lib to a science is like trying to hide a parachute under your blouse.

This chapter doesn't pretend to be all inclusive, either. There is no way that it could be because each ad-lib comes from left field and may violate all the rules that went before it. Thus, it creates new rules and the art form is ever expanding and improving.

All of the suggestions on ad-libbing are only that—suggestions. I hope that if you're a poor ad-libber, this chapter might make you fair. If you're fair, perhaps you'll become better. If you're a great ad-libber, then I want to read the chapter you write.

The glory of the ad-lib is its spontaneity. It has to feel as though it's happening here and now. That's much more important than the comedic value of the line. A top-of-the-head line doesn't have to be that funny if the moment is right.

To illustrate (and we'll refer to this example throughout the rest of the chapter), suppose you were presenting a trophy at a bowling awards banquet. The announced winner steps to the lectern, you hand him the trophy, and the bronzed figure at the top falls off the trophy, clunks on the table, and hits the floor with a clank. *Anything* you say at that moment will get a laugh. *Anyone* can ad-lib then. Will the line have to be among the funniest ever conceived? Certainly not. The accident is so hilarious that it will get the big laugh. What you say will just piggyback on that humor, but it will recapture your audience. It will bring them back to center stage and refocus their attention on the award rather than on the bouncing statuette.

That's why fearing an ad-lib is like being afraid of having your teeth cleaned at the dentist. It's not unfounded, but it's futile. You can't safely avoid either.

There will be times when you'll have to ad-lib. Some speakers may object, saying, "My talk is precisely written and diligently rehearsed. It is absolutely flawless. There's positively no room in it for improvisation." Many speeches are that meticulously conceived and executed. Nevertheless, your audience and your surrounding will never be that perfect.

Try giving that inflexible a presentation in an auditorium where the lights go out because of a faulty circuit breaker. I defy you to continue with your prepared speech as a waiter trips with a tray of dishes and gets up covered with embarrassment and chocolate mousse. Let me see you stick with your script when one of your well-rehearsed gestures accidentally hits the microphone and knocks it to the floor with an electronically amplified thud that almost deafens your listeners. These things happen to the greatest speakers and during the most unforgettable orations.

These nuisances *demand* ad-libs. Why? Because you have to maintain control. You're orchestrating this audience. You're in charge. Any unforeseen disturbance creates tension in a crowd. Humor, as we learned earlier, is among the best ways to eliminate tension.

If your presentation is as finely tuned as you claim, then you won't want anyone to miss a syllable of it. Therefore, any distraction has to be met, conquered, and disposed of, so that it doesn't interfere with your speech any more than it already has.

Of course, even though certain occurrences require an ad-lib, you can introduce a funny line any time you want to; however, it may not get the same reaction without the proper set-up. What I mean is, that unless the situation is obviously unplanned, the audience may just assume it's part of your program. If it's funny, fine. However, it won't have built-in laughs going for it like the broken trophy incident did.

I once saw George Gobel performing. As he sang and accompanied himself on guitar, his voice suddenly cracked. He said, "I just swallowed a fly." As he coughed and sputtered, he managed to call offstage for a glass of water. The water was late in coming and Gobel continued to try to clear his throat. Finally he did, without the water ever arriving. He shouted offstage, "Never mind. I'll just let him walk down."

The audience loved that gag. They laughed and applauded. I suspect, though, that Gobel swallowed that same fly at just about the same time in every performance. I didn't believe it was accidental, and didn't accept the "ad-lib."

Accepting my premise for the moment, and supposing there were people in the audience who had seen the show before, they wouldn't appreciate that line as much as those who believed it was a genuine top-of-the-head quip.

Understand, I'm not condemning George Gobel for deception. For all I know, it might have been real, but even if it weren't, it was well designed and it worked. I'm just using it as an example to show that genuine, believable, spontaneity will help a comedy ad-lib.

Later on in this chapter we'll talk about the prepared ad-lib. For instance, we may even steal Gobel's bit. Suppose you're talking and you get a tickle or a sudden frog in the throat. You might ask for a glass of water, drink it, recover and say, "That's much faster than waiting for him to walk down." But more on that later.

Let's investigate some of these magic moments that cry out for our off-the-cuff cleverness. When are we practically obliged to resort to the ad-lib?

WHEN THERE'S A DISTURBANCE THAT DISRUPTS YOUR PRESENTATION

It's important to maintain control of an audience. An audience is only human. Should there be a loud crash, bang, crumble from the kitchen area, they're going to turn and look regardless of how dynamic a speaker you are. You have to allow them that weakness. Then you have to draw their concentration back to you. (Remember the question from my fellow writer? "How long did it take you to *get them back?*")

There's a caution that should be pointed out here. Be careful that your comment doesn't come off as a whining, complaining, or a snide remark. Some speakers are insulted by any disturbance. "How dare they drop dishes while I'm on?" This attitude could promp a sarcastic remark which only produces more discomfort in your audience. You take an ill-timed disturbance and make it worse.

Accidents can and do happen. When they do, no insinuating remarks can erase them. The best advice is to get out of the situation as delicately as possible and file away some ideas to keep this sort of thing from happening again.

You do yourself a disservice by being nasty about it because you'll lose some audience attention. What's worse is—you serve notice that your message is not powerful enough to overcome this tiny setback.

Many years ago, I listened to a radio personality address a meeting of our plant's Management Association. I don't know exactly when it was, but Russia and China were making headlines with their border disputes. As this gentleman spoke, someone in the kitchen did drop a pile of dishes. The noise was so loud it was impossible to ignore. The speaker poised as his audience laughed at the disturbance. At just the right time, he said, "I see Khrushchev's not the only one that's having trouble with China."

The timing was perfect. He got laughter and an ovation. He also got our attention for the continuation of his talk.

WHEN SOMEONE TOPS YOU: REMARKS FROM THE AUDIENCE

There will be times when people shout from the audience at precisely the wrong time. It's particularly annoying for a humorist when the intruder shouts a hilarious line. You have to reclaim your audience. This is not an ego thing. It's just sound speaking technique. You're the ringmaster at this circus and you have to hold on to your whistle. It's important that you have the last word.

Of course, we're only speaking about uninvited comments from the audience. Many speakers make it a practice to invite their audience to participate. That's fine and audience remarks then should be welcomed. In fact, any sort of flip retort here might inhibit your listeners from any further participation.

When remarks from the audience are disruptive, though, you have to reestablish your authority. This doesn't mean you have to chastise the offender. Often the remark is genuinely funny. Both you and the rest of the audience are amused by it. It's all right then to applaud this person's creativity. Johnny Carson sometimes acknowledges remarks against him with that wistful look of his. Bob Hope always has a look and then a comeback.

My humor style is in the form of bragging. I'll build myself up and then inadvertently do a put-down. This style encourages the audience to play along with me. Sometimes during a question and answer session, I'll get some pretty aggressive questions. Many of them are clever and get big laughs from the rest of the audience. When this happens I'll let the laugh build while I put on my comedy offended look. Then I'll have ad-libs like:

"I spend three weeks writing this speech, and then she gets the big laugh."

Or, I'll use the name of the group to feign annoyance. For instance, if I'm addressing a group of engineers, I might counter with:

"If there's anything I can't stand, it's an engineer who ad-libs."

These sort of comments don't offend the person. (I can't do that, since I encouraged it.) In fact, it pays them a small tribute. Nevertheless, it does get the spotlight back on me, so that I can answer whatever question accompanied the ad-lib.

WHEN YOU MAKE A MISTAKE

This happens to the best of us. We "fumpfer" a line, or we get lost in our notes, or we forget the name of the association we're addressing. I don't know about all other speakers, but when it happens to me I feel a flush of embarrassment. It's a physical thing. I get warm, maybe redder than normal, I sweat a little heavier, and I lose concentration for a beat or two. It's a dangerous moment.

I had a basketball coach in high school who would allow us one mistake. Anyone was entitled to one mistake, whatever it might be. What he campaigned against were mistakes that happened in pairs. A player would make a mistake at one end of the court, be humiliated by it, try to overcompensate to make amends, and immediately commit another, even more stupid error. This player then had to face an angry coach.

An audience is like that coach. They'll forgive us our trespasses. They know we're human. All we have to do is admit it to ourselves.

There are some who say that Nixon would have continued in office after Watergate if he had just admitted what happened. The unforgivable was trying to deny it.

You'll do some dumb things at the microphone, too. Humiliation will surge through your body, and you'll hope against all logic that no one in the audience noticed it. They did.

The best thing to do is take a moment to compose yourself. Give them a moment to enjoy your *faux pas*. Then dismiss it with some cute ad-lib and move on.

I once got horribly lost in a speech. My mind went almost totally blank. I say almost totally blank because there was one thought in there. It was the thought that I didn't know what I was going to say next.

The audience saw that I was floundering, and there was a mixture of amusement and sympathy among them.

I recovered enough to ask, "Has anyone here ever heard me speak before?" A few hands went up. I pointed to one young lady and said, "You have?" She said, "Yes." I then asked, "Can you please tell me what I'm supposed to say next, because I don't have the foggiest idea."

While they laughed at my admission, I took out my notes and continued my talk.

This discussion has covered a few of the whys of ad-libbing, and some of the whens. Obviously you want to know the hows.

Let's take two incidents as a basis for studying ways of formulating ad-libs. One, the broken bowling trophy, I've already outlined. The following is an incident that actually happened to me.

I spoke at a banquet in a beautiful hotel dining room. The audience was seated at several round tables and over each table was a beautiful, ornate chandelier. During my speech, the chandelier at the front table to my right began to blink on and off. The custodians noticed it and worked frantically at the switch box to control it, but nothing could be done. I either spoke with a flickering light or in total darkness.

Now, how do we get ad-libs out of these two situations—the broken trophy and the flickering chandelier?

1. TAKE TIME TO THINK

Don't rush. Don't be afraid of silence. Even though these incidents disrupt your fabulous talk, they are funny and ironic. Milk them.

The trophy falling apart is a sudden, unexpected happening. That's what comedy is made of. Allow it to grow. The incident itself will get laughs, so you'll have to wait for them. Then with a confused look, you might glance down to where the trophy has fallen. That will generate more laughs. Then you might look at the part of the trophy you still have in your hands. This will draw attention to how silly it looks and get more response from the audience. A look to the frustrated recipient might get even more. All of this depends on the situation and the person making the presentation.

I guarantee, though, if that were Tim Conway presenting the

awards, the laughs would go on interminably before he would even say a word.

The chandelier incident doesn't lend itself to pauses or delays because it is not so sudden. It's more an ongoing disturbance, so should be handled differently.

However, in those situations where the delay applies it will serve two purposes. It will allow you time to think of the appropriate ad-lib, and when it's delivered, the long delay and look will enhance it.

2. LOOK FOR THE PAINFUL TRUTH IN THE SITUATION

In searching for an ad-lib, the first element you might explore is the truth. Often, just a simple statement of the truth will provide the irony you're looking for.

We have to be careful, though, because we're looking for the *real* truth, not the truth that we've been conditioned to believe. We have all become so adept at disguising the truth that we sometimes can't find reality under all the camouflage.

During questions and answers on the *Carol Burnett Show,* Carol was frequently asked if she would have her children on the show. Carol said, "No. My mother never put me on her show. Why should I put them on mine?"

Basically, that's a true line and it gets laughs mostly from shock value. We don't expect a mother to say anything so harsh, therefore we laugh at it.

Take a moment and investigate some of the cold-blooded truth in the trophy incident. I'll list a few, but you should search out others.

- It's poorly made.
- The hosts were cutting costs.
- The winner didn't really deserve the win.

These might prompt some ad-libs; you might go to rivals. If this were a Knights of Columbus bowling league, you might say:

"That's the last time we buy trophies from the Masons."

Or:

"I think the trophy just expressed its own opinion about your bowling."

Do the same now with the chandelier disturbance.

- They didn't pay their electric bill.
- The light doesn't like your talk.
- The lights are trying to walk out on you.

Your lines might be:

"This is the last time I work for a group that can't afford to pay their electric bill."

"I've had people walk out on me before, but never an entire chandelier."

3. STUDY HOW THIS DISTURBANCE AFFECTS YOU

Once I did a banquet for the place I worked in. It was held immediately after quitting time. The microphone was set too high and every time I tried to get close to it, it whistled. The custodians were adjusting it while I approached it about four times, and each time it whistled loudly. Finally, when I got safely to the microphone, I said, "When you have to come here directly from work, you don't get a chance to shower."

I took an awkward situation and turned it against me. It's an effective ad-lib method, and you can do it either of two ways . . . either with humility or false braggadocio.

Let's see how you can ad-lib with the trophy incident both ways:

"I seem to have the Midas touch. Everything I touch turns to automobile mufflers."

"I'm sorry about that, but when I tell jokes, *everybody* falls down laughing."

And the chandelier incident:

"How do you like that? When I speak even the lights start to doze off."

"I must really look great tonight. Even the lights are winking at me."

4. STUDY HOW THIS DISTURBANCE AFFECTS YOUR HOSTS

Don't be afraid to go for the jugular. Attack your hosts, attack authority. Be careful, though, that it's done in a spirit of fun and it's obvious that you're kidding. You don't want to come off here as a whiner or a complainer. Neither should your line appear as an indictment against the host association.

For example, in kidding about the chandelier incident, I said, "This is the last time I'll work for a group that can't afford to pay their electric bill." It was obvious that paying the bill wasn't the problem. Therefore, no one in the audience believed my line. It was accepted as being pure fun.

However, there's a different situation if you're using a flip chart easel and it collapses in the middle of your presentation. Now a reference to how cheap the hosts are might be taken as a sarcastic remark because the stand definitely was faulty.

In the trophy fiasco, you might attack the organization gently with a line like:

"The organization wanted to present you with something that would last."

5. STUDY HOW THE DISTURBANCE AFFECTS YOUR AUDIENCE

Everyone in the audience is probably aware of the disturbance and therefore they become a part of it. Don't let them off the hook. Again if it's done in a spirit of fun, you can include them in your extemporaneous remarks.

This line would have worked well when the lights blinked on and off a few times:

"Oh, I forgot to tell you. Any time I feel I deserve a standing ovation, I'll blink the lights on and off."

With the trophy, if you knew the winner well, you might say:

"Apparently, just like you, this trophy has a screw loose."

Or a more general audience comment would be:

"Next time have the heavier drinkers sit in the back. Someone's breath just melted the glue that holds this thing together."

These hints may give you a slant or a direction, but you'll still need the joke itself. Here's a tip that may help you to formulate extemporaneous jokes quickly."

FILE AWAY WHAT GOES ON BEFORE YOU AT THE BANQUET

Many things that happen before you begin your speech can be fodder for your humor. This doesn't require any intricate memory feats, or an inordinate amount of concentration. You simply have to be attuned to your surroundings. Be observant and aware. Your mind will store information and present it to you when you require an ad-lib.

I once spoke before a group of personnel managers and was attentive at the cocktail party before the banquet. I gathered that shop stewards were the avowed enemy of this group.

During my talk I asked for questions from the audience, and one member got a bit playful with me. He asked a question that had a friendly put-down incorporated into it. The audience laughed, and he was a big hero. I pretended to be insulted and said, "He'd make a perfect shop steward, wouldn't he?"

It was an easy joke, but they loved it because they knew it was spontaneous, and it applied to them.

It's interesting that it works both ways, too. Had this been a shop stewards' gathering and the same situation occurred, I might have said, "You can always spot the ones who are going to go into management, can't you?"

PREPARED AD-LIBS

Although the real beauty of an ad-lib is in its spontaneity, certain ad-libs can be prepared beforehand. Why? Because some incidents can be foreseen. They have happened before and you know they'll happen again. As good as you are at the platform, you will "fumpfer" a line. Someone will shout out from the audience. If you do a question and answer session, you will get repeating questions. You know better than anyone the things that happen to you on the platform more than just on rare occasions. You should prepare a few ad-libs for those times.

The old comics used to say after a "fumpfer," "My tongue got in the way of my eyeteeth and I couldn't see what I was saying."

I have one for anyone who shouts from the audience: "Thank you very much, but I do a single."

There are also some situations that you can create and have lines ready for them. For example, suppose you are doing some audience participation routine and you're going to ask someone when his birthday is. If he hesitates in replying, you might say, "Are these questions too tough?" If he proudly blurts out the answer, you could say, "You said that like you're very proud of yourself. Do you want a medal for knowing when your own birthday is?" Or he could do or say something that you've never encountered before. Just do a take and ride with his momentum.

Ad-libbing can be fun and beneficial. Don't let it frighten you away. It's not that difficult, and at the right moment it can get big laughs from your audience—and help you keep or regain their attention.

What to Do When the Humor Fails

THE QUESTION THAT'S MOST ASKED at humor seminars is: "What do I do if my jokes fall flat?" It's the fear most speakers have about using comedy. It's not unfounded because that's a horrifying feeling to be standing up there with egg on your face. Nevertheless, it's an apprehension that's exaggerated.

On a vacation trip back to my hometown of Philadelphia, I was asked to give a luncheon talk at a retirement home for nuns. Any readers who studied in the Catholic schools know that a request from a group of nuns amounts to a command performance. As I said in my routine that day, "I couldn't say 'no' to a group of nuns. I was afraid to. I don't want to be sent to Hell on a technicality. Besides, the last time I turned the nuns down, it snowed in Philadelphia in July—but only in my hotel room." So, I did the talk.

None of the room preparations were what the National Speakers Association would recommend. The room was a cafeteria with a podium set in the center. The tables were not tightly grouped. This was not to be an after-luncheon speech, but a *during*-luncheon talk. It's not only difficult, but unhygienic to make people laugh while they've got a mouthful of food. They don't appreciate it and neither does the person sitting opposite them.

I wrote original material about the Sisters and being raised in the Catholic schools. I also did some material about living in a Catholic household. All of it was respectful, and, I thought, funny. It got, at best, chuckles.

I muddled through it somehow and the only positive thought that crossed my mind during this performance was that at least they won't ask me back here on my next vacation trip. Finally, the talk ended to polite applause.

Then I was invited to go through the cafeteria line and enjoy lunch with some of my family and friends who were there also. I settled down to my meal and couldn't get to eat it. Practically every nun stopped over to tell me how much she enjoyed this talk. Each of them told me how one routine or another stirred fond memories of her Catholic upbringing. Some of them passed on anecdotes that related to my speech.

A speaker can generally tell when the post-presentation niceties are routine and when they're sincere. These were genuine.

I was honestly astounded. I got very little laughter or audience response, but I was a success.

This was an unusual circumstance. I've had audiences that responded very little and meant every minute of it. A few of them may have shook my hand afterward and said, "We really enjoyed it," but none of them ever wanted me to darken their podium again. But some crowds are not demonstrative. Nuns who have not only taught, but lived discipline all their lives, would naturally be somewhat reserved.

The point is that laughter is not the only goal of humor. Everyone who uses humor certainly wants the approval of hearty laughter, but it is not always absolutely necessary.

Had I surrendered that day to my own insecurity and self-pity and thrown away the rest of my talk, the performance would not have been as successful as it eventually was. It's an important point to keep in mind and we'll talk more about it later.

We should briefly pause here and recall the purpose of this book and your objective in reading it. We both want to add some humor to your presentation because it will be beneficial in many ways. We're not interested in turning you into a Las Vegas comedian. To a comedian, laughter is imperative. To a humorist, audience response is a frill. To a speaker using a dash of humor, it's not that important at all.

Speakers don't use humor as an end in itself. They use it to refresh their audience, to help them remember outstanding points, and to make themselves more likable to their listeners. Laughs aren't necessary for these.

Let me give you an example. Suppose a learned professor is giving a serious lecture on a complicated subject. He is doing a magnificent job, but his audience is absorbing so much knowledge that the educator senses that they're weary. He tells them a horribly corny joke. They groan rather than laugh. Mission accomplished. This lecturer has provided his recess. The listeners may hold their noses and wave their arms at him to never tell another joke again, but meanwhile, they've been mentally refreshed. They're now ready to get back to the serious theme and absorb more data. That's why the professor is there and that's why his joke served him well.

I will have to concede, though, that if you're going to use humor, you'll want laughs in return. You'll expect them and probably be shattered if you don't get them. How do you handle that situation?

1. PREPARE FOR FAILURE, BUT DON'T PREDICT IT

When you step to the microphone, you should be prepared for the worst. However, you must avoid making that a self-fulfilling prophecy. There's a difference between being prepared for disaster and expecting disaster.

Each time you address a group, you should expect that group to love you. You should be ready to give them the best talk you're capable of giving. If you're going to use humor, you should use it well, wisely, and effectively. And you should get laughs. That should cover 99.9 percent of your speeches. Now we're going to discuss what to do for the other 0.1 percent of the time.

If you ever want to see jokes fail, watch Johnny Carson's monologue for a few nights. Carson does fresh material each night without benefit of break-in time. His show is live, so he doesn't have the luxury of editing. Some of his jokes have to miss, but to his credit he turns them to his advantage. He has fun with the flops.

Occasionally, some of your humor won't work, either. You should be prepared to turn that to your advantage.

The first thing I recommend is that you be ready with "savers." Savers are just that: some comments that can save you from total disaster after your humor flops. Another way of putting it is, the joke flops but you don't.

Let me give you a few examples:

Before a presentation, I may casually ask if there are any members of the association who are famous for telling bad jokes. There's usually one. Often, I don't even have to ask. Since I'm billed and publicized as a comedy writer and speaker, it often comes out when others are speaking at the microphone which member tells the corniest jokes. I file that information away and then use it after a weak joke like this:

"That's the last time I ever buy a joke from   (NAME)   ."

If there is no bad joke teller, I may just file away a name that the people know and have kidded earlier. Then the saver after the bad joke may go:

"   (NAME)   told me that would really be a biggie.
I think I'm going to start not listening to him from now on . . . just like you people do."

Or you can just do general savers without any input from the group you're addressing. After a joke flops, you might take an index card from your pocket and complain:

"Well, that's the third time that joke didn't work. (Tear up the card and throw it away.)

Sometimes circumstances will just present a saver to you. One banquet I spoke at was preceded by a cocktail party. At that party, the main topic of discussion was the singer who entertained at the banquet the night before. Suffice it to say she was *Dolly Partonish*.

I kept one idea in the back of my mind and after one gag didn't get much response, I paused, glared at the audience, then said:

"Oh sure. You would have laughed at that joke if I was built like the girl that sang last night."

Some comics have more intricate saver systems. One night club performer even tells a story in his routine that he knows never gets much audience response. Then he uses that later as his saver.

Let's say that the punch line of the bad story is, "That was no lady, that was my wife." He'll deliver the punch line and then be surprised that it didn't work and repeat it for the audience, questioning why they didn't laugh at such a great joke. Can they all hear all right? Is the microphone turned on?

Now that the punch line is set in their minds, he can use it later. He'll tell a joke that doesn't get a great response and he'll say:

"Don't you get it? . . . that was no lady, that was my wife."

Bob hope tells what he learned about using savers when he was playing vaudeville:

> While I'm on the subject of how to get laughs, there's a line between being smart and too smart. People like a simple type of humor, too. Sometimes I'd tell a bad joke, make a wry face at myself for telling it and say, "My brother writes my jokes. Someday I'm going to go up into the attic and loosen his straight-jacket."

You may be able to write some savers of your own (if you had sense enough to buy my previous book on writing humor), or you might get some from joke books or services. (Bob Orben's *Current Comedy* or some of his many joke books usually have a few.) Another good way to build a repertoire of savers is to be aware of them and notice when professional comics use them.

It's nice to have them, but it's nicer never to have to use them.

2. KEEP YOUR COMPOSURE

The tendency is to overreact. The jokes are a failure, therefore my speech is a failure, therefore, I'm a failure.

To begin with, all your jokes haven't failed because you haven't told them all yet. People that do a lot of humor often have had the experience of bombing for a bit and then turning the audience around with one joke. After that, everything they say works. That can happen at any time. I've worked with comics who had mediocre nights, but their ending was so powerful that people would leave the theater with a good impression of them. Remember, we discussed earlier that if people like you, they'll be more ready to laugh at your material. In this case, folks like the comic at the end. They must have mentally decided that now they liked the stuff that they didn't laugh at earlier.

Be aware, also, that as a speaker, your humor is used for reasons other than to simply generate laughter. So you shouldn't base your evaluation on whether a particular joke works or doesn't work. What's important is the cumulative effect. Did your *sense of humor* impress this audience? Did it help them to hear what you were saying? Did it help them to remember it? Those are the things that are important to you. Consequently, the success or failure of one piece of material is not that important.

A speaker using comedy is like a baseball player up at bat. He doesn't have to get a hit every time he steps to the plate. It's the average that counts. Should he strike out this time at the plate, he has to forget it. He can't let it hurt his performance for the rest of the game.

Tennis players are a good example, also. They're also more volatile than most baseball players. They don't expect to win every point, just enough over the course of the match to defeat the opponent. However, we often see one lost point affect them so much that it hurts their play for the rest of the match.

Speakers can't allow that to happen. You have to accept whatever response the audience gives you, stay cool, and continue with what is really important—the rest of your presentation.

3. DON'T RUSH

It's no fun to attempt humor and have it backfire on you. Show business people have grim metaphors for it. "I died."—"I bombed."—"I laid an egg." None of these is very appealing. So, when we're experiencing this, we naturally want to stop experiencing it. We want to get it over with as soon as possible. Consequently, we rush.

That's a mistake. It's no fun to have a serious operation, either. Yet, we don't tell the doctor to rush through it because we want to get it over with. We do just the opposite. We say, "Doc, take as much time as you like, but just make sure you're doing it right."

Jokes, stories, anecdotes, even one-liners, have a natural rhythm. Jack Benny's stories had an agonizingly slow pace to them at times. I'd often find myself saying, "Get to the punch line, please." Of course, when Jack got there, it was well worth the wait; in fact, it needed the wait.

Henny Youngman has a clipped delivery that wastes no time. He crowds in a lot of jokes and moves on to the next one before you get a chance to be too judgmental about the one you just heard. Changing the pace of either would destroy them.

You, whether you know it or not, also have a built-in rhythm. The humor you use is best delivered at a certain place.

Okay, you're telling a story and it doesn't seem to be working. To rush ahead with it is going to destroy any chance it might have of survival. Resist the temptation. Try to keep Bill Gove's admonition in mind. "Be responsible *to* your audience, but not *for* your audience." Tell this story the best you know how. Keep the rhythm and the pace that feels natural to you. If the audience still doesn't like it, that's an entirely different problem.

4. DON'T CHANGE

This is quite similar to what we just discussed. The tendency in this trying situation is to escape, so you'll sometimes drop material, or you'll try to rewrite it while you're speaking. This generally destroys any chance you have of ever making the material work.

Presumably, you put time and effort into this piece of material. It is failing, but there is no way you can improve it in just a moment's time. There is no way you can concentrate on the changes while you're delivering it. Tampering with it while on the platform is a sure way to guarantee its continued failure.

Do it as written and as well as you know how. If it fails, then study it afterwards. Make required changes while you have a cool head and the time to devote your full efforts to it.

Any piece of comedy can always be improved, but not while you're at the mike.

5. WAIT FOR YOUR LAUGHS

We devoted a goodly portion of Chapter 17 to this, but it's worth repeating here for a slightly different reason. In the earlier chapter we were talking about letting folks know where the jokes are. Here we're talking about bombing.

We have the temptation when our material isn't working to try to outwit an audience. We do a joke and then quickly move on as if to say to them, "I knew that joke wouldn't get a laugh anyway, so I'll just keep going." Fight that temptation.

In writing for television sit-coms, it seems that half a writer's time is spent explaining jokes to performers. They don't believe it's funny, and we try to convince them to try it. Often, we'll have the power to get them to use the line, but not the persuasion to sell the comedy of it. What they'll do in retaliation is read the line as written, but not allow room for the laugh. They're saying to the viewers, "I don't expect a laugh here."

Sometimes their ploy will work. They'll go so fast that no one even realizes a joke went by. Sometimes, though (and it's a delight to writers), the laugh will come anyway, and they'll be caught stepping on their own laughs.

As painful as it is, leave room for the laugh. If none comes, the audience feels as awkward as you do. They deserve to. Why should you suffer alone? If they're made to feel a little guilty this time, perhaps they won't be so cavalier the next time.

Sliding by a punch line just to cover your own embarrassment is criminal. It's allowing the audience to control things. It's also serving notice to them that this piece of material in your talk is not good. It's much better to send out the message, "This material is good and I'm going to allow you some time to realize that. If you still choose not to appreciate it, that's your decision, but you're making a grave mistake."

I know I quoted Bob Hope in Chapter 17, but I'm going to save you the trouble of paging back. I'll repeat it here. I think it's that important.

> One of the things I learned was to have enough courage to wait. I'd
> stand there waiting for them to get it for a long time. Longer than
> any other comedian has enough guts to wait. My idea was to let
> them know who was running things.

6. KEEP GOING

I mentioned earlier that when I was starting out as a humorist, I had done a fantastic selling job to have a recording studio tape some of my appearances to make a comedy album. The owner who was sacrificing the time and money showed up at the first taping. I bombed.

I not only bombed, but I knew I bombed. In fact, I knew while I was bombing that I was bombing. So I just surrendered. I gave up on the audience and just repeated the words so I could put them and me out of our collective misery.

As the technicians were packing the gear at the end of the evening, I tried to convince the boss that we should continue. I recited a lot of platitudes like, "We can't give up after only one defeat,"—"When the going gets tough the tough get going," and a few others. He listened patiently, then taught me a great lesson. He said, "You just did everything you're telling me not to do. You stood up there on stage and flat out quit."

He never made another tape and my recording career was over.

He was right. Anybody can win over an easy audience. It's the tough ones that require more effort. It's not easy and you won't always win over the crowd. But, at least, when the performance is over you can say, "I did everything I could and tried every trick I know."

It's not only important to feel good about your failures, but if you hang in there throughout, a proportion of them will turn into triumphs.

7. DON'T GIVE UP ON IT

Even if you're called on to practice points one through six every time you try comedy, don't abandon it. It's worth more effort.

Phyllis Diller has told me many times that her first efforts at stand-up comedy were disastrous. She'd cry after each performance. It's interesting, though, that even in the retelling of it, she never gave up. She has never said, "I felt like quitting." She always says, "I realized how much I had to learn."

Phyllis obviously stayed with it, learned a lot, and is a glorious comedienne today. Speakers won't have that gigantic a struggle. We're only going for a dash of humor and we have our polished speeches to fall back on. The benefits of humor are so great for us, though, that we should be tenacious. We should have that determination of Phyllis Diller and continue to learn and improve. Eventually, your style and sense of humor will find its way into your talks and you'll reap the benefits.

Learn from Your Speeches

ALL GOLFERS, PROFESSIONAL or amateur, scratch player or 23 handicapper, go to school on their opponent's putts. Let me explain that for the nongolfing reader.

Greens in golf are rarely level and most putts are not straight. The undulations in the green, and sometimes the grain of the grass, will cause the ball to curve or break one way or another. These elements are not easily recognized by the naked eye. But golfers will study a putt from every angle, trying to make the best guess possible. Regardless of how carefully they study conditions, though, their estimate of how much the ball will curve is always a guess.

There are times when your putt will be in the same relative position of the golfer who putts before you. You can watch this putt and "go to school" on it. You see how his putt rolls and take most of the guesswork out of your putt.

As a speaker you should "go to school" on your own performances. Every speech you give should improve your next one.

The comedy stars that we laugh at and admire today weren't always big stars. One evening while I was delivering some comedy material to Bob Hope's house, I chatted with Mr. Hope as he was going through some files in his office. He handed me a little booklet and said, "Look at this." It was the original "Playbill" from the Broadway play, *Roberta*. That show was produced in 1933 and was a turning point in Hope's career. The one paragraph biography said simply that Bob Hope was a protege of Roscoe "Fatty" Arbuckle and had won some notoriety in the Cleveland area doing Charlie Chaplin impersonations.

Another time Hope told me a vaudeville producer had spelled his name wrong on the posters. Hope went to the gentleman and pointed out the error. The guy shrugged and said, "Who'll know?"

It's logical, but seems strange that a personality who is now recognized all over the world was ever an unknown. All of them were, though.

Of course, they were unknown because it takes time to be discovered. A reputation grows and builds and it has to start from practically nothing. However, there is another reason why these folks were not always giant stars. At one time, they didn't deserve to be.

Frank Sinatra is a fantastic showman and a technically polished vocalist. He wasn't always. Paul Newman is a fine actor today, yet when his first film, "The Robe," was to be shown on television, he paid for his own full page newspaper ads to urge people not to watch it. He was that embarrassed by his performance.

Practically every skilled performer that you can name grew into that proficiency by self-analysis and steady improvement. There are no shortcuts.

In 1924, Hope and his partner, Lefty Durbin, signed to perform in Fred Hurley's tabloid shows. These were shows that travelled the small town vaudeville circuit. They were mini-musical comedies and each performer had to be versatile and play many different roles.

Hope left the company in 1926, but he speaks fondly of the training the tab shows provided:

> There's no possible way to measure the value of the Hurley years, the poise and seasoning they gave me. I remember when I landed the part of Huck Haines in *Roberta* and played it without falling apart on the first night the producers didn't know how many openings I'd been through.

Don't be too harsh a critic of your comedy and delivery. You haven't yet reached your peak.

On the other hand, if you're getting a goodly quotient of laughs, don't get complacent. You can get even better.

Humor has to continue to grow and change. You have to adjust along with it and learn to improve. Even if you never change a word of your script, your performance can improve because you should constantly be learning more about yourself and your audiences.

In my first year in the humor business, I did a benefit show for a Catholic Church. I wrote material that applied to this group alone and the opening night was very successful.

The second night, though, I accidentally learned a valuable lesson about comedy timing that I still use. I had just delivered one of the strongest jokes of the routine and it got a nice big laugh. When I was going to continue my monologue, I got a frog in my throat. I covered my mouth, stepped back from the microphone, and coughed slightly.

The audience thought that I was overwhelmed with my own joke and was laughing at it a second time. They laughed harder and applauded.

A friend of mine in the audience complimented me on the technique. I confessed it was a cough and not a laugh, but it was going to be a laugh from now on. It was and each performance it drew applause from the audience.

Let's discuss some of the mechanics of studying and learning from your own performances.

The first commandment is: "Thou shalt not let thyself off the hook." The tendency of most performers and speakers is to blame someone or something else. When I was hanging around nightclubs writing special material for comics, I'd be amazed at how many performers would come backstage after a lackluster performance with the same complaint, "That's a lousy audience. They don't want to laugh."

These strange people would come home from work, hire a babysitter, get dressed up, then spend a tiny fortune on dinner and a cover charge so they could sit there and NOT be entertained.

Later I saw the same phenomenon when I joined my first television writing staff. All of the writers would gather to watch the taping of the show on a closed circuit monitor. When the comedy wouldn't work, we had hundreds of excuses. "The actors are not delivering the lines right." "The director missed the shot." "The costumes are wrong for this sketch." "The scenery ruins the jokes." All of these excuses let us off the hook. We were now free in good conscience to return to our typewriters and write material that was no better than the stuff that had just failed.

The comedian should have asked himself, "How can I make these people laugh?" We writers should have recognized that we had to endure poor acting, directing, costuming, and set designing, and set our sights on writing material that transcended all of this.

Understand, you may be right when you blame circumstances for a weak performance, but you gain nothing by doing that. You'll learn more by being overly critical of your own performance than by being too forgiving.

Understand, too (and this is most important) that being severe on yourself does not mean becoming depressed and frustrated. No, it's rather a cold-blooded, unemotional appraisal of your work. It's not dwelling on the past and what could have been. It's looking forward to the future with great optimism and learning what you can do to make your next performance more sparkling.

Circumstances can have an effect on your speech. The way the tables are set. The distance between the tables. The room lighting. The sound system. All of these can hurt your performance. There is no question of that. However, you will gain more by dwelling on your performance under those conditions, than by dismissing the whole situation as not worthy of study because "the lighting was bad."

Let's suppose you're a speaker who can only get laughs in a room that is set up with theater-style seating, a hand-held microphone, bright lighting, and a raised stage. Under those conditions, you're magnificent.

That's commendable. But suppose the group you're speaking to today only has a fixed microphone on the lectern. You don't do as well. So you dismiss it, saying, "With a hand-held microphone, I would have been brilliant."

Why not study this performance and perhaps learn what you can do to be brilliant even with the fixed microphone. You may not be as good as you could be with the hand-held mike, but you may be better than you were today.

Which would you prefer to be, a speaker who is magnificent under ideal conditions, but terrible otherwise? Or a speaker who is magnificent under ideal conditions, and pretty damned good under any conditions?

I know some performers who evaluate themselves immediately after each performance and make up a PPP—Post Performance Plan. That means they write a few reminders to themselves of things they should do before their next performance.

Some of this can be self-improvement like "practice eliminating nonwords like unh, ah, oh-uh, and the like." The reminders can also affect the externals, too. For example, suppose this speaker just had to work with a fixed microphone when she prefers a hand-held. She might remind herself to include this point in her letter accepting the speaking assignment. "I would appreciate a detachable microphone." This might assure her of the right conditions thereby making her a better speaker.

Whatever plan you adopt, it's wise to critique yourself soon after your appearance. Thoughts are fresh in your mind then, and your emotions are still reacting. If you gave a poor speech, you'll feel that inside and want to correct it. Your energy will be directed toward enthusiasm. If you wait too long, your attitude may change to, "Oh, it wasn't that bad. I'll just let it ride."

What's most important is that you adopt some form of review. What form is not that important, so long as it works for you. Every speech you give is a valuable lesson, and it would be a pity not to mine some of these riches.

Listed below are five evaluating techniques that speakers use. Some I like and some I don't. Those are personal judgments. I'll list them all with my preferences and prejudices and the reasons. You can try them and see which one or which combinations work best for you. Or, of course, you can come up with your own unique method.

YOUR OWN REACTIONS

Speaking is two-way communication. Not only do you communicate with an audience, but they also transmit emotions back to you. It's almost impossible to give a speech and not feel how you're doing.

I once sat in an audience to hear a friend give a presentation. He was very nervous beforehand and, at the start of his talk, things went wrong. The sound system went out and then the microphone broke. The engineers had to switch systems and experiment with it throughout the first two or three minutes of this presentation. It was terribly distracting, but what was worse, it totally destroyed this man's confidence. He never recovered.

After the talk, most people over-compensated. They heaped praise on the speaker to make him feel better, which was so obvious, it only made him feel worse.

When I saw him in his room about ten minutes later, he was on the verge of either tears or the worst anger fit in history. I walked in and said, "Boy, you were lousy."

That statement was so bold and so obviously true that he took a fit of laughter. We then talked about the disaster and how to prevent its ever happening again.

The point is, my telling him he was lousy was no great revelation. He knew that himself. Anyone who deals with an audience gets feedback. Mercifully, it's not always as extreme as this, but that's why it takes immediate analysis. You have to capture it and get it on paper while it's there, because, unless it's as traumatic as this example, it's quickly forgotten.

Review your speech and remember which pieces worked. When did you feel they really appreciated your humor? When did you feel you were losing them? Did you feel that a certain piece of material was good but could have been better? Jot down for later study any emotions that you felt during your speech.

These are gut reactions and they may be wrong. If you note them, though, you can corroborate them or refute them with other analysis. However, they are very valuable because they are pure interaction. They're removed from any circumstances or outside intervention. It's the interaction between a speaker and an audience.

AUDIENCE COMMENTS

After most speeches, you'll get a different kind of audience feedback. The speech is now over and people will approach you and offer comments. They can be very revealing.

You'll get an immediate inkling of how well the talk went over. It's fairly easy to separate the polite compliment from the sincere. If most people are simply being courteous, you'll know your talk was ordinary. If the comments are sincere, you were probably a hit. If the comments are guarded or noncommittal commendations, you can safely assume you were a flop.

Noncommittals are words of praise that have no meaning. "You were interesting." "Our members were really surprised by you." "You did better than last month's speaker." All of these are saying, "Don't bother leaving your card. We won't ever want you back."

How many people come up to meet you and shake your hand afterwards, and how long they'll wait to meet you will tell you how much they liked you.

If people have nothing good to say, they might approach you out of a sense of civility. But if there is a group ahead, they won't wait long. They'll be looking for any chance to avoid you. If they go out of their way to chat with you, you were a smash. (Except, of course, for those who want to sell you something.)

The comments they offer can be revealing, also. If each person mentions a certain story as appealing, you know you've got a valuable piece of material.

EVALUATIONS

This is a formal handout that many speakers swear by. Some even offer a free gift, such as a pamphlet or tape, but only to those listeners who hand in a completed evaluation form as they leave the auditorium.

The evaluation form is a questionnaire the speaker has prepared asking people to rate things such as: Appearance, Speech Content, Humor Content, and a number of other items.

I'm not an advocate of this because I feel it can be a distraction. Rather than listening to you, folks are mentally composing their evaluation comments.

If you introduce it after your talk it's an imposition. No matter how good a speaker you might be, an audience still cherishes that moment when they are "liberated." They want to get out in the lobby for a cup of coffee, or go to the rest rooms. They definitely won't want to stay and do paperwork.

I object, also because I think they're almost impossible to translate. They have no real meaning. For instance, if you ask an audience to evaluate your appearance on a scale of 1 to 10, a 4 from one person may be equal to an 8 from another person. Unless you know each individual member of the audience, it's hard to rate their ratings. The speakers who use them will argue that you do get an overall feel for what people thought of your performance. That's true. But to me, it's an awkward way of getting the feedback. Besides, I feel a good performer should be able to sense, as we discussed in the two previous sections, how an audience is reacting.

They can be helpful, though. I was advised once to drop the question and answer period that I generally employ at the end of my talk. A person I respected felt it was gimmicky. I enjoyed the thing so much that I was reluctant to drop it.

Then I spoke to a local chapter of the National Speakers Association. They passed out evaluation forms as standard procedure. Most people noted that the Question and Answer period was the most enjoyable. I kept it in.

TAPES

Professional speakers could not exist today if the cassette recorder had not been invented. We would wither away and have to go back to working for a living. Many tape every performance and listen to it looking for places to improve.

I don't. First of all, I generally find it awkward. I don't like to go to a lecture with a mechanical device and then have to push several buttons before addressing the audience. Half way through my talk, I don't want to stop and flip the tape to the other side. I want to just talk to the crowd, get my share of laughs (maybe two or three standing ovations) and move on to the President's reception for cocktails.

Secondly, the few shows that I have taped, I rarely listened to. When I did listen, they weren't that beneficial to me. I wound up enjoying the good parts and ignoring the bad. That's the opposite of what is necessary for improvement.

I also dislike tapes because studying them takes too long. If you give an hour presentation, it takes an hour to listen to the playback. Unless you're very organized, it takes forever to find just one selection to review.

They can be revealing, though, because the tape is unbiased. It reports just what it recorded. If you use the phrase, "You know" 847 times during your speech, it will haunt you 847 times during the playback. Perhaps you should work on eliminating it. I just commended myself on the question and answer period of my talk. However, in listening to a cassette, I noted that I begin the answer to every question exactly the same way: "unk . . ."

Despite my prejudices, tapes can be very beneficial. I would suggest that you tape a few typical presentations for study and then employ the following suggestion. It has many of the same benefits, and is much less time consuming.

ASSISTANT'S NOTES

Furnish someone a script or an outline of your talk and ask him to rate the audience reaction. Rate the audience laughter on a scale of 1 to 5 for you. Now this doesn't have the same drawback that I pointed out under "Evaluations" because you're only dealing with one person here. A 2 to this person will always be a 2 and a 5 will always be a 5.

Of course, even this person's judgment is only an estimate, but it will furnish you a fairly accurate graph of the audience reaction.

This will now help you corroborate or refute your own predictions of how your humor should be working. For instance, you may have several small jokes which you hope will lead up to a big punch line. In our numbering system, you might expect to have three 2's leading up to a 5. If your three 2's lead up to a 3, you might want to reconsider that punch line.

I have three stories on one subject that I expected to build in a 3, 4, 5, sequence. Several evaluations of this type showed that it was going in a 5, 4, 3, direction. I reversed the order.

The nice part of this method is that it furnishes you a quick, readable, graph-like evaluation of your performance. You can put this on a table and study it because the entire presentation is before you. Pieces can be rearranged and repositioned for more effectiveness. You can see spots where you lost your audience, and then liven that portion of your talk up with something that gets a bigger reaction.

I hope this book has convinced you to try some humor in your speaking. Comedy is a delicate art, full of surprises. It takes constant dedication to keep it sharp and crisp, but it's worth it.

A light sprinkling of humor throughout your discourse has many benefits. Your ideas will be communicated more effectively and retained more completely. Isn't that the whole purpose of your getting up to talk in the first place? And what's sweeter still, you're presentation becomes painless. No, it goes beyond painless. It's pleasant.

It's fun from both sides of the lectern. One of the most memorable compliments I ever received after a successful talk was from a gentleman who said, "You know what I liked most about your talk? You seemed to be having more fun than anybody in the room." Since hearing that I try to live up to it every time I approach a microphone. That spirit of fun is infectious. It captivates an audience and allows the speaker to hold their attention in his hands. Also, if I'm having a good time, I know for a fact that at least one person in the auditorium is enjoying my talk.

Bob Hope's theme song, "Thanks for the Memories," has a line that applies to all speakers. It reads, "You may have been a headache, but you never were a bore." Don't you be a bore, either. Add some humor.

Questions and Answers

"QUESTIONS AND ANSWERS" is a favorite part of any speech I give. That's probably because I don't have anything to memorize, and the structure of the program is determined solely by those who raise their hands and make the queries. I just sit back and go with the flow.

So this is my chapter to relax and give some top-of-the-head replies to those questions I frequently hear.

QUESTION: My message is very important and I deliver it with some intensity. Wouldn't humor in this instance be in the way?

ANSWER: There's a joke about a man who was drafted and notified to report for his physical. The doctor told him to remove his shirt. "I don't have to remove my shirt," he said to the doctor. "I just want to get over there and start tearing up the enemy. Just let me at them with my bare hands I'll rip 'em apart." The physician said, "That's fine, but I have to check your heart." "My heart is good enough to stomp on them jerks and that's all I want. Just give me a gun and some grenades and turn me loose," the man screamed. The doctor said, "You're crazy, man." The guy said, "Don't tell *me,* Doc. *Write it on the paper.*"

Sometimes our own fervor is counterproductive. The listeners can mistake it for fanaticism and pay no attention to your message.

Intensity tempered with just a little humor shows people that you're dedicated, but have a balanced outlook. Your message will be better received.

QUESTION: If I have a serious message, why do I need humor?

ANSWER: Because seriousness is exhausting. Exercise is good for our bodies and minds, but most of us avoid it because it's boring. We tire of it. So we're constantly on the lookout for ways of making it fun.

A valid message can tire a listener if it's delivered with unremitting earnestness. It's up to the speaker to inject some fun into the proceedings, to keep the audience alert.

A sprinkling of humor throughout a serious talk allows the listeners a moment of relaxation. It refreshes and revitalizes their minds. It delays the mental fatigue so that they remain attentive to each of your points.

QUESTION: In a tense business situation, how do I get things off to a lighthearted start?

ANSWER: In this situation, the truth generally works best. We've grown so accustomed to using euphemisms and outright lies that we've almost come to accept them as truth. Consequently, when we come right out and express the truth, it's refreshing enough and humorous enough to merit a chuckle.

I remember an occasion when I was to address a crowd of 300 business people. I was scheduled to arrive for a cocktail reception at 6:30 and begin my presentation at 7:30. My plane was delayed, and those people waited over two hours for my appearance. I was introduced, approached the podium to polite applause, looked at the crowd and said, "Boy, I'd better be good."

None of those people would have said that, but practically everyone was thinking it. It was a simple statement that said what had to be said. It told them that I knew I had put them through an ordeal and that I knew how they felt. And it said it all with a smile.

I remember a supervisor in a business situation who gathered us together. We suspected it was for a chewing-out. The boss began with, "Some of you may be thinking that this is going to be a group reprimand. You're right."

QUESTION: In a situation like the one you described in the last question, how do we know what will and what won't relax people? How can we avoid saying the wrong thing?

ANSWER: Put yourself in your listeners' place. Find out what they're thinking. In most business situations, especially ones where there is some apprehension and tension, the listeners' thoughts are fairly obvious. Humor, then, is "what oft was thought, but ne'er so well expressed."

Avoid stating your own thoughts. That tends to polarize an audience. If tension existed before, and the audience discovers you're at the microphone to defend your position, they'll take offense.

Study your audience. Figure out what they're thinking. Even if it is in stark opposition to your own thinking, you can turn that polarity to your advantage.

The humor that's generated from that approach will be eloquent and meaningful.

QUESTION: Are there different types of humor for different situations?

ANSWER: Yes. Let me give an example from personal experience. It has nothing to do with show business or speaking, but will illustrate how some humor is tasteful even in unhappy circumstances.

At my grandfather's funeral, we were all concerned about Grandmom and how she would bear up under the grief. Many old friends came to offer their sympathy, and each one brought back memories which intensified her sorrow. But she was blessed with a beautiful sense of humor, and when the grief was becoming too much for her, she turned to us and said, "If your grandpop could sit up and see all the people who came to his funeral, he'd drop dead."

We laughed, she laughed, and probably somewhere Grandpop laughed. It was neither disrespectful nor out of place.

The right kind of humor can generally be found for any occasion. However, it's a seat-of-the-pants operation. You'll have to decide when and how much and which type.

One word of caution, though: If you're in doubt, don't do it. Humor is a powerful tool, but it can backfire. It's better to do without it than to use it unwisely.

QUESTION: How do you know which kind of humor is appropriate?

ANSWER: I sometimes think that humor is 90 percent psychology. To discover which kind is appropriate, you have to get into the minds of your listeners and find out what they want said, then say it in a funny way.

Probably more important than which style of humor is appropriate is *when* is it appropriate. Timing, in this sense, is very important in your use of humor. As speakers, we should learn when interrupting our message with a touch of humor will enhance it and when it will damage it.

To illustrate, let me go back to my favorite pastime once again— tennis. The way I play the game, there are lots of laughs. Jokes and wisecracks are very much a part of the game, because my playing partners and I are not very good at any other part of the game. But even then, timing is important. There is a right time and a wrong time to joke. Between points, the banter is welcome. During the point, it's rude.

Golfers observe the same courtesy. They enjoy joking about the bad play of one another, but never while the player is making a shot.

QUESTION: Are there some people who simply aren't funny, don't have a sense of humor, and can't do comedy?

ANSWER: I don't believe so. Everyone has a sense of humor. Some people may be more difficult to reach with comedy, but everyone laughs at something. I believe that if you have a sense of humor, you can also use humor effectively. Each person, though, has to find his own brand of humor and employ that.

An element of fear enters into the use of comedy, though. Experimentation is necessary to find the right style of humor and the correct stories to tell. In experimenting, we sometimes fail. That failure produces an apprehension the next time we try to tell a joke or story. This can escalate until we avoid using humor altogether.

I traveled with Bob Hope on his Christmas tour of Beirut in 1983. He told hundreds of jokes that the sailors and marines loved. Once in a while, though, he'd read one off the cue cards that just sat there—no reaction. It didn't fluster him. He'd just tell the cue card man, "Throw that one overboard." That line would get laughs.

Use a comedy style and stories that reflect your own attitudes and that you're comfortable with. Relax and enjoy your own stories and your audience. If it fails, you've learned something, and even humor that fails produces results for a speaker. It relaxes the audience and it shows them that you have a balanced outlook. It's catastrophic only when your whole presentation is geared for comedy.

The most spontaneous humor is among friends. Treat each audience as your old friends and you'll have no trouble delivering effective humor.

QUESTION: Are there any secrets to telling a funny story?

ANSWER: First of all, it's important to note that not all humor is jokes or stories. It can simply be an attitude, a style of speech, mannerisms—almost anything. Bill Cosby, for example, is a very funny man, but his routines aren't built around funny lines, per se. The humor comes more from the way Bill says something rather than what he says.

However, if you *do* tell jokes, I can recommend that you know where the humor is and know where you're going as you tell the story.

The punch line is all-important, and it generally comes at the end. So you must know your ending and build to it. Everything you say in your storytelling should serve only to enhance the ending.

In television, we run across a certain problem often. The person delivering the straight line studies only that line, with no regard for the punch line to follow. As a result, it's easy to blow the setup line. Let me give you a dumb joke as an example.

HE: Can you tell me how long cows should be milked?
SHE: Same as short ones.

Admittedly, it's not a blockbuster, but if it's going to be a joke at all, it has to be done correctly. If someone doesn't understand the ending, he might read the setup line as:

HE: Can you tell me how long to milk a cow?

The joke is ruined.

So, in any story you tell, find out where the humor is and make everything you say in the telling of it head toward that ending.

In addition—and this is not a secret, but a word of advice—no joke or story is carved in stone. If you hear it or read it one way and feel that it is funnier with a different wording, either along the way or at the punch line, try it. Change the thing; make it your own.

QUESTION: Where's the first place to look for humor?

ANSWER: Always look first in the truth. When I began writing for Phyllis Diller, she would mark up the pages with comments on the jokes that she didn't select. On one she wrote, "This just isn't true. If it isn't the truth, honey, don't send it to me."

This sounds surprising because Phyllis does zany, outlandish, bizarre lines, yet each of them is based on truth.

The truth can be stretched, reversed, exaggerated, distorted, but it is where humor is based.

Art Holst, an NFL referee and a very funny speaker, tells a story about a game he was officiating. A strange formation was employed by one team. When it happened he immediately threw a penalty flag. He adds, though, "Not too high." It's a funny line, and truthful.

In trying to generate humor, look first for the truth, the facts. Then find clever, interesting, surprising ways of stating the truth.

QUESTION: What do you do when the humor doesn't work?

ANSWER: The first thing to do is own up to it. I watched a performer taping a television show once and one of the jokes was pretty stale. The audience groaned and then booed. The performer said, "See where you're booing now? When this show airs, there'll be a big laugh in there."

The audience got a big laugh out of that, and a bad situation was turned into a good one.

Work harder when the humorous material is failing. There's no guarantee that a story or a piece of business will work every time or with every audience. However, you should give it your absolute best. If material fails, make sure it's the audience's fault and not yours.

You'd be surprised, too, at how often one good bit of humor can turn an audience around. So don't surrender too early.

Also, you should accept an occasional weak show and learn from it. Why was it weak? How can it be improved? Maybe it should be delivered in different ways to different audiences?

We have devoted a whole chapter to this topic, so review it.

QUESTION: Do you ever get an unreceptive audience? If so, what do you do?

ANSWER: Most audiences want to hear what you have to say and want to be amused. However, for various reasons, some are simply unresponsive.

There really isn't much you can do about it. By definition, these folks are the villains. It's not the speaker's fault.

Earlier I quoted Bill Gove, who says, "You should be responsible *to* your audience, but not *for* your audience." As a speaker, you have an obligation to be on time, to be prepared, and to deliver your material as best you can. If your listeners choose not to receive it, it's out of your hands.

However, you must be sure of two things: First, that this is truly an unresponsive audience. Don't take the easy way out and blame each substandard performance on the listeners. There are times when it may be your fault and you should be learning from the experience.

Second, almost the opposite of the first, don't be too quick to change material just because it fails once or twice. If you have good humorous material that is honed and polished, it's not wise to change it around just because this one audience didn't appreciate it.

QUESTION: Should conditions be controlled to make humor more effective?

ANSWER: Whenever possible, yes. I recently did a television show where the star did an opening monologue that got a lukewarm reception at best. It was taped during a holiday weekend and the house was less than half filled. The people were scattered throughout the studio, leaving lots of spaces. The producers decided not to try to bunch them all up front for fear that once they got up, some of them would leave.

The star was not happy with the taping, so we retaped the opening monologue two days later to a packed house. The very same monologue played so well this time that the performer admitted it was his best response in years. The only thing that had changed was the seating.

Humor is delicate; many things can affect it. I perform better from a raised platform. I like the audience close to the stage, not separated by a dance floor. I like the lights to be dimmed. Comedy plays better to a house that is packed than to one that is half empty. I'd rather have a small, crowded room than a big room with spaces. If there are empty seats in the auditorium, the people should be bunched together rather than scattered. The laughter seems to spread faster that way. The sound equipment is important: People can't laugh if they can't hear what you say.

You should try to arrange as much of this as possible in advance. Tell the organizers the type of arrangements you prefer.

It won't always be possible to secure the ideal conditions. You'll have to compromise one way or another. It's important then to accept the conditions you have and perform to your maximum. The poor conditions you have to endure are your problem. Don't make them the audience's.

I've heard speakers bore listeners with their repeated moaning about the auditorium, the lighting, the microphone, or whatever. The audience doesn't really care. Just do the best job you can with the conditions you've got.

QUESTION: Does humor belong in the business world?

ANSWER: Humor belongs anywhere where there is stress. It's the greatest nonprescription antidote for stress. A sense of humor also gives a clearer, more balanced view of the facts. This alone makes decision making, which is so crucial in business, that much easier.

A sense of humor and a good working use of humor are as important to executives as they are to speakers. A discreet mixture of wisdom and wit produces likability. If you think about who you like to be around, you'll probably discover one reason is that they're *fun* to be with. This by-product of humor helps salespeople and executives.

Humor also gets people—employees, superiors, and clients—to listen more attentively. So much dialogue in the business world is predictable that it's easy to shut it out of our minds and not really hear it. A breath of originality makes your message more palatable and gets more attention.

People not only hear what is said with humor, but they remember it longer and better. The uniqueness of wit makes it memorable.

QUESTION: How does humor help relieve stress?

ANSWER: I may be out of my league with this reply, since I'm neither a doctor nor a medical expert, but I will answer from my own experience and observation of others.

Let me begin by telling a story about something very enlightening that happened while I was taking a group tennis lesson. A young woman in the class was at the net hitting volleys. One of the balls bounced off the edge of her racket and hit her directly in the mouth. Naturally, she let out a yell, dropped her racket, and held the wound. The teaching pro come to her calmly and said, "How bad does it hurt?" She replied with the standard, "I'm all right." He wouldn't let her off the hook that easily, though. He said, "Tell me exactly how much it hurts." She said,

"Well, it hit me right in the face. It really hurts." He asked, "Like being burned with scalding water?" She replied, "Not that bad." He said, "Like a bee sting?" She admitted it wasn't that bad. Finally, through several questions and answers, she decided that it wasn't a "hurt" at all, but rather a "sensation."

We all tend to intensify and magnify pain and suffering. This player was forced to analyze what she was yelping about and discovered that it wasn't worth all the yelping. It *actually* didn't hurt that bad.

The teacher forced her to see, recognize, and accept the facts. We've said that that is what humor is: seeing, recognizing, and accepting the facts as they are.

All of us have setbacks in our business and personal lives. We dwell on them and magnify and exaggerate them just as this tennis player did. When we look on them with a sense of humor, we see them more clearly. Recognizing and accepting the actual facts tends to reduce the stress of the situation.

It's useful to note that the teacher in our story didn't eliminate the hurt or make it go away. He simply focused on the actual pain and eliminated the magnification of it. So humor doesn't eliminate the large or small annoyances in our lives. It simply minimizes the stress of them.

INDEX

Other Books of Interest

General Writing Books

  Beginning Writer's Answer Book, edited by Polking and Bloss, $14.95
  Getting the Words Right: How to Revise, Edit and Rewrite, by Theodore A. Rees Cheney $13.95
  How to Become a Bestselling Author, by Stan Corwin, $14.95
  How to Get Started in Writing, by Peggy Teeters $10.95
  International Writers' & Artists' Yearbook, (paper) $10.95
  Law and the Writer, edited by Polking and Meranus (paper) $7.95
  Make Every Word Count, by Gary Provost (paper) $7.95
  Teach Yourself to Write, by Evelyn A. Stenbock $12.95
  Treasury of Tips for Writers, edited by Marvin Weisbord (paper) $6.95
  Writer's Encyclopedia, edited by Kirk Polking $19.95
  Writer's Market, edited by Bernadine Clark $18.95
  Writer's Resource Guide, edited by Bernadine Clark $16.95
  Writing for the Joy of It, by Leonard Knott $11.95
  Writing From the Inside Out, by Charlotte Edwards (paper) $9.95

Magazine/News Writing

  Complete Guide to Marketing Magazine Articles, by Duane Newcomb $9.95
  Complete Guide to Writing Nonfiction, by the American Society of Journalists & Authors, edited by Glen Evans $24.95
  Craft of Interviewing, by John Brady $9.95
  Magazine Writing: The Inside Angle, by Art Spikol $12.95
  Magazine Writing Today, by Jerome E. Kelley $10.95
  Newsthinking: The Secret of Great Newswriting, by Bob Baker $11.95
  1001 Article Ideas, by Frank A. Dickson $10.95
  Stalking the Feature Story, by William Ruehlmann $9.95
  Write On Target, by Connie Emerson $12.95
  Writing and Selling Non-Fiction, by Hayes B. Jacobs $12.95

Fiction Writing

  Creating Short Fiction, by Damon Knight $11.95
  Fiction Is Folks: How to Create Unforgettable Characters, by Robert Newton Peck $11.95
  Fiction Writer's Help Book, by Maxine Rock $12.95
  Fiction Writer's Market, edited by Jean Fredette $17.95
  Handbook of Short Story Writing, by Dickson and Smythe (paper) $6.95
  How to Write Best-Selling Fiction, by Dean R. Koontz $13.95
  How to Write Short Stories that Sell, by Louise Boggess (paper) $7.95
  One Way to Write Your Novel, by Dick Perry (paper) $6.95
  Secrets of Successful Fiction, by Robert Newton Peck $8.95
  Writing Romance Fiction—For Love And Money, by Helene Schellenberg Barnhart $14.95
  Writing the Novel: From Plot to Print, by Lawrence Block $10.95

Special Interest Writing Books

  Cartoonist's & Gag Writer's Handbook, by Jack Markow (paper) $9.95
  The Children's Picture Book: How to Write It, How to Sell It, by Ellen E. M. Roberts $17.95
  Complete Book of Scriptwriting, by J. Michael Straczynski $14.95
  Complete Guide to Greeting Card Writing, edited by Larry Sandman (paper) $7.95
  Complete Guide to Writing Software User Manuals, by Brad McGehee (paper) $14.95
  Confession Writer's Handbook, by Florence K. Palmer. Revised by Marguerite McClain $9.95

Guide to Greeting Card Writing, edited by Larry Sandman $10.95
How to Make Money Writing . . . Fillers, by Connie Emerson $12.95
How to Write a Cookbook and Get It Published, by Sara Pitzer, $15.95
How to Write a Play, by Raymond Hull $13.95
How to Write and Sell Your Personal Experiences, by Lois Duncan $10.95
How to Write and Sell (Your Sense of) Humor, by Gene Perret $12.95
How to Write "How-To" Books and Articles, by Raymond Hull (paper) $8.95
Mystery Writer's Handbook, edited by Lawrence Treat (paper) $8.95
Poet and the Poem, revised edition by Judson Jerome $13.95
Poet's Handbook, by Judson Jerome $11.95
Programmer's Market, edited by Brad McGehee (paper) $16.95
Sell Copy, by Webster Kuswa $11.95
Successful Outdoor Writing, by Jack Samson $11.95
Travel Writer's Handbook, by Louise Zobel (paper) $8.95
TV Scriptwriter's Handbook, by Alfred Brenner $12.95
Writing and Selling Science Fiction, by Science Fiction Writers of America (paper) $7.95
Writing for Children & Teenagers, by Lee Wyndham. Revised by Arnold Madison $11.95
Writing for Regional Publications, by Brian Vachon $11.95
Writing to Inspire, by Gentz, Roddy, et al $14.95

The Writing Business

Complete Handbook for Freelance Writers, by Kay Cassill $14.95
Freelance Jobs for Writers, edited by Kirk Polking (paper) $7.95
How to Be a Successful Housewife/Writer, by Elaine Fantle Shimberg $10.95
How You Can Make $20,000 a Year Writing, by Nancy Hanson (paper) $6.95
Profitable Part-time/Full-time Freelancing, by Clair Rees $10.95
The Writer's Survival Guide: How to Cope with Rejection, Success and 99 Other Hang-Ups of the Writing Life, by Jean and Veryl Rosenbaum $12.95

To order directly from the publisher, include $1.50 postage and handling for 1 book and 50¢ for each additional book. Allow 30 days for delivery.

Writer's Digest Books, Department B
9933 Alliance Road, Cincinnati OH 45242
Prices subject to change without notice.